PROBLEM SOLVING

PROBLEM SOLVING

Concepts and Methods
for Community Organizations

Ralph Brody, Ph.D.

Federation for Community Planning
Cleveland, Ohio

HUMAN SCIENCES PRESS, INC.
72 FIFTH AVENUE,
NEW YORK, N.Y. 10011

Copyright © 1982 by Human Sciences Press, Inc.
72 Fifth Avenue, New York, New York 10011

Printed in the United States of America
23456789   987654321

Library of Congress Cataloging in Publication Data

Brody, Ralph.
   Problem solving.

   Includes index.
   1. Community organization.   2. Social work administration   I. Title.
HV41.B69   361.8   LC 81-7221
ISBN 0-89885-078-9   AACR2
ISBN 0-89885-079-7 (pbk.)

Dedicated to Phyllis, Lisa, Mike, and Diane

CONTENTS

INTRODUCTION

People involved in community organizations spend hundreds of hours each year in meetings trying to solve problems. Many of these hours are fruitful and productive, with group discussion leading to well conceived problem statements, specific objectives, and strategies to implement action plans. But often, too many hours are spent in frustration arising from an inability to adequately define problems or develop workable strategies.

To be sure, some problems faced by community organizations are intractable—inadequate housing, high unemployment, and increasing crime, to name a few. Resolution of these problems may require more than any one organization is capable of doing on its own. No magic formula or set of techniques can guarantee the solution of tough, complex problems, and a certain healthy skepticism ought to be directed at anyone proposing quick answers to difficult community situations.

Despite these caveats, the thesis of this book is that a conscious, consistent, systematic planning approach can enhance the capability of organizations to solve problems. Such an approach can provide an organization with effective ways of thinking about problems, determining which ones it wants to deal with, and pinpointing ways in which it can more efficiently concentrate its energies. By understanding the basis of problems, taking advantage of current opportunities, and anticipating future events, an organization sharpens its capacity for achieving desired results.

I have written this book out of a strong personal conviction that the gap between theory and practice in community problem solving must be bridged. As a teacher of undergraduate and graduate students in community planning and organizational theory, and as a community organizer, planner, and program administrator, I have become increasingly aware of the importance of relating conceptual ideas and problem-solving techniques to real world, firing-line situations. What students and practitioners want and need are concepts that aid them in understanding complicated community problems and methods that can help them be more effective.

This book emerges in part from problem-solving workshops I conducted for students and professionals involved in human services and community programs. The workshops confirmed that students and professionals from a variety of settings want information about problem solving and are eager to try out ideas not ordinarily available in most courses. Health nutritionists want to understand how to write proposals, human service administrators want to learn about parliamentary procedure, and health planners want to understand how to conduct group discussions to elicit ideas. This book is an outgrowth of these workshops.

In determining the topics of the book, I was guided by two factors. The first was based on what students and professionals have told me they want to know more about; the second was information and techniques I have drawn on to help me in dealing with community problems. I have used most of the techniques presented in the book in sessions with boards of trustees, community planning groups, professional staff, and citizens' groups.

The book is therefore written for students and professionals who are or intend to be involved in varied organizational settings:

> Professional staff and volunteer community leaders of boards of trustees or public advisory committees concerned with community issues such as day care, mental health, foster child welfare, youth development, aging, health, public welfare, and vocational programs.
>
> Professional staff and volunteer community leaders involved in community planning councils, United Way organizations, neighborhood groups, and advocacy bodies concerned with consumer needs, housing problems, women's issues, and racial injustice.
>
> Undergraduate and graduate students in social welfare planning, urban studies, health planning, and public administration.

The examples used in the text to illustrate different techniques are drawn from both public and voluntary agencies. For the most part, the problem-solving methods can easily be transferred from one organizational context to another. Where necessary, I have indicated some of the limitations inherent in the techniques.

Each technique is presented in sufficient detail so that the reader will be able to use it without necessarily requiring the services of an outside consultant. I have prepared a review checklist that serves as a summary of the elements of the problem-solving process as developed in the book. I have also provided exercises, keyed to each chapter, that can be useful to students or group participants. I urge readers to use the exercises (or others developed by the group itself) because I believe that people learn best through directly experiencing the material.

Frequently the problem-solving process is outlined in a simple, systematic sequence of steps: defining the problem, setting objectives, identifying and assessing alternative approaches, implementing one of the solutions, and evaluating results. But the real world often does not permit such a completely rational planning model. People will differ on the problem definition or decide part way through the process to reconsider their problem selection, objectives, or implementation strategies. They may not have anticipated all contingencies or find they may have to make decisions with insufficient information. The real world of problem solving is both demanding and dynamic.

The format of this book reflects both the systematic and dynamic aspects of the problem-solving process. Chapters 1 and 2 describe the process of formulating the problem and setting objectives. Chapters 3 through 6 discuss internal decision-making processes, including the functions and structures of decision-making techniques. They highlight both the creative and analytical decision processes. Chapters 7 through 10 focus on the strategies involved in considering and carrying out action plans. Special attention is given to considering alternative action proposals, conducting negotiations, developing methods for tracking activities, and identifying ways of obtaining funding for projects. Chapter 11 describes ways to review efforts and results. The Epilogue identifies survival strategies.

This book combines concepts with techniques and can be read in the sequence I have outlined. Or readers can concentrate on those sections that are most relevant to their particular needs. Readers primarily concerned with internal decision-making processes, for example, may wish to concentrate on those chapters that describe parliamentary procedures or creative problem-solving techniques. I believe many readers will find it useful to refer to the book when they are involved in a situation requiring a specific method.

A number of people have contributed specific suggestions to the book: Cathy Barber, Leslie Brooks, Bruce Campbell, Elsie Day, Joe Ferrante, Gerda Freedheim, Joe Garcia, Burt Griffin, Chris Herbruck, Frank Kimber, Lynne Kweder, Pat Langmack, Robert McGraw, Kay Raffo, Judy Sherman, Stanley Wertheim, Marilyn Williams, Nancella Wilson-Harris, and Sidney Josephs.

I also want to thank Marvin Rosenberg, Yosef Katan, Lois Swack, Roberta Steinbacker, and Kul Bhushan for providing me the opportunity to test out earlier versions of the manuscript in their classrooms or workshops, and to Leona Bevis and Richard Streeter who encouraged the development of the book in a creative work atmosphere.

Phyllis Brody and James Huston were most helpful in reviewing earlier drafts. And I want to express my appreciation to Rose Alexander, Roslyn Bucy, Tammy Junke, and particularly Marcie Levy whose attention to details and ability to maintain a positive spirit through numerous rewrites helped me in the preparation of the manuscript.

I have learned much in writing this material, and I hope you will too.

Ralph Brody
January 1982

Chapter 1

FORMULATING THE PROBLEM

When people in a community are concerned that a discrepancy exists between a current situation and a desired end, they have taken an initial step toward identifying a problem.[1]

Discussion of a problem may begin with a general idea that something is wrong, as illustrated by the following examples:

"Our schools are deteriorating."

"We have a welfare problem."

"Teenage pregnancy is reaching epidemic proportions."

"There is a conflict between the suburbs and central city."

But many people have a tendency to stop the problem formulation process at this point. Having broadly stated the problem, they want to rush into action and seek immediate solutions without giving sufficient forethought. To begin to deal more effectively with a community problem, they should understand (1) the process by which it becomes a community problem, (2) the background of the problem, and (3) the theoretical perspectives to the problem. Because poorly thought-out statements set the stage for poor solutions, community people must resist the tendency to spend too little effort on defining and understanding problems in their eagerness to seek answers.

EMERGENCE OF A COMMUNITY PROBLEM

Although some individuals in a community may be dissatisfied with a given situation, this by itself does not constitute a community problem. A condition may be troublesome, but people may adapt to it, alter their community institutions and practices to cope with it, even change their values to accommodate it. For example, for a number of years alcohol abuse was not considered a community problem, although many individual adults and youngsters were suffering the consequences of alcoholism. Similarly, individual women privately suffered inequality until the women's movement articulated it as a public issue. Private troubles experienced by certain unemployed individuals, pregnant teenagers, or elderly poor do not necessarily become community problems.

A community problem exists when a considerable number of people identify a condition that must be changed. Obviously, the problem has to have some basis in reality. This is the reason that facts about the situation must be gathered, although different people (and experts) may argue about how to interpret these facts. A problem becomes a community problem when individual discontent becomes a broadly felt concern.

Awareness is thus a first stage in the development of a community problem. Accompanying this growing awareness is the gaining of community legitimacy. The problem moves from a fringe group to become more widespread as the public media write and talk about it, foundations become interested in funding pilot projects, politicians endorse proposals to deal with it, and voluntary and governmental funders provide financial support for programs. Examples of current community interests include drug abuse programs, housing for battered women, child abuse programs, group homes for the mentally retarded—all of these programs began with a collection of individuals deeply concerned about a target population who then formed organizations that worked to influence the broader community and the country first to be aware of the problem and then to do something about it. The significance of this discussion is that one of the most important, and often difficult, steps in the problem-solving process is that of making individually experienced, latent concerns known to a broader segment of the population.

Understanding the Background of the Problem

Most community problems are sustained by a wide variety of factors, and some are more influential than others. The challenge is to locate the major factor(s) that have an effect on the problem requiring correction. To meet this challenge effectively, it is essential to research the background of the problem and gather relevant facts about it.

Developing a thorough understanding of the problem demands an intensive review of the literature on the problem and discussion with those experienced in dealing with it. Is it transitory or ongoing? Is it limited to a few people or widespread? Who in the community defines it as a problem and who does not? Does the problem reside in the individuals and families or is it related to status and distribution of power? These questions are among those needing to be explored.

For example, a group may be interested in developing community-based residences for recently released mentally ill patients. The group would need to have a solid understanding of the theories and concepts of how people recovering from mental illness can have an optimum living situation that will aid their recovery. Then, too, in anticipation of dealing with the community, it would need to be aware of the sociological and psychological concepts of community resistance. Further, it would have to become knowledgeable about legal precedents for establishing group homes and financial requirements. In short, a community group thoroughly investigates all facets of the problem.

Gathering facts about the community condition is also crucial. In the group home example, it would be essential to know how many people from a locality were likely to be needing the facility, where current group homes were located, how community decisions were made, and what other attempts have been made to obtain a group home.

Depending on the particular problem under consideration, information can be obtained from various sources, including census data, employment statistics, housing surveys, or records from schools, courts, and human service agencies. Local community planning agencies in health, human services, and mental health usually issue periodic reports. State and federal agencies also issue reports with certain information that has local relevance. Those experiencing the problem may need to be surveyed. And service providers, funders, and academic experts may need to be contacted.[2]

In gathering data on the problem, the group may be faced with two difficulties: obtaining too much information that may prove to be irrelevant and identifying too little information from normal sources. Good judgment must be used to distinguish *noise* (meaningless data) from information that helps in analyzing a problem. Similarly, when data is not easily obtainable, concerned individuals may be required to use ingenuity, functioning like good investigative reporters by checking out leads. With the advice of knowledgeable researchers, special studies may need to be conducted as part of the fact-finding process.

Clarifying the Theoretical Perspectives of the Problem

Those dealing with a problem tend to limit their perspective to the conceptual methods in which they have been trained. The world is viewed through the lenses of a particular academic discipline or body of thought, which then forces any given problem to be viewed and dealt with in a particular way.

In dealing with the problem of alcoholism, for example, psychoanalytically oriented people will identify intrapsychic conditions as the major factors to be dealt with; behavior modification proponents will select immediate reinforcement; social psychologists will examine social pressures. In examining the problem of unemployment, to use another example, some may consider the problem as residing in the individuals and therefore propose educational and training remedies, whereas others would see the problem in the structure of the economy, thus seeking alterations in economic policies. It is no wonder that discussion of community problems is often confused; participants in the discussion use different definitions and assumptions but often fail to make these explicit. Consequently, they talk past each other. It is essential, therefore, that the theoretical perspective be made explicit and that consideration be given to its appropriateness in the problem formulation phase.

REFINING COMMUNITY PROBLEMS WITHIN AN ORGANIZATIONAL CONTEXT

In the discussion of community problems, emphasis has been placed on examining a community problem without reference to organizational constraints or realities. The advantage of this initial approach is that it can in general free people to concentrate on the special needs of the population.

Certainly, some situations and some organizations permit a wide latitude in identifying and selecting community problems. Multiissue organizations, such as community action commissions, neighborhood organizations, health and human service councils, and women's coordinating councils, have a broad mandate to tackle a variety of problems. Normally they do not have constraints of running programs, and frequently they have the ability to advocate changes. They can be open to a full exploration of a wide variety of community problems.

Other organizations may have a more narrow focus and they may be constrained by their mandate, funding requirements, and bureaucratic regulations. They may have programs to run, services to provide, and political expectations to meet. Mental health centers, welfare departments, and city-sponsored human resource departments all operate under these constraints. Hence, potential problem solvers must be aware of both community and organizational factors that could effect the problem.

Regardless of the nature of an organization—whether single purpose or multiissue, primarily involved in running programs or advocating for problem resolution, functioning individually or joining with other groups—it must be able to develop a clarity and precision about the problem before embarking on a course of action. To achieve this clarity, it should arrive at a refined problem statement that avoids vague and ambiguous terms, answers certain basic questions, avoids too narrow a view, clarifies organizational perspectives, and identifies key factors that could have an impact on the problem.

Avoiding Vague and Ambiguous Terms

Initially, groups tend to express a general problem in vague and ambiguous terms. Vague terms have too little meaning. If a problem definition states that welfare grants are "too low," the meaning is not clear unless "too low" is defined as, for example, being 72% of the state-determined minimum level of decency. Ambiguous terms have multiple meanings.[3] If concern is expressed about people on welfare, for example, does this refer to the elderly receiving Supplemental Security Income (SSI) benefits, families receiving Aid for Dependent Children (ADC), or general relief for single adults and childless couples? Unless the terms are defined precisely, one cannot be certain what is meant by "people on welfare."

In Table 1–1. problem statements, as they might have been initially expressed, are illustrated with key words italicized. Then the revised

Table 1-1. PROBLEM STATEMENTS

Initial Problem Statements	Revised Problem Statements
(1) *Racism* in public schools *exists*.	Textbooks do not provide an accurate picture of black people in history.
(2) *Teenage unemployment* is *high*.	Unemployment for those inner city black youth age 16-20 is 38% as compared to 6% unemployment for adults.
(3) *Sexism* in higher education *exists*.	Only 10% of administrative posts in higher education are occupied by women.

problem statements are shown as they might read with the key words defined. It should be kept in mind that, depending on the particular problem situation and community context, other revised statements are possible.

The revised problem statement spells out definitions of key terms and gives concrete examples of the problem. To achieve precision in a problem statement, two methods can be considered. One way is to add the phrase, "as evidenced by." This is illustrated below:

> Racism in public education is evidenced by the absence of descriptions of black leaders in high school history texts.
>
> The problem is that teenage unemployment is high as evidenced by a 38% unemployment rate for inner city black youth aged 16 to 20 compared with a 6% rate for adults.
>
> Sexism in higher education exists as evidenced by the fact that only 10% of administrative posts in higher education are occupied by women.

Asking Basic Questions

Another way of obtaining precision is to break a problem into its component elements by asking a series of basic questions. The answers to these questions can help to pinpoint more exactly the nature of the problem. The following basic questions can serve as a guide to many problem situations:

> What is the problem?
> Where does it exist?
> Who is affected by it?
> When does it occur?
> To what degree is it felt?[4]

In Table 1–2. these basic questions for five citizen-identified problem issues affecting local communities are listed: (1) a dangerous increase in levels of air pollution, (2) a decline in the quality of education, (3) substandard housing, (4) an increase in the number of gas stations, and (5) an increase in the number of taverns. By specifically answering each basic question it is possible to develop a problem statement, recorded at the bottom of the chart. Of course, some of these questions may not be appropriate for all problem issues, and modification should be made depending on the context. For example, if a problem is related to lack of services for deaf persons, identifying a particular neighborhood may not be relevant, since the existing services for the deaf may be located throughout the community. With this qualification in mind, a refined problem statement would therefore incorporate answers to the appropriate basic questions.

Time spent defining the problem will result in changing fuzzy problem statements to sharp, clear statements that can then be used later to identify possible areas for special attention and work effort.

Avoiding Too Narrow a View of the Problem

Although it is desirable to develop greater precision of the problem statement, at the same time it is important to avoid a too narrow or limited view of the problem, thereby restricting the range of options to deal with it. The basic mission of the organization can itself be one major factor in restricting a view of the problem. A welfare agency will be concerned with income issues, a health agency with community health problems, a day care group with early childhood issues. And yet other aspects may impinge on any of these broad problem areas. For example, housing problems may affect welfare recipients, mental health problems may affect which people are seen at health agencies, or transportation problems may have an impact on day care. When people have special needs that are unrelated to the central mission of the organization, these may be ignored. The result is fragmented programs based on what the organization provides rather than comprehensive programs based on client and community needs.[5] Hence, premature narrowing of a problem can be, in large part, affected by how the organization perceives its own set of boundaries.

Another restricting factor occurs when a premature solution is built into the problem statement.[6] Defining the problem as, "Where should we build the new building needed to handle more clients?," is narrow and presupposes a solution (new building) to the problem of inadequately serving all clients. Compare this with the question, "How can we serve the increased demand from clients?" If the group leaps too quickly to define the problem as, "Where do we get money to hire additional staff during the peak client demand period?," then this would likely be a narrower view than, "How do we obtain urgently needed short-term staff resources?," which opens up such options as dollar-a-year volunteers, lend-lease staff from industry, or providing staff with incentives for taking vacations at nonpeak periods.

Both the organization's mission and the premature inclusion of a solution in the problem statement can serve to inappropriately delimit the problem.

Table 1-2. PROBLEM IDENTIFICATION WORKSHEET

	INCREASING AND DANGEROUS LEVELS OF AIR POLLUTION	DECLINE IN THE QUALITY OF EDUCATION	SUBSTANDARD HOUSING	INCREASE IN THE NUMBER OF GAS STATIONS	INCREASE IN TAVERNS
What is the problem?					
Where does the problem exist?	In Ward 36 Tremont area City of Cleveland	In the Amherst Elementary School District	In the census tract 18 area of the City of Cleveland	In the census tract 12 area of the City of Cleveland	In the Union area
Who is affected by the problem?	1,000 residents residing in this geographical area	500 pupils attending these schools	Approximately 100 homes are considered to be substandard quality	200 area families living in this area	1,200 citizens of this community
When does the problem occur?	Increasing problem in the past 2 years	Identified as a problem in 1976, but probably existed before 1976	Housing standards have continued to decline over the past 10 years	Increases have occurred in the last 4 years	Increases in the past 2 years

Table 1-2 (cont'd.)

To what degree/extent is the problem felt?	Air pollution levels have increased by 75%	Low rating on national academic scores	75% increase in homes designated as substandard in the area by city housing inspectors	An increase of 4 gas stations in the area	100% increase (3 additional taverns)
Problem statement	In the past 2 years the air pollution level has increased 75% in the Ward 36 Tremont area of the City of Cleveland affecting 1,000 residents.	A decline in the quality of education for 500 pupils in the Amherst Elementary School District is evidenced by low ratings on national academic scores.	A continued decline in housing in the census tract 18 area of the City of Cleveland is evidenced by a 75% (75 homes) increase in the number of homes designated as substandard dwellings by the city.	An increase of 4 gas stations in the census tract 12 area of the City of Cleveland in the last 4 years has become an increasing concern for the 200 area families.	Residents in the Union area are concerned about 3 new taverns in the past 2 years.

Clarifying Organizational Viewpoints

Different people will have different perspectives on the problem or issue. Before a problem can be dealt with intelligently, these perspectives must be expressed and a decision made as to which aspect of the problem will be given attention.[7] Organizational affiliation and roles will be one major way perspectives of a problem are influenced.

Situation: A group of people have been called together to discuss "the day care issue." These are day care providers representing sponsors from social agencies, owners of proprietary (for profit) organizations, parents, and the human service agency that pays for day care for low-income persons. After 3 hours of discussion, the following perspectives are distilled from the meeting:

Parents:	The problem is that a parent is not able to distinguish the quality of one day care center from another.
Social Agency Sponsor:	The problem is that the human service agency is threatening to cut back the daily rate paid on behalf of low-income parents, thereby affecting the quality of service.
Proprietary Agency:	The problem is that the human service agency is not willing to pay additional money for clients on our waiting lists.
Human Service Agency:	The problem is that we cannot adequately distinguish between the high-cost agency and a low-cost one, both of which meet basic standards. Should we pay more money per day for fewer children served (and perhaps get higher quality service) or pay less money per day for more children (but then perhaps lower the overall quality)?

Rarely does each party to the discussion articulate its perspective as explicitly as is described here—unless each subgroup is specifically asked to express its view of the problem beginning with the sentence, "The problem is. . . ." This selection of the particular perspective is crucial because it will affect potential remedies. If the parents' perspective is selected, for instance, then the group might develop a checklist for parents. If, however, the human service agency's perspective is chosen, then an approach would be to develop an evaluation instrument that attempts to compare one agency with another for determining funding rates. Until these different perspectives of the problem are articulated and clarified and a conscious decision made on which one will be given concentrated attention, the group decision process will flounder. As a particular perspective on the problem develops, those with different viewpoints will have to decide whether or not to "buy in" to the problem as it is eventually defined.

Another factor influencing problem perspective is the value orientation of the participants—what they consider to be important. In their deliberations, members of the organization should determine who feels that the problem exists. Who owns the problem? The answers will invariably indicate that certain significant people or groups do (or do not) perceive "the problem" to be a problem. Who sees day care centers as being insufficient? Welfare grants as being too low? Board of trustees and staff as having a poor relationship? In other words, from whose perspective is the problem seen as a problem? If those people who should be seeing the problem do not do so, then this perspective will affect how the problem will eventually be described.

Identifying Key Factors

As stated earlier, because any given community problem is likely to have many contributing factors, members of an organization can benefit from reviewing all the possible factors that could affect it. Suppose, for example, an organization develops the following problem statement: In our community approximately 150 abused or neglected children who suffer physical and emotional damage are identified each month.

Below are listed some factors considered as contributing to the problem:

(1)   Parents lack parenting knowledge and skills.
(2)   Parents have severe emotional problems.
(3)   Parents do not know where to seek help.
(4)   Parents feel socially isolated.
(5)   Insufficient foster homes exist to permit temporary placement.
(6)   The agency is unable to provide sufficient staff to work with parents.
(7)   Staff is inadequately trained to work with emotionally needy parents.
(8)   Parents have inadequate financial resources.
(9)   Parents have unrealistic expectations of children.

Examining Factors

Following the listing of factors (in the example above a dozen more factors probably could be identified), the next step is to examine them to determine which are more crucial than others and which might more easily be affected by the organization. Here a sorting out process needs to take place. Some factors may contribute to other factors, e.g., lack of knowledge about normal growth and development leads to unrealistic expectations about a child's behavior. Some factors may not be directly related to the organization's mission, e.g., inadequacy of financial resources. Some factors reside in the target population, e.g., parents have emotional problems, whereas other factors may reside in the organization, e.g., lack of staff training. A group considering these various factors would explore their meanings and relationships by combining some with others and omitting duplicates.

Selecting the Factor(s)

The difficult decision now needs to be made as to where the organization can have an impact. In making the selection, an organization sets boundaries on those aspects of the problem with which it will deal. As a consequence of the review of multiple contributing factors, the organization becomes aware that whatever its selection, certain parts of the problem may not be addressed. In the example of abused children, if the most pressing factor identified is the lack of foster homes and an agency decides to devote energies to this factor, ignoring for the time being the others, it runs the risk of not solving the problem completely but only ameliorating it (see Chap. 6, Avoiding Traps of the Problem-Solving Process).

Narrowing the Problem Focus

The danger of narrowing a general problem area too soon, thus resulting in prematurely selecting a solution, was discussed previously. Also the reality that different people will bring different perspectives that can influence problem selection was discussed. But once the general problem area is determined, it is essential to begin sorting it into specific problems that can be dealt with by the group and analyzing those factors that contribute to the problem.[8] An analysis of the general problem area, specific problems, and contributing factors is illustrated in Figure 1–1.

Suppose for example, a community committee is composed of volunteer leaders and foster care staff that is concerned about the lack of foster homes, which has been identified as one of several factors related to abused children. Obviously, even this factor is too broad, so the group begins to analyze the general problem and determines that specific problems include the following: (1) insufficient foster homes resulting in monthly waiting lists, (2) insufficient

Figure 1-1. ANALYZING THE PROBLEM

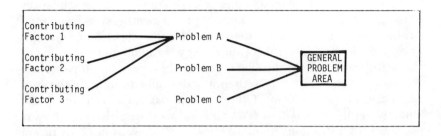

staff to handle large caseloads, (3) payments to foster parents that have not been increased in 5 years despite inflation, and (4) concern by current foster parents about how to handle problem situations. Each of these specific problems has in turn contributing factors that affect the problem and on which the community committee may wish to concentrate its efforts. The community committee identifies limited public information about foster care, insufficient follow-up on those who do make inquiries, and inadequate orientation for those interested in foster care as being related to the problem of insufficient foster homes. The breakdown of the problem analysis, in part, would look like Figure 1–2.

For the moment, the community committee has decided to concentrate on insufficient foster homes and the attending contributing factors. In time, it could concentrate on one or more of the other specific problem categories.

Figure 1-2. FOSTER CARE PROBLEM ANALYSIS

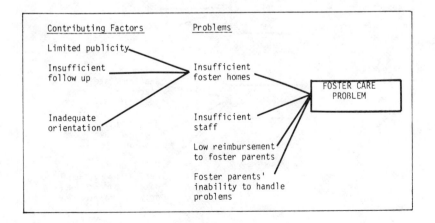

Expressing the Consequences of the Problem

Sometimes a problem statement clearly conveys the consequences of the problem, but often it does not. If group members are developing problem statements only for their own use, then describing consequences may not be necessary, for they have a common understanding of the significance of the problem. But if they need to convey their problem statement to others, then it is desirable to indicate the consequences of the problem.[9] Otherwise the risk is run of being asked what the significance is of such statements as, "More girls who run away are put into institutions than are boys," or "There is not a sufficient number of day care centers," or "The board of trustees and the staff have different ideas about how to run the agency."

In the problem analysis phase, consequences are defined as unfavorable conditions the organization wants changed. Just as there are likely to be several contributing factors affecting a general problem, so there may be a number of consequences that emerge from the problem, as illustrated in Figure 1–3.

By identifying one or more specific problems and their contributing factors on the one hand and their consequences on the other, the organization is now able to make explicit the target for its efforts to change conditions. It knows precisely what it wants changed. By articulating consequences, the group will know later (after it has carried out its action plan) to what extent it has been on target in resolving the

Figure 1-3.   CONSEQUENCES OF THE PROBLEM

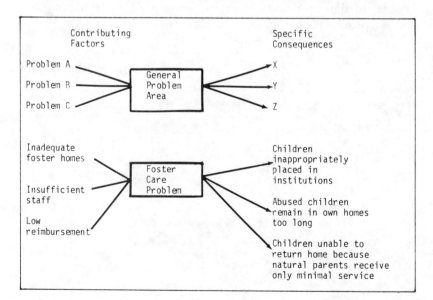

precise problem. In the problem illustrations provided earlier, a community organization would document in its analysis, for example, the consequences of substandard housing or increased gas stations. As Figure 3 shows, if an organization has elected to concentrate on the insufficiency of foster homes because of the consequences of children being placed in institutions or remaining in abusing home situations too long, then it is now prepared to establish objectives and consider action plans designed to deal with these consequences. Later the organization can or will be able to evaluate to what extent its efforts resulted in a reduction of these specific unfavorable conditions.

DETERMINING PROBLEM PRIORITIES

Because most organizations have limited time, energy, and money, an organization must purposefully select which problems and contributing factors it will concentrate on and which ones it wishes to postpone. The organization must select priorities (first things) for focused attention. Since it is unlikely that an organization will be able to give equal attention to all problems, it should explicitly identify posteriorities (last things), i.e., those problems which it will ignore for the present by placing them at the bottom of a list. Of course, at some later time those specific problems initially put aside may become priorities.

By establishing priorities, the organization is faced with a dilemma. On the one hand, by establishing boundaries around its area of concentration, it can focus its resources so as to assure potential resolution. It avoids spreading itself too thin in diverting its members and staff from doing so many things that none of them are done well. It concentrates on the few critical issues or problems on which it can have an impact. In the illustration on foster homes, the organization might elect to concentrate only on the need for more foster homes because to try to campaign for increased per diem rates and training for foster parents at the same time could result in its not being able to deal effectively with its priority problem. After it successfully concentrates its energies and resources (sometimes called the *critical mass*) on one problem, it can then move on to other issues. Indeed, an organization may purposefully establish a sequence or phasing process as it moves from one aspect of the major problem to another.

On the other hand, by limiting the priority focus to only one of several problems, the organization may not be able to fully resolve the general problem because of the cumulative effect of specific problems. Problems are so often intertwined that unless they are all dealt with, only limited success can be anticipated. In our example, unless the foster care reimbursement rate is raised, staff are increased, foster parents are given tangible support, and counseling is given to natural parents, concentrating efforts to recruit more foster parents may not be sufficient to cope adequately with the broad problem. Similarly, a program designed to deal with teenage unemployment may not prove successful unless simultaneous attention is given to the school system from which a constant stream of new school dropouts is emerging.

There is no easy, simple answer to the dilemma of whether to concentrate on one problem at a time or all problems together. But the problem analysis will help the organization to be clear and purposeful about what aspect of the overall problem it is, or should be, addressing. With this realistic appraisal, the organization can determine to what extent it will likely affect the problem, and this in turn will prevent it from overselling the potential impact of its project.

AN APPROACH TO PROBLEM SELECTION

The selection of a problem priority can occur informally through group consensus or, under some circumstances, by the organizational leadership (see Chap. 3 and 4 on consensus and continuum in decision making). When, however, an organization wants to determine systematically its priorities, then it may wish to undertake a formal ranking process. This formal ranking can be used to determine priorities among several major problem areas (e.g., day care, foster care, employment, housing) and also to select specific problem categories within a general problem area. For example, within the general foster care problem should the organization select insufficient foster homes, low reimbursement rate, or lack of staff training?

The organization can determine its priorities by undertaking a preliminary review of two elements: (1) importance of the problem, and (2) potential for success.[10] At this point in the problem identification and selection process, the organization may be undertaking a preliminary, and perhaps even a superficial, review of the array of problems it could consider. It is preferable that an organization, confronted with a number of problem issues, would conduct an in-depth analysis of each one before determining its priorities. In reality, organizations do not generally have the resources or the patience to conduct an intensive review of each of several problems before determining which one to concentrate on. Since at this stage the organization's decision is tentative, it should be prepared, based on new information, to reconsider its priorities later. (See Chap. 7 for more discussion on feasibility of undertaking a course of action.)

The following suggested basic criteria can assist an organization in determining priorities:

Importance of the Problem:

Number of people affected by the problem
Importance of a solution to the survival or enhancement of the organization
Significance of the problem to those served by the organization
Impact of the problem on the community

Potential for Success:

Anticipated commitment of organization members
Potential support of other organizations
Availability of resources: staff, volunteer time, funding
Availability of technical knowledge
Popularity of the issue in the community
Potential support of the media

Depending on the particular problem(s) under consideration, the organization may want to modify the criteria. Most organizations will tend to concentrate their preliminary decisions about the selection of priority problems based on the *importance* element. Equal attention should be paid to the *potential for success* element, however, for this deals with the issue of feasibility. Organization members may determine that it is highly desirable to work on a problem, but the feasibility of doing so may be quite limited. Conversely, an organization may determine that the possibility of success may be high for a problem that is not important enough to merit the organization's effort. Some might argue that excessive concern with feasibility will cause the organization to continue what it has always done and to be cautious about taking risks. Others in the organization might stress that with limited resources, the organization must focus on those problems it has the best chance of succeeding with. In their deliberations members will have to determine the balance of the *importance* and *success* elements in deciding where to devote their efforts.

Members of the group should be asked to rank each problem from 1 to 10, with 1 being the lowest and 10 the highest for both the *importance* and *potential for success* elements. Individual scores are than tallied to give an aggregate group score on each of the elements. Shown in Table 1–3. are the results of one organization's rankings. Note that some issues (education and housing) on the final priority ranking do not correspond with the numerical outcomes.

Because highly subjective and intangible factors are being dealt with, the results of adding the *importance* number and the *success* number would result in a tentative priority ranking. The ranking process should only be used as a tool in the decision process, and decisions

Table 1-3. RANKING THE PROBLEM

Problems	IMPORTANCE Member Scores		POTENTIAL FOR SUCCESS Member Scores		TOTAL	RANKING
	A B C D E F G H I		A B C D E F G H I			
(1) Air pollution	9 8 6 7 8 8 10 9	7 = 72	7 9 10 8 8 8 6 5	7 = 68	140	(1)
(2) Education	6 5 4 4 4 6 4 5	4 = 42	6 7 5 9 6 6 4 7	4 = 54	96	(3)
(3) Housing	6 7 5 8 4 4 6 5	5 = 50	3 5 4 4 6 5 6 4	5 = 42	92	(2)
(4) Foster care	3 5 4 6 1 1 5 2	3 = 30	3 2 5 2 4 1 5 4	3 = 29	59	(5)
(5) Increased number of taverns	5 6 4 7 2 2 5 4	4 = 39	4 5 4 6 1 2 3 3	5 = 33	72	(4)

should not be made mechanically. After all, numbers represent preliminary guesses, and therefore the result of adding one factor to another gives only a rough estimate of which problems should be selected. After reviewing the outcomes of the scores, the organization may decide not to use the numerical ratings in determining the final priority rankings. The hypothetical organization illustrated in the chart chose to override the numerical ratings, after further discussion, by selecting housing as a second rather than a third priority.

It is possible, of course, to conduct this process of ranking problems on the basis of *importance of problem* and *potential for success* without quantifying the elements as we have described. Indeed, because the process is somewhat mechanistic, individuals may be reluctant to use numerical ratings. This reluctance is understandable, but the technique can make explicit the ingredients that should be considered, especially when the organization is limited in its ability to address several problems at the same time. The technique also disciplines the organization to consider quite early in the decision process not only the desirability of dealing with a problem, but also the feasibility of doing so.

Summary

A social or community problem is defined by an organization as a deviation between what should be and what actually is. Typically, members of an organization experience an uneasiness or discomfort with a situation and this is expressed as a general problem statement. Usually this is a vague and ambiguous position requiring further revision and refinement. The process of developing a greater in-depth analysis of the problem involves the following: (1) defining or clarifying abstract, vague terms; (2) being aware of whether the problem statement is too restrictive because of the mission of the organization or because the problem prematurely focuses on a solution; (3) under-standing how different people or groups might have different pers-pectives; (4) narrowing the problem focus by selecting within a broad problem area specific contributing factors; (5) articulating consequ-ences of the problem so that impact can later be assessed; and (6) ranking problems for priority consideration.

Diagnosing and formulating problems is a dynamic process. New information and new circumstances may require redefinition and re-finement of the problem. What may start out as a broadly defined problem may later be narrowed or vice versa. New or different re-sources may stimulate the organization to take directions different from those originally intended. Thus, as the organization enters into other stages of the problem-solving process it must be prepared to make conscious changes in its problem focus.

Chapter 2

SETTING OBJECTIVES

ORGANIZATIONAL PURPOSE, GOALS, AND OBJECTIVES

Once a problem is selected and defined it should be possible to set objectives that are statements of what the group intends to accomplish. The yardstick for success then becomes the extent to which an organization accomplishes its objectives. By setting objectives that are related to a problem, the organization can later assess whether it was fully or partially successful or a failure in resolving the problem. Before discussing objectives in detail, the differences between organizational purpose, goals, and objectives will be highlighted.

The organizational purpose is the general mission, the reason for being, of the organization. It usually remains unchanged and is general enough to cover all aspects of the organization. An example is, "The general purpose is to increase the human services to people of the community."

Organizational goals represent broad statements of what the organization wants to accomplish. Goals provide a general direction for commitment to action. They are global descriptions of a long-term condition toward which the organization's efforts will be directed. Goals are ideals, they are timeless—and they are rarely achieved. Examples of goals' statements are the following:

"reduce crime in the community,"

"upgrade housing,"

"improve interracial relations,"

"provide information to low-income clients,"

"prevent teenage illegitimate births,"

"eliminate child abuse and neglect."

It can be seen that goals, while perhaps inspiring members of an organization to strive for ideals, are unamenable to clear definition and measurement.

Objectives, in contrast to goals, represent relevant, attainable, measurable, and time-limited ends to be achieved. They are relevant because they fit within the general mission and goals of the organization and because they relate to problems identified by the group; they are attainable because they are capable of being realized; they are measurable because achievement is hopefully based upon tangible, concrete, and quantifiable results; and they are time limited because the organization specifies the time frame within which results can be achieved. Objectives provide the clear-cut targets for organizational accountability.

THE RELATIONSHIP OF AN OBJECTIVE TO A PROBLEM STATEMENT

Earlier it was observed that objectives are related to problems. Note these differences between a problem statement and an objective:

(1)   The problem statement expresses a situation in negative terms; something is wrong. An objective states a desirable situation to be achieved. It is intended to correct the problem.

(2)   The problem statement can reflect a larger condition than will normally be achieved by an objective; an objective is related to realistic, achievable accomplishments, which may mean that the problem is not entirely eliminated.

Examples of the distinction between problems and objectives follow:

(1) *Community Situation:*

The problem is 100 deteriorated homes.
The objective is that 30 homes will be rehabilitated in 1 year.

(2) *Organizational Situation:*

The problem is that 20 paraprofessionals are not performing at the expected job performance level.
The objective is that (after special training) 15 paraprofessionals will conduct the expected number of outreach interviews.

DIFFERENT KINDS OF OBJECTIVES

Three kinds of objectives—operating, process or activity, and impact objectives—are used by community organizations:[1]

(1) *Operating objectives* convey the intent to improve the general operation of the organization. Examples include the following:

to sponsor four in-service training workshops in the next 3 months for 40 staff,
to obtain a pilot project grant of $10,000 within 4 months,
to increase the size of the membership by 150 within the coming year,
to reduce staff turnover from 20% annually to 10%.

Operating objectives are essential because they enhance the way the organization functions. They are a means to the end for which the organization was established: providing in-service training, obtaining a special grant, or increasing membership are interim steps to help an organization achieve results.

(2) *Activity objectives* (sometimes called process or production objectives) indicate the organization's counting of activities provided or services rendered. Examples include the following:

to serve 300 clients in the program year,
to conduct 680 interviews,
to provide 17 neighborhood assemblies.

What the organization actually accomplishes in the way of activity objectives (e.g., actually serving 273 clients) is called its *output.*

Impact objectives specify outcomes to be achieved as a result of program activities. Whereas activity objectives reflect the amount of effort to be expended, impact objectives detail the return expected on the investment of time, personnel, and resources. Impact objectives focus on results. Examples include the following:

to place 20 adoptable children in adoptive homes,
to increase the number of foster children reunited with their
natural parents from 40 to 50.

Actual results of impact objectives (e.g., placement of 17 children)
are referred to as *organizational outcomes*. Because impact objectives
are the most difficult to delineate, their formulation will be described
in more detail.

FORMULATING IMPACT OBJECTIVES

General Criteria

While considerable flexibility can be used to prepare impact objective statements, the following criteria are suggested:

(1) Generally use a strong verb that describes an observable
    change in a condition. "To reduce," "to improve," "to
    strengthen," and "to enhance" are examples.

(2) State only one aim with one specific result. An objective
    which states two aims may require two different imple-
    mentations, and confusion could later occur about which of
    the two objectives was achieved. "To reduce the recidivism
    rate by 10% and obtain employment for 20 former delin-
    quents" is an example of an objective with two aims.[2]

(3) Be certain that the objective is realistic. Do not, for example,
    promise to reduce significantly illegitimate teenage preg-
    nancies through a program designed to work with 100
    youngsters in a community which experiences 5,000 illegiti-
    mate births a year.

(4) Be clear about the difference between activity and impact
    objectives, as highlighted below:

Activity objective:	to provide training to 100 unemployed persons
Impact objective:	to obtain jobs for 40 out of 100 persons trained
Activity objective:	to provide counseling to 200 alcoholic people
Impact objective:	to resolve the drinking problems of 80 of the 150 persons seen in three or more interviews

Standards of Performance

Standards of performance are the criteria used to assess the success (or failure) of the organization in meeting its objectives. Without such standards, fuzzy, meaningless abstractions will result. If, for example, the objective is, "To improve police/community relationships," how would it be known at the end of the year whether, and to what extent, the objective has been achieved? Two kinds of standards of performance can be used to document achievement:

> (1) *Standards determined in advance* are criteria that answer the question, "How will we know when we have achieved our objective?" In the following objective statements, the italicized phrases show the predetermined standard indicators:

to insure in the next program year that *90% of those children placed in foster homes remain in the same home or are returned to their parents,*

to insure that in the next year *80% of the children will experience only one day care mother,*

to increase in the next year *group homes for the elderly by eight homes in the Forest Heights community,*

to reduce the *waiting list for day care openings from 250 to 200* in the next year.

Each of these objectives has a clear indication of whether or not success is achieved. Usually this will reflect a measurable amount of change.

(2) *Performance standards not predetermined* are expressed in abstract terms that will require further definition and exploration. When it is initially difficult to specify objectives in concrete terms or estimate expected results (either because of lack of experience or because the technology of measurement is undeveloped), then objectives can be formulated by defining major characteristics. For each term used in the objective statement, a concrete and observable performance indicator can be specified. That is, abstract terms are made operational even though performance standards are not preestablished. The following is an example of this process of working to define abstract terms:

> The objective is to provide *adequate* and *humane* social services to 2,000 residents of the community. *Adequate* is defined as the number of people accepted for service compared to the number

turned down, the length of waiting period, the number of clients indicating travel to the program, and the hours of the program. *Humane* is defined as the number of people who express satisfaction/dissatisfaction with the way they were treated.[3]

Such ambiguous and fuzzy words and phrases as "acceptable," "adequate," "appropriate," "as soon as possible," should be avoided, or, if used, then they should be defined.

PREPARING OBJECTIVE STATEMENTS

To attain precision in the preparation of objective statements, it is helpful to break down the major elements of most impact objective statements into the desired situation (what), the target population (who), the degree of change (extent), and the time frame (when).

WHAT: The desired situation or condition to be attained, the factors to be changed. Example: reduction in truancy rate.

WHO: The target population to be served (it is helpful to distinguish target population from total need or risk population). Example: Out of 800 projected exoffenders released in the coming year, the program will be geared to an expected target population of 70, of whom 45 actually will experience an impact by being helped to obtain jobs.

To clarify the distinction of the various populations, consider Figure 2–1.

Figure 2-1. POPULATIONS: RISK, TARGET, AND IMPACT

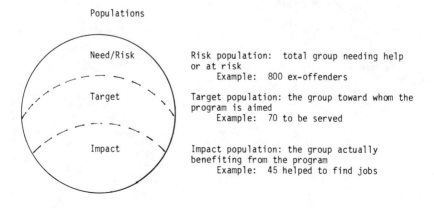

Populations

Risk population: total group needing help or at risk
    Example: 800 ex-offenders

Target population: the group toward whom the program is aimed
    Example: 70 to be served

Impact population: the group actually benefiting from the program
    Example: 45 helped to find jobs

The value of making distinctions between impact, target, and risk populations is that this will provide a clear perspective on the extent to which the organization will be making a dent in the overall community problem. Of course, in some instances an organization may not have accurate information on the total risk population, e.g., the number of families needing day care.

EXTENT: The degree of change to be achieved. This can involve the number or percent of the target population expected to achieve the intended outcome (impact population). Example:

Seventy percent of the target population will show improvement in their relationship with their children.

Eighty percent will express satisfaction with the program.

WHEN: The time frame in which the objective is to be achieved. Example: within 1 year.

The format of Table 2–1 gives examples of objectives with predetermined standards.[4]

The written objective statements would be as follows:

to decrease *delinquency* (defined as acts judged to be delinquent by a juvenile court judge) by 50% in 1 program year;

to increase the number of voter registrations in *inner city neighbor-*

Table 2-1. FORMAT FOR MEASURABLE OBJECTIVES-EXAMPLES OF PREDETERMINED STANDARDS

DESIRED SITUATION	TARGET POPULATION	EXTENT OF CHANGE	TIME FRAME	MEASUREMENT INDICATORS
Decrease delinquency	50 high school dropouts	50%	1 program year	Court decisions
Increase the number of voter registrations	Inner city neighborhoods	Between 700 and 850	3 months	Specified wards
Improve school performance	First offenders	50% of the cases served	1 program year	Teacher evaluations
Improve personal adjustment	Ex-mental hospital patients	75% of the cases served	1 program year	Psychological tests

hoods (defined as wards 3, 7, 8, and 10) by between 700 and 850 in 3 months;

to improve *school performance* (as indicated by teacher evaluations) of first offenders in 50% of the cases served in 1 program year;

to improve *personal adjustment* (as determined by specially constructed psychological tests) of ex-mental hospital patients in 75% of those served during 1 program year.

It is important that the organization be clear and precise about defining whatever abstract terms it uses in an objective statement. To aid in this precision, it is helpful to define fuzzy or abstract terms in as concrete a manner as possible. In the objective statements written above, measurement indicators of abstract terms are shown in the parentheses.

Measuring Change

As noted previously, impact objective statements should begin with a verb that expresses a change in a situation (e.g., to increase or reduce . . .). This is intended to identify something to be achieved. Ideally, this emphasis on striving for change should be included in objective statements which have a basis for comparing planned change against actual accomplishment. But sometimes precise performance standards are not possible because the organization has not had previous experience in documenting change. It would then express an objective statement without reference to a standard to be achieved, as illustrated below:

to increase school attendance rates of delinquents,

to rehabilitate as many homes as possible.

It is understandable that an organization embarking on a new program and with only limited experience in recording results would be reluctant to specify targets for change in advance. The organization may fear the risk of making a guess that could later be questioned by its members or a funding body. Moreover, it may fear that each year there will be the expectation that it reach perpetually higher levels of achievement. (Example: If a community housing organization rehabilitates 7 houses this year, then next year it will have to rehabilitate 10 houses.) Realistically, an organization may achieve a plateau of success. It is suggested that when it is not possible to determine precise performance standards in advance or when an organization has reached a plateau, the organization should include in its objective statement a *zone of success* or reasonable range it hopes to achieve. (Example: to rehabilitate 7 to 10 homes.) This preserves the advantage of having objectives that contain targets to be achieved and yet permits the organization some flexibility. Deviations from the range would then invite special organizational review.[5] To be meaningful, then, objectives should be both realistically achievable and have sufficient stretch that they inspire organization members to achieve at their highest performance level.

Substituting Activity Objectives for Impact Objectives

Under some circumstances an organization may not be able to develop impact objective statements because the state of the art is insufficiently developed or because it lacks the ability to adequately and accurately measure results. Under these circumstances, organizations may have to resort to using *subjectives* to indicate their intended accomplishments. *Subjectives* are defined as statements of intended accomplishments that cannot be documented directly. Instead, organizations may use verifiable activities that, if accomplished, would lead logically to impact objectives.[6] The organization must make explicit how it sees the accomplishment logically flowing from the performance of activities. Thus, the *subjective* statement, "to improve interracial relations," may be presumed to occur with the publication of newsletters and weekly community meetings. Similarly, the statement, "the provision of homemaker services," may be presumed to achieve the nonverifiable objective of preventing older people from going into nursing homes or being hospitalized. The group should articulate the underlying assumptions to show how the implementation of the activities is related to intended results.

Reporting Results

For most objective statements involving populations served by a program, it is possible to identify the degree of change in terms of percentages. That is, a comparison can be made between the impact population that benefited from the program as compared to the target population that experienced the program. This comparison can be expressed in ratio format, with the impact group in the numerator and the target group in the denominator.[7] In reviewing and working with a variety of agencies and programs, the following four possible kinds of measurement indicators expressed in ratios have been identified:

(1) *Improvement of total number of program participants*	*Impact*
Total number of program participants	Target
Example: *In a vocational program, the total number of persons becoming employed*	*Impact*
Total number completing job training	Target
(2) *Average number of episodes, rate, or score of participants at time #2*	*Impact*
Average number of episodes, rate, or score of participants at time #1	Target
Example: *Average annual arrest rate on felony and drug charges at time #2*	*Impact*
Average annual arrest rate on felony and drug charges at time #1	Target
(3) *Total number of persons who maintain their progress or who avoid regression*	*Impact*
Total number who evidence progress initially or who participate in the program	Target
Example: *Number of persons able to maintain adequate nutrition rating 1 year after enrollment*	*Impact*
Number who complete special education program Example: *Number of elderly persons who maintain independent living*	Target *Impact*
Total number of persons seen by homemakers	Target
(4) *Total number of consumers who rate service as satisfactory*	*Impact*
Total number of consumer responses	Target
Example: *Total number who rate counseling services as meeting their needs*	*Impact*
Total responses to the survey	Target

The advantage of using a ratio is that quantitative results can be translated into percentages for easier review and analysis. As can be seen from the examples shown above, the particular ratio used to document achievement of objectives should be based on its relevance to the particular situation. (For more detail on reporting results, see Chap. 11.)

SOME COMMON QUESTIONS ABOUT SETTING OBJECTIVES

The previous section highlighted the preparation of impact objectives for two reasons. They are what human service organizations are primarily in business for: to produce change in the clients or the community. And they are more difficult to document than are operating or activity objectives.

Frequently organizations lose sight of impact objectives as they concentrate on activity and organizational objectives. So it is strongly urged that organization members keep the setting of impact objectives in the foreground. At the same time, it is understood that members have a number of concerns that are not limited to impact objectives alone. Based on the author's teaching and consultation experiences, some commonly asked questions about all three types of objectives can be identified:

(1) Q: How broadly or narrowly should objectives be written? For example, suppose funding for a transportation program for elderly persons has been eliminated. Should the objective be to obtain funding or to develop other ways of improving older persons' access to social services?

   A: The determination of objectives should flow from an analysis of the problem and how broadly or narrowly it has been defined. If the organization has defined the problem as how to increase access to services (of which transportation is one approach), the objective can be written more broadly than if the problem focus was on transportation alone. Hence, it is essential that the group conduct a problem analysis before setting objectives.

(2) Q: Should achievement of objectives be the sole basis on which to assess whether an organization should receive additional funding from its funding source?

   A: The review of accomplishment of objectives should not be used to reward for success or punish for failure for two reasons. First, organizations will tend to select data that reflect positively on them and ignore information that does not show them in a positive light, if their funding depends on this information. Second, without an experimental design, it is difficult to be certain that the program intervention was the main reason for improvement in the situation. The primary value of reviewing objectives is for the organization's internal review. This review of accomplishments works best when those responsible for the program are self-motivated, because internal motivation enhances self-appraisal and self-control and eventually leads to self-corrective action.[8] It can, of course, have limited use for funders as long as they are aware of inherent limitations.

(3)   Q: Should the organization devote considerable time in determining whether every objective should be labeled as *impact, activity,* or *operating?*

       A: The distinction has been made to assist in understanding the objective-setting process and to foster greater interest in impact objectives. The bias reflected in these pages is that, in general, accomplishments of operating and activity objectives are not sufficient indicators of the success of most community organizations. But if the labeling process results in lengthy debates and immobilizes members of a group, preventing them from setting any objectives, then the process has become self-defeating. The group must determine when the objective-setting process (intended as a tool, not as an end in itself) interferes with, rather than enhances, the problem-solving process. The group should have a clear rationale for the selection of its objectives.

(4)   Q: Many organizations, though concerned about their impact on their clients and the community, are faced with internal problems requiring resolution. How should this be dealt with?

       A: The principles involved in setting objectives are the same regardless of whether the group is dealing with impact or operating objectives. For example, a voluntary organization is concerned with the lack of communication between the board of trustees and the staff. The objective could be stated as, "To increase communication between board and staff so that by the end of the year staff members would have had an opportunity to report to the board on their activities." At the end of the year, the organization can review the extent to which it has achieved what it set out to do.

(5)   Q: Organizations may be well intentioned in wanting to set objectives, but somehow do not manage to do so. Why?

A: Many reasons can account for an organization not being able to set objectives and track its achievement. One of the most significant resistances is that members will be held accountable for results. This accountability can be threatening—unless members see that accounting for the achievement of objectives offers the organization an opportunity to evaluate progress and take corrective actions. To insure an investment in the objective-setting process, those accountable for achieving objectives should be involved in setting them.

(6) Q: Is there a logical way of relating goals with objectives and activity and organizational objectives with impact objectives?

A: Often, but not always, this is possible to convey, as illustrated below:

> Goal: To improve foster care services
>
> Impact Objective: To decrease the number of children waiting each month for a foster home from an average of 150 to 170 to an average of 100 to 120
>
> Activity Objective: To conduct a recruitment campaign that will increase the pool of prospective foster parents from 10 to 50
>
> Operating Objective: To convince the county commissioners to hire two additional staff to recruit foster parents

As can be seen from this illustration, some objectives can become a means to other objectives. These can be designated as *feeder* or *interim* objectives because they help in the achievement of the major impact objective. The advantage of keeping the logical relationships in mind is to make explicit that the achievement of an interim activity objective is not an end in itself, but a means to an end.

(7) Q: Can the achievement of some objectives interfere with the achievement of others?

A: Yes. It is quite possible that objectives can compete and even conflict with each other. For example, the objective statement, "To improve recording of staff accomplishments," may actually reduce the effectiveness of the agency's services, as staff devote more time to documenting their services, thereby giving less time to serving clients. Another example, "To reduce organizational costs," may result in not achieving the objective of serving more people, since part of the cost reduction may affect public information about the organization.   Hence, organizations need to weigh the consequences of achieving various objectives.

(8) Q: Should an organization work on several objectives at the same time?

   A: For any given problem situation, an organization may decide to have multiple objectives. In establishing the goal, "To improve quality of foster homes," an organization might set the following objectives:

   > to increase foster parent understanding of children's needs by providing training to 60% of all new foster parents within 1 year,
   >
   > to reduce the number of foster home replacements by 30% in the coming year by more actively dealing with foster parents' concerns,
   >
   > to increase availability of staff contact time with parents from an average of one time per month to twice per month.

   All of these objectives are desirable, but faced with limited resources, an organization may have to choose whether it can undertake all of them simultaneously or defer some until a later time. It might even abandon some objectives because, as desirable as they may be, the organization has neither the current capability nor the likely potential of obtaining resources to undertake them. Hence, it may have to determine priorities for its objectives.

(9) Q: Is it possible that an organization may become so invested in establishing an objective and then later recording its achievement that members lose sight of more fundamental considerations?

   A: If, as described earlier, an organization establishes an objective to increase the number of foster homes, and then concentrates its resources on foster home recruitment, it may in fact obtain more foster homes. But before the organization becomes too self-congratulatory, it should determine whether the achievement of this objective sufficiently deals with the problem. Suppose, for example, the targeted number of foster homes are obtained, but they are of poor quality. Or suppose that despite the increase in foster homes, the pool of abused and neglected children continues to grow. Thus, though an organization must strive to achieve its objectives, it should not be blinded to other fundamental issues. (For a more detailed discussion of evaluating the achievement of objectives, see Chap. 11.)

Summary

In summary, the following steps should be considered in preparing objective statements:

(1)   Relate the objective to the problem with which the organization is concerned.
(2)   Distinguish between goals and objectives.
(3)   Distinguish between three major objectives: operating, activity, and impact objectives.
(4)   Establish impact objectives in concrete, quantifiable terms.
(5)   Develop indicators of performance that specify the following elements: the situation to be changed, the target population, the level of change expected, and the time frame.
(6)   Report results using a ratio or percentage format that relates impact to target populations.
(7)   Compare actual with projected results to determine degree of success.

Chapter 3

DECISION MAKING IN ORGANIZATIONS

Functions, Structures, and Participants

Usually problem solving in community organizations occurs within some kind of group process. Although occasionally individuals may grapple with a problem and make a decision to expedite action, typically a task group is involved because it has special advantages. Through group participation, members increase their identification with the goals of the organization, become motivated to implement plans they helped to develop, pool their expertise and wisdom, divide up their responsibilities, and develop their leadership potential.[1]

While task groups can be highly effective, they can also have serious drawbacks. The idea that a camel is a horse put together by a committee is familiar to anyone who has spent long, frustrating hours in ineffectual group processes. If task groups operate under impossible constraints, if they are badly led and have ineffectual procedures, if they are composed of inappropriate people or too many people, and if they have little power to implement their ideas, then the group process will deteriorate. Indeed, task groups can spend considerable time on trivial matters, develop imprecise plans, and permit responsibility to be diffused.[2] Task groups should not be formed when one person can do the job, when the tasks are beyond participants' capabilities, and when situations require speedy action.

The purpose of this chapter is to identify ways task groups examine functions, structures, and participants involved in the problem-solving process.

FUNCTIONS OF TASK GROUPS OR COMMITTEES

For purposes of this discussion, the term *task group* is used synonymously with *committee,* since usually the main purpose of a committee is to accomplish some task or function. The most common functions of committees are the following:

Studying the problem: Committee members or staff undertake to precisely analyze a problem.

Reporting information: Individuals or subcommittees provide the necessary intelligence that later may become the basis for decision making. Reports can include facts gathered or studies conducted.

Coordinating: Several groups work on the same issue and need to develop ways to complement their efforts.

Distributing work: Assignments must be clarified and distributed to group members.

Solving problems: The group identifies a problem and considers several alternatives.

Making decisions: The group makes a decision or recommendation from among alternatives. Those making a decision may or may not be the same as those identifying the problem.

Ratifying decisions: The leader or manager proposes a decision and the group is asked to sanction it. Many large organizations which have several committees use their boards of trustees primarily as ratifying bodies.

Monitoring: The group reviews progress toward resolving the problem.[3]

A committee can be established to undertake only one of these primary functions, but most carry more than one, although not necessarily at the same time. That is, a committee may study a problem, then gather facts, then decide on recommendations, following which it will implement action and monitor results. It is important that the group be aware of its primary function(s).

COMMITTEE STRUCTURES

The form that an organizational group takes should follow its function.[4] The questions to be asked initially are: "What is the group's basic purpose?" "What objectives are to be achieved?" Following this, the form or structure can be developed. Decision-making structures can take several forms.

Executive committees usually consist of officers of a board of trustees and other specially selected persons who act in emergencies or conduct specified decisions as designated by their board, such as budget decisions. Usually an executive committee acts in the interim between board meetings. The bylaws of the organization specify composition and role of the executive committee.

Standing committees are permanent bodies that implement the group's program and business. Standing committees meet regularly to decide upon recurrent situations. Examples would include finance, program, personnel, and membership committees.

Special committees or ad hoc ("for this case only") groups are appointed to consider particular issues. They fill a temporary need and are dissolved when their work is finished. Special committees might be designated in the following ways:

Study groups are intended to examine an issue and make recommendations.

Task forces are intended to accomplish a certain action within a specified time period.

Work groups are intended to develop a plan for implementation by the organization.

Joint committees are groups consisting of members from other committees or organizations who work together on a joint project of interest to their respective parent organizations.[5]

COMMITTEE MEMBERSHIP

Because who the members are will influence how effective the group will be, attention should be paid to their selection, their personal satisfaction, and the use of their time.

Selection of Members

Chairpersons and committee members should be selected purposefully on the basis of the kind of results intended. If, for example, it is anticipated that a committee report will encounter resistance from a board of trustees, then careful attention should be given to selecting committee members who are creditable to the board. If it is desired that a community institution be challenged, then people who are inclined toward advocacy should be selected. If an eventual outcome requires acceptance by a professional organization, then highly respected professionals should be placed on the committee. If funding recommendations are likely to occur, then those with knowledge about funding sources and procedures should be chosen. If a controversial issue is likely to arouse organizational divisiveness, then those representing different viewpoints should be purposely selected to work out their differences. If it is important to have representatives from key constituencies, then members should be chosen on the basis of their affiliations, such as unions, business, or university. If the group is likely to deal with complex issues, then the selection would be made to combine highly creative thinkers who can start with fresh and original ideas with those who have had experience and knowledge in dealing with the problem.

Of course, it is not always possible to be certain of the anticipated outcomes of the committee process, and therefore people may be selected who will make limited (or negative) contributions. But careful assessment of the mission and potential projects of a proposed committee generally are good indicators of the desired characteristics of potential members. The selection process may be time consuming, but it is time well spent.

Membership Needs

People's motives for participating in community organizations will vary: Some become involved because they think it will give them status, others because they hope it will provide social relationships, and others because they anticipate it will provide them with power. Most, presumably, participate because they want to make a contribution to the community and at the same time experience some personal growth. They want to work on problems they are concerned about. They also want to feel a sense of pride in achieving something meaningful for the community. Because of this common need for members to feel that they are working on significant and achievable projects, previous chapters on problem definition and on setting objectives stressed identifying problems that lend themselves to success and determining doable objectives.

Initially, a committee may not function as a group working toward common objectives, but as individuals oriented to their own special concerns. This self-oriented behavior can take various forms. Some want to use the group to satisfy their need for control and influence. They may resort to excessive arguing, ridicule, and/or hostile humor— under the guise of intellectual debate. Others seek acceptance from other members and the chairperson and may passively acquiesce to decisions. And others may develop a wait-and-see attitude, avoiding an investment until they see whether the group is responding to their interests. Every group goes through a testing process of growing pains in which members determine whether to form into a cohesive unit or remain a collection of individuals. Hopefully, the sense of common purpose and growing trust helps members transcend their individual orientation and allows them to work on mutual concerns.[6]

Use of Time

It is often said that if an important job is to be done, one should ask a person who is already busy to do it. Usually, highly competent people in community work are already actively participating on some project. Those who are likely to make contributions to the organization are under time constraints—some may already be overextended and "overcommitteed." The following are some suggestions designed to make the best use of their valuable time:

(1)   Reading material, including minutes of meetings, should, if possible, be sent out in advance of meetings.
(2)   Meetings should be time limited. An ending time of a meeting should be set, to be violated only under extraordinary circumstances. Usually, meetings should last no longer than 1½ to 2 hours. If the meeting is extended beyond the normal limit, the group runs the risk of people quietly leaving and feeling annoyed that their departure prevents them from participating in significant decisions.
When it is important that a meeting be concluded by a specified time, the following "timed agenda format" could be observed:
(a)   Members of the group agree on an ending time.
(b)   Those who have agenda items state them to the group. The chairperson and the group determine the length of time to be devoted to each item.
(c)   Someone in the group is designated as timer. That person announces when time is to be concluded and the next item is to begin.
(d)   Under exceptional circumstances the group could agree to extend the time period of one item by subtracting time from another item.

(3)   To keep meetings on target, the chairperson should establish ground rules that distracting and irrelevant ideas will be
avoided so that the main business of the group can be
conducted within agreed upon time limits.

(4)   Not all of those who have something to offer to a group
need to be members of a committee. Some people with
special contributions (e.g., fiscal or legal expertise) can serve
as advisors or consultants, without necessarily becoming
ongoing members. They can be individually interviewed, or
they can be invited to participate on a time-limited basis in
group deliberations.

(5)   Meetings should be called only when it is essential that the
group come together to deal with important matters. Some
people will attend meetings because they feel obligated to
do so or because they enjoy social contacts or the prestige of
the group. But most are not likely to attend meetings unless
they have a strong sense of urgency that their contributions
are needed. Meetings in which the predominant style is
reporting by a few to the rest of the passive audience will
result in declining attendance. For people who are busy,
meetings should offer opportunities to grapple with problems or actively make decisions.

At times, groups may have a special need to meet for an extended
period to review complex or highly charged issues. The determination
of whether this extra time demand is a problem for busy people should
be discussed with them.

ROLE OF THE CHAIRPERSON

Committees require that tasks be accomplished within a context of
good social relations. For committee members to sustain their commitment they must feel they are moving successfully to accomplish their
tasks within an atmosphere of good interpersonal relationships. The
chairperson plays a crucial part in helping the group achieve optimal
functioning in regards to both relationships and tasks accomplishment.

Dealing with Conflict

Though good relationships do not necessarily guarantee that tasks
will get done, when people become preoccupied with their own concerns, they become unable to give to the group. A chairperson must

therefore be concerned with how to minimize the tendency for relationships to become deteriorated and how to repair those that are damaged.

Conflict between members is a significant factor in the breakdown of group relationships. In all community organizations, conflict is inevitable as individuals and groups compete for influence or resources.[7] Moreover, people have differences about values, priorities, and goals, giving rise to pressure groups, rivalries, contests, and personality clashes. The task of the chairperson (and other leaders of the group) is to blend these differences into a coherent whole. As one author put it, a group is like a car equipped with an accelerator, clutch, and brake; operate them simultaneously and to their limit and there will be a lot of noise and no movement. Coordinate them and manage their interactions and progress will be achieved.[8] The chairperson, then, faces the challenge of resolving problems of competing forces so that the organization can move forward—this is the politics of an organization.

To carry out this necessary political process, the chairperson needs to distinguish between productive and disruptive conflict. Productive conflict in the form of argument and competition can benefit the group because members are stimulated to come up with creative ideas and willingly invest of themselves. The chairperson understands that through the clash of ideas, positions become sharpened, facts are obtained, and proposed methods are clarified. Establishing the ground rule that members must actively listen to other viewpoints, the chairperson encourages debate and avoids premature consensus (see Chap. 4). The chairperson has to discern at what point the clash of positions requires harmonizing. Sometimes it is necessary to let the argument continue until the contesting parties work out their differences so as to avoid arriving at a compromise that is not acceptable to anyone. At other times the disagreement becomes so destructive that a compromise must be worked out.

Competition for the scarce resources of the organization, too, if kept within bounds, can be constructive. It can serve to channel energies and establish higher standards. When resources are limited, each unit of the organization is compelled to make its best case to establish a track record that invites confidence and to win the support of other units within the organization for its position or project. But if competition results in either increasing the power of one group at the expense of others, or in enhancing self-aggrandizement of certain individuals or subgroups, then the group is likely to experience destructive hostilities, jealousies, interpersonal friction, and low morale. The organization becomes a battleground, and task accomplishment is of secondary importance. Sensing destructive competition, the chairperson should work to keep the competing forces within boundaries by insuring consistent ground rules for making decisions, by exploring ways in which different parties can have a sense of winning, and by working to reconcile divergent interests.[9]

Beyond normal and sometimes constructive debates and competition, other forms of conflict, if not given concentrated attention by the group and the chairperson, can result in serious breakdown of cooperation. Destructive fighting often occurs over boundaries. Usually in boundary disputes, one group is perceived by another as encroaching on its territory or sphere of influence. Refusal to cooperate is an attempt to deter this perceived encroachment.[10] Such disputes can occur within professional organizations as one unit resents the intrusion of another in its area or within voluntary organizations when two committees compete over who takes responsibility for a particular issue. In such situations two avenues are open for action by the organization's leadership: (1) clarifying respective roles and responsibilities of the disputing parties or (2) developing a coordinating mechanism (e.g., joint committees) or coalitions.

Of even more serious concern are conflicts over principle and ideology. One faction in a neighborhood organization wants primarily to provide services; the other faction wants to be involved in community politics. One faction in a mental retardation citizens' group wants to work on a cooperative relationship with the state department; the other faction wants to embarrass state officials. These major ideological differences are latent in all organizations; but they can turn into full blown schisms when ambitious leaders of one or the other faction intensify feelings or when the organization is at a crossroad of having to make a choice between opposing ideologies.

The chairperson can neither ignore these battles, nor take sides without jeopardizing the leadership role. The only recourse is to seek a genuine compromise between the two opposing parties, based on a synthesis of the positions. Any other approach risks the organization's future, if only because ideological disputes arouse passions all out of proportion to the practical interests involved. Hence, the chairperson must work to bring the factions together, force them to work out a mutually acceptable compromise, and then strongly support that compromise.[11]

Moving the Group Forward

If a community committee is to make progress, a strong chairperson is essential. Just as it is important to carefully select members of the group, so the chairperson's selection should be well thought out. An effective chairperson coordinates, molds, and applies the thinking of individual members to group decision making. The following functions reflect proper leadership roles of the chairperson:[12]

Formulates or Agrees to a Previously Formulated Purpose of the Committee   Before a committee is formed, its mission or *charge to the committee* should be developed, preferably by the parent organization to which the committee is accountable. Usually the chairperson is appointed by the parent organization and participates in the formulation of the charge. Included in the charge to the committee are the expected results and time period within which it will operate. Occasionally, the parent organization may have only a general idea of a committee charge, in which case the committee develops its own charge, subject to approval. An example of a committee charge is as follows: "The charge of a housing task force is to determine if a housing office for the elderly is needed in the community. If the committee determines the housing office is desirable, then it will examine the following:

> whether the service should be located in one place or in several,
> what the functions of the housing office should be,
> sources of financing,
> anticipated costs,
> sponsorship,
> how it is to function.

The committee should provide a preliminary report in 3 months to the board."

Prepares the Meeting's Agenda   Through a written agenda all members know what topics have to be covered. If many topics have to be covered within a designated time period, the chairperson may wish to obtain the group's approval of a time schedule of items. The agenda should distinguish information reports from decision-making items.

Insures That Issues are Thoroughly Studied   Members cannot be expected to intelligently decide on issues without adequate knowledge and assurance that the matter has been thoroughly analyzed. The chairperson is therefore responsible for seeing that appropriate information is transmitted to members.

Helps the Group Clarify Ground Rules   If at all possible, the chairperson should open the first meeting with a discussion of what the intended outcomes are, what roles are expected of members, and what ground rules are to be observed. Before beginning to work on a problem, group members should consider how they will be working together as a group. Among questions to be considered at the initial meeting(s) are the following: Are we each committed to working on the issue or undertaking? Can we give the time necessary to accomplish the work? How is the work to be distributed? The first meeting should begin to make explicit the extent to which people believe strongly enough in the problem or project to tackle it. At the initial session(s) the chairperson helps clarify the demands likely to be made on group members, so that those who feel they cannot make the required investment have an opportunity to withdraw—and those who decide to remain agree to a contract, in effect, to fulfill obligations of committee membership.

Defines Specific Tasks to Members   The assignment should include when tasks would be accomplished. It is preferred that the delegation of tasks not be done in an arbitrary manner but involve the commitment of the members in undertaking their assignments.

Adheres to the Agenda   Since members will often stray from the subject under discussion, the chairperson must tactfully but firmly keep meetings from going off track.

Encourages Open and Free Discussion   To gain commitment from members, the chairperson invites different viewpoints, paraphrases them to make certain the group is aware of these differing views, and encourages participants to listen to each other. In this open atmosphere, all ideas are deemed worthy of consideration. By using questioning techniques (discussed in the next chapter), the chairperson draws out and controls the flow of discussion.

Summarizes Ideas at Different Points in the Discussion   The chairperson reviews which points the group has already covered and what different ideas have been stated so that as decision points are reached the group is operating with full information. By synthesizing different views, the chairperson draws out tentative generalizations and themes leading to a possible consensus.

Moves the Group to Closure on an Issue.   Following full debate and evaluation of proposals before the group, the chairperson helps the group to make a decision. The chairperson asks, "Are we ready to decide?" or "We have identified three possibilities—which do you prefer?" As discussed previously, if a compromise is necessary, the chairperson works with opposing factions to arrive at a reconciliation, being careful not to arrive at a premature consensus.

Keeps Good Human Relations Paramount   The chairperson gives credit to people who have proposed good ideas and acknowledges when people have performed an assignment well. While the chairperson may express a personal opinion, this position is not used to manipulate issues or members.

The chairperson does not try to manipulate the group with a hidden agenda, for members quickly catch on that they are being used. If the chairperson is not sincere in problem solving and is merely trying to sell a conclusion, members will resent being used as a "rubber stamp."

Occasionally, the chairperson may wish to ask group members whether they are satisfied with the way meetings are progressing and ascertain from them suggestions for improving how meetings are run.

Seeks to revitalize the group   The chairperson is aware of the natural tendency of most organizations to wind down. Typically, when an organization begins a project members conscientiously attend meetings. But if the project is long-term, members tend to lose interest or be diverted to other efforts. The chairperson attempts to offset the tendency of members to become stale by encouraging the influx of new people, rotation of assignments, and consideration of new ideas. All groups benefit from these kinds of revitalization processes.

CONTINUUM OF DECISION MAKING

The determination of who makes decisions, leader or group, is based upon several factors: (1) the leader's (manager's) preferred style of operating, (2) the nature of the organization, (3) the problem being worked on, and (4) the group members' preferred style of functioning. The term *contingency theory* has been developed to express the idea that there is no one approach to decision making—it all depends on the people involved and the context in which the decision has to be made.[13] For example, a local welfare agency involved in routine distribution of food stamps based on formal rules developed by state or federal government would function differently in its decision-making pattern than members of a research team. Decision making in the welfare agency would be greatly constrained by regulations promulgated by legislative mandates; the research team might function in a collegial style because of few constraints from administrative heads. Hence, the group and the leader will develop a decision-making approach that is appropriate to the organization, the task, and the people involved.

It is usually possible to identify a continuum of influence in relation to the leader (chairperson or manager) and the group.[14] At one end of the continuum the leader exerts considerable control and at the

other end the leader follows the dictates of the group, as Figure 3–1 illustrates.

Briefly explained, the continuum consists of the following:

1. The leader reviews the problem, sets the objectives, considers the alternatives, and presents a decision to the group, which then carries out the decision.
2. The leader takes major responsibility for the problem analysis and then tries to overcome resistance by convincing members of the group of this position.
3. The leader has developed a proposal and then must respond to questions by the group to clarify the implications of the decision.
4. The leader presents a tentative position, but the group becomes involved in making modifications.
5. The leader presents the problem, hears solutions presented by the group, and then makes a decision. Although ideas are drawn from the group, the leader has the ultimate decision-making responsibility.
6. The leader defines the problem and sets limits (e.g., "We can spend a maximum of $2,000"). The group then reviews alternatives and decides on a solution.
7. The group makes decisions within organizational limits. Here the group identifies and diagnoses the problem, develops alternatives, and decides on solutions. The leader participates with no more authority than any other group member.
8. The group makes decisions and may even override the leader's wishes. The leader implements the group's decision.

Figure 3-1. CONTINUUM OF INFLUENCE

(1)	(2)	(3)	(4)
Leader makes decision; group accepts	Leader must convince group before gaining acceptance	Leader presents decision, but must respond to questions	Leader presents tentative decision, subject to change by group

(5)	(6)	(7)	(8)
Leader presents problem and, after input from group, makes decision	Leader defines limits within which group makes decision	Leader and group jointly make decisions within organizational constraints	Group makes decision and leader implements

Clearly, at one end of the continuum the group has limited discretion while at the other end, members' concerns and discretion are paramount.

Several points should be made about this continuum of decision making. First, it is important that the leader and group be clear about the degree of decision making actually being given to the group. If group members feel that they have the power to make decisions, only to have them subsequently overridden by the leader, they will become resentful about the so-called democratic process. The leader and the group should understand *who* can decide *what*.

Second, how the decision-making process gets played out will depend on a number of interrelated factors: (1) the extent to which the leader is personally inclined to share in the problem-solving process with the group members; (2) the need as perceived by the leader and group members for group members to invest in the problem-solving process and their capacity to do so; (3) the traditions and norms of the organization in fostering participatory versus authoritarian decision making; (4) whether the nature of the problem is such that a group can significantly deal with it; and (5) whether there is sufficient time to permit a group decision process.

The more group members are involved in a decision-making process, the more likely it is that they will develop feelings of team work and cooperation, thereby increasing their motivation, commitment, and contribution to the group. This is why, generally, authoritarian leadership is not successful. Group members may have to take the initiative with an authoritarian leader to make explicit their concerns about leadership that is not consistent with their fully participating in the decisions of the organization.

STAFF ASSISTANCE TO COMMUNITY ORGANIZATIONS

Those community organizations that have staff available to assist in the decision-making process ideally work out a collaborative partnership. Volunteers and paid staff share common goals, determine mutual objectives, and complement each other in carrying out tasks.[15]

This ideal description may not always hold up in reality because tensions occur between staff and volunteers when roles are ambiguous, when one or the other perceives interference with their functioning, or when one takes on tasks that the other considers its responsibility. Tension will also occur when either volunteers or staff feel that the other is not appropriately assisting them in carrying out their role. When these problems take place, organizations will be hampered in their problem-solving capacity. Their energies become concentrated in the intramural battles rather than on the objectives for which they were established.

This discussion will briefly describe two major staff-volunteer relationships that can affect the problem-solving capacity of community organizations: an organization director's relationship with the board and staff relationships to committees.

Relationship of Executive to Board of Trustees

If properly involved, board members can contribute to the problem-solving capabilities of a community organization because they may offer needed expertise in technical areas, attract financial and other resources, know about the community and certain target groups, critically review organizational efforts, and represent the organization to the community.

A major problem affecting the problem-solving capability between the director of an organization and the board is confusion about roles and responsibilities. At one extreme, a board of trustees may be used by an executive to affirm decisions and policy staff have predetermined. Staff screen out important information, offer no options for decision making, use board meetings to report how well they are doing, and have the general expectation that the board will not challenge or question policies. Under this situation, the chairperson is usually weak and malleable. Decision making by the board is perfunctory as members are passive and uninvested. When the time comes to marshall support during a special crisis, members of the board are often unable to rise above their usual lethargy.

At the other extreme, a board may become excessively involved in day-to-day operations, make decisions about hiring and firing staff, and direct the executive on how to administer the organization's programs. As a consequence of this style, either the executive and the board will experience considerable tension if the executive attempts to preserve personal perogatives, or the executive is reduced to an ineffectual administrator.

It is outside the purview of this book to discuss in depth the general functioning of boards, but Table 3–1 can give some insight as to how the board/executive can complement each other to facilitate proper decision making in a community organization.[16]

To perform their responsibilities well, boards of trustees of community organizations require good staff backup. Staff working with boards should make certain that board members understand the organization's mission, participate in key decisions involving the setting of goals and objectives, assist board members in establishing priorities, and present options and alternatives for board action.[17] Then boards

Table 3-1. DIVISION OF RESPONSIBILITIES

	Board	Executive
Policy issues	Determines all major policies	Presents options (and indicates preferences)
		Implements decisions
Operations and programs	Determines general framework and procedures; may help in the design if members have expertise	Runs day-to-day operation Proposes programs
Fiscal matters	Approves budget Determines spending guidelines	Administers budget within guidelines
Staff	Sets general policy for hiring and firing Determines personnel policies	Hires and fires staff Authority and supervision over staff
Goals and objectives	Approves or vetoes	Recommends to the board
Evaluation of results	General responsibility for monitoring	Also responsible for monitoring

can become vitally involved in examining community problems and making decisions.

Relationship of Staff to Committees

Staff working with committees can assist in the following:

selecting qualified members to match potential assignments,
defining purposes and goals,
encouraging leadership skills of the chairperson,
carrying out assignments, including providing necessary background information, working with the chairperson to develop meeting agendas, preparing minutes, and drafting reports,
helping to relate to other community committees,
dividing assignments into manageable tasks.[18]

Two possible problems can occur in staff-committee relationships: staff members can do too much or too little. Because staff are sometimes more knowledgeable than volunteers and are working on the issues on a day-to-day basis, they may tend to take over the decision-making process. As one experienced community organizer has pointed out, community groups should be watchful of professional staff attempts to bypass members and to do work for them rather than with them.[19] A major responsibility of staff is to work with people to develop their own capabilities.

Staff can also do too little. Because volunteers generally do not have time for extensive research of community problems, data gathering responsibility often falls to staff. Moreover, the arduous task of writing committee reports is generally done by staff—with the understanding that committees will always have the prerogative of making revisions. Although not commonly done, staff reports to committees can be made more useful if options are identified with consequences delineated for each option. This spelling out of possible alternatives can help focus and sharpen committee decision making.

Staff Roles in Working with Committees

What are the most suitable role behaviors of staff working with community organizations? Obviously there is no one answer to this question because organizations, staff, and situations differ so greatly. An aggressive, advocacy role may be quite appropriate in one situation and counterproductive in another. To be effective, staff working with community groups must be conscious of their own styles and of the impact different approaches can have on the decision-making process.

Facilitative Style   As group facilitator, the staff nurtures the inherent capability of community members and encourages them to articulate their own ideas and actions. Staff take special pride in seeing volunteer members grow in their confidence to do things for themselves.

Entrepreneurial Style   Like the executive or entrepreneur who organizes and manages a business, staff functioning in the entrepreneurial style takes pride in originating program or project ideas and seeing that they are brought to fruition. Feeling a profound sense of ownership in the proposed project, staff works at influencing and persuading community volunteers to accept its ideas.

Advocacy style   To carry out this role, staff perceives the organization as the client, in much the same way as the attorney becomes the advocate for the client. Staff aggressively promotes the group's concerns.

Depending on the particular situation, staff will shift roles, becoming, at times, entrepreneur, facilitator, or advocate.

Chapter 4

FACILITATING THE DECISION-MAKING PROCESS

DECISION BY CONSENSUS

In the previous discussion of the chairperson's role, the term *consensus* was sometimes used. Consensus occurs after all members have had an opportunity to voice their opinions and can then arrive at a decision that almost everyone can support. The process of arriving at a consensus is a free and open exchange of ideas which continues until agreement has been reached. The process insures that each individual's concerns are heard and understood and that a sincere attempt is made to take them into consideration in searching for a resolution. This resolution may not reflect the exact wishes of each member, but since it does not violate the deep concerns of anyone, it can be agreed upon by all.[1]

Consensus, then, is a cooperative effort to find a sound solution acceptable to everyone. It is not a competitive struggle in which an unacceptable solution is forced on the losers. Usually, those initially expressing disagreement finally consent to go along with the prevailing viewpoint even though they may not fully endorse it. With consensus as the pattern of interaction, members need not fear being outsmarted or outmaneuvered. They can be frank and authentic in the decision-making process.

In some groups, decisions are not made unless there is a "Quaker consensus," i.e., decisions are not made if even *one* member of the group vetoes the action. Then either discussion continues until that one member acquiesces, or the group delays its action. Usually, however, complete unanimity of opinion is not absolutely essential and is rarely achieved.

Decision making by consensus works best when members of a group have established trust in each other. In such a climate, having disagreements is seen as a natural and acceptable means of searching for a range of opinions and ideas rather than as reflections of interpersonal hostility. Frequently through consensus a group will collectively arrive at better decisions than those individually arrived at by any one member.

Some suggestions for arriving at a consensus include the following:

> encouraging group members to listen to and try to understand viewpoints that may differ from their own;
>
> discouraging an "I win/you lose" mentality and encouraging a climate, especially when an impasse is reached, that allows everyone to come out ahead;
>
> encouraging people who disagree to continue hammering out their differences.

Groupthink—A Danger of Consensus

In some situations consensus occurs either because members want to avoid conflict or because they feel pressure to conform. Some feel that they must show group loyalty by agreeing with the group's position, even though they fear the consequences of the group's action. Called *groupthink*,[2] this arises when members strive to avoid what they fear will be harsh judgments of their peers; consequently, they adopt a soft line of criticism. Members give priority to being amiable as they seek concurrence even on issues where there may be fundamental differences.

Groupthink is most likely to occur in strongly cohesive groups where criticism is not the norm. Members suppress their deviant thoughts and may minimize, even to themselves, their own misgivings. As a result, the group develops the illusion of unanimity. One danger of groupthink is that when members are pressured to give in, the resulting diluted decision greatly weakens what might otherwise have been a strong stand, position, or program. Another danger is that unvoiced criticisms may result in decision making or action taking which might later prove to be detrimental because these are not supported (and may even be sabotaged) by group members.

Ways to prevent groupthink include the following:

Positions presented for consideration to the group by a subgroup should, if possible, include alternative choices.

Members should be encouraged to be devil's advocates to make sure positions are defensible from a variety of angles.

Discussions should be held with people who are not part of the deliberations, including knowledgeable people outside the organization.

Scenarios should be thought out about how different people would react to the ideas under discussion.

Members should be encouraged to express reservations.

The disadvantages of encouraging dissenting opinions before consensus is reached are that discussions can become divisive, prolonged, and inconclusive. When action is required during a crisis, such dissension may prove especially difficult to deal with. Organization leaders and members must weigh the trade-offs involved in fostering too quick a conformity on the one hand and an atmosphere that encourages provocative clashes on the other.

Using Questions to Facilitate Discussion

If group members feel that their ideas are wanted and that their thinking will contribute to a common group objective, then they are more likely to become involved in thinking about the problem and participating in its solution. One of the most useful techniques a chairperson can employ to enrich discussions is to ask pertinent questions. Although the chairperson is primarily responsible for directing the flow of ideas through questions, any member of the group may at times assume the role of questioner. Listed in Table 4–1. are types of facilitating questions, the rationale for using them, and examples of each.

DECISIONS THROUGH PARLIAMENTARY PROCEDURE

Parliamentary procedure is based on the democratic principle of majority rule, which requires that the minority abide by the will of the majority. In turn, the acceptance of majority rule by the minority is based on the willingness of the majority to permit the minority to

Table 4-1. FACILITATING QUESTIONS

TYPE	RATIONALE	EXAMPLES
Opening questions	To get the group started	"What do you think the problem is?" "What facts do we need before considering this problem?" "What is your experience in dealing with the problem?"
Information questions	To obtain facts or evoke opinions	Who, what, where, when, why, how...?
Leading questions	To suggest an answer within the question	"Given the nature of the problem, couldn't we do the following...?" "Is this the only solution worth considering?"
Justifying questions	To move members of the group to justify their reasoning and to challenge ideas	"Why do you think so?" "How will this solve the problem?" "How can we be sure it will work?"
Hypothetical questions	To introduce the chairperson's ideas into the discussion without having the idea attributed to the chairperson	"Suppose we try... what would happen?" "In another community they tried this approach. How do you think it would work here?"
Questions that consider alternatives	To compare two or more possible courses of action	"Which of these approaches do you consider the best?"
Clarification questions	To add understanding to the discussion To make general and abstract ideas more understandable To shift from small details and trivia to the core issue	"What do you mean by interorganizational relationships?" "Before discussing the details of the proposed program, shouldn't we decide what we want to accomplish?"
Questions that stimulate	To encourage new ideas from the group	"Are there any other ways we can deal with this problem?" "In addition to the 3 proposals already mentioned, what do you think about this idea?"

Table 4-1 (cont'd.)

Questions that promote participation	To stimulate people to present their ideas	"Could we hear from you who have not spoken?"
		"How do these ideas sound to the rest of you?"
		"Bill, could you give us your ideas?"
Questions that limit participation	To reduce the involvement of overactive participants	"Since not everyone has had a chance to speak, could you hold your comments until later?"
Questions that focus discussion	To help the group review where it is in the discussion	"Where do we go from here?"
		"Have we crystallized a position?"
Closure questions	To encourage the group to make a decision	"Have we spent enough time on this topic?"
		"Can we shift to another area of concern?"
		"Have we agreed upon the following?"
Evaluation questions	To help the group assess itself	"Why do you think we are blocked on this particular issue?"
		"Can anyone suggest how we can improve our discussion process?"

express its views before action is taken. Parliamentary procedure also assures that deliberations will proceed in an orderly fashion so that discussion can be crystallized into group action. Decisions must be made in the face of conflicting interests among members. For parliamentary procedure to work effectively, there must be a basic belief in the organization, despite major differences. Thus, parliamentary procedure provides the rules under which group discussion and group action can occur.

This section on parliamentary procedure is a digested version of one developed by O. Garfield Jones entitled *Parliamentary Procedure at a Glance*.[3] It is based on the assumption that, for most organizational meetings, exhaustive knowledge of parliamentary procedure is not necessary, but that an understanding of basic concepts can facilitate group discussions and action. Those interested in more extensive examination of parliamentary procedure should consult the basic, *Robert's Rules of Order*.[4]

For most organizations involved in making decisions about service and community problems, parliamentary procedure is not a preferred method because it is much too formal and intensifies adversarial, win/lose relationships. It tends to solidify opposing forces, to lower the losing faction's commitment to the decision (unless those in the minority have very strong investment in the organization), and to set in motion future competition over other issues. It also discourages exploration of innovative ideas in a free and open manner because people tend to take sides early in the discussion.[5] For organizations that require a formal way of conducting business or for large assemblies, the following pages should cover the salient points about parliamentary procedure.

Clarification of the Procedure of Motions

The main motion is the principal resolution that the organization is discussing. Because having more than one primary idea before the assembly at any one time would cause confusion, the main motion has the lowest rank or precedence. It can be moved only when there is nothing else before the group.

Table 4–2. ranks the most commonly made motions by order or precedence. Not that the main motion and the motion to repeal are ranked lowest on the chart. They yield to all the motions above them.

When a main motion is before the assembly, any motions above it may be moved. For example, motions may be made to amend the main motion, postpone consideration, close debate, rise for information, or to adjourn. These motions also take precedence over the main motion because they either apply to it, or, as in the case of the motion to adjourn, are of such urgency to the assembly that they must be voted on immediately regardless of what else is before the group.

It is possible, of course, to have many motions before the assembly at any one time, provided they are offered in the correct sequence. For example, if a main motion has been moved, then an amendment can be made to that motion. Also, a motion to postpone to a certain time, a motion to close debate, a motion to table, and, finally, a motion to adjourn can all be made. While technically this could happen, the chairperson and the majority may be concerned that this is a result of manipulation by the opposition, and the chairperson may choose to ignore some of the motions until other motions before the assembly are voted upon. Of course, if members are dissatisfied with the chairperson's decision, they can appeal it.

Classification of Motions

Motions can be classified as follows:

1. *Privileged motions* are of such importance to the assembly that they must be acted upon immediately. They are undebatable be-

cause of their high rank. The reason the motion to adjourn is privileged is that in the event of an emergency it can be acted upon at once.

2.   *Incidental motions* are of two kinds: either they arise out of a pending motion and must be decided before any business is taken up or they are connected with that business of the assembly that must be attended to immediately. Most incidental motions are undebatable. Points of order, parliamentary inquiry, and requests for information do not require group action but are usually decided by the chairperson.

3.   *Subsidiary motions* are intended to affect the main motion by modifying it, delaying action on it, or otherwise disposing of it. They supercede the main motion and must be dealt with before the main motion.

4.   The *main motion* or question is the primary idea before the group. Often an idea will be presented to the group and discussion will take place before a motion is made. Sometimes this helps to identify and refine the main issue. But frequently this procedure results in unusually long meetings and a vague attempt at consensus. It is usually better for a motion to be made early in the discussion so that members have a specific, concrete proposal to which they can react. As was stated previously, there can only be one main motion before the group at any given time.

Discussion of Common Parliamentary Procedures

Common parliamentary procedures are discussed below.

Adjournment.   When the time for the next meeting has been determined (as is usually the case in most organizations), then the motion to adjourn can be moved at any time and must be voted upon at once because it is not debatable. If, however, no time has been set for the next meeting, then it is not a privileged motion, can be moved only when there is no other business before the group, and is debatable. In this circumstance, it yields to a motion to fix the time for the next meeting.

Question of Privilege.   Usually questions of privilege (not to be confused with privileged motions) are related to the rights and comforts of the group. Accordingly, they are given immediate consideration, regardless of what else is before the assembly. For example, a member may even interrupt another speaker to complain about the lack of proper ventilation or request visitors to leave because of the confidential nature of the discussion. The chairperson decides immediately whether or not the special privilege is to be granted.

Table 4-2. COMMONLY USED PARLIAMENTARY MOTIONS

Motion (Second Required?)	Example	Interrupt Member Who Has the Floor	Chair Must Recognize	Debatable	Vote
(1) Fix time of next meeting (Yes)	"I move that we adjourn until next Tuesday at 4:00 P.M."	No	Yes	No	Majority
(2) Adjourn (Yes)	"I move we adjourn."	No	Yes	Not when Privileged	Majority
(3) Question of privilege (No)	"I rise to a question of privilege to request that the visitors leave the room."	Yes, if necessary	No	No	Decided by the Chair
(4) Point of order/ Parliamentary inquiry/Request for information (No)	"The motion is out of order because there is already a main motion on the floor."	Yes	No	No	Decided by the Chair
(5) Appeal (Yes)	"I appeal the decision of the Chair."	Yes	No	No	Majority

Motion (Second Required?)	Example	Interrupt Member Who Has the Floor	Chair Must Recognize	Debatable	Vote
(6) Withdraw a motion (No)	"I desire to withdraw my motion." Chair: "If there is no objection, motion is withdrawn."	No	Yes	No	Majority if any members object to the withdrawal
(7) Motion to head count or ballot (No)	After a vote by sound, "I call for a vote by a show of hands (or by ballot)."	Not Applicable	Yes sounds close	No	
(8) Lay on the table (Yes)	"I move we table the main motion."	No	Yes	No	Majority
Take from the table (Yes)	"I move we take from the table...."	No	Yes	No	Majority
(9) Close debate (Yes)	"I move we close debate" or "I call for a previous question."	No	Yes	No	2/3 Majority
Limit debate (Yes)	"I move debate be limited to 5 minutes for each speaker."	No	Yes	No	2/3 Majority

Table 4-2 (cont'd.)

Motion (Second Required?)	Example	Interrupt Member Who Has the Floor	Chair Must Recognize	Debatable	Vote
(10) Postpone to a certain day (Yes)	"I move we postpone consideration of this motion until the next meeting."	No	Yes	Yes, only to proprietary of postponement	Majority
(11) Refer to committee (Yes)	"I move we refer this question to the Program Committee." (Note: can be amended; for example, size of committee and method of selection.)	No	Yes	Yes	Majority
(12) Amend (Yes)	"I move we amend by adding (or striking out, inserting) the words...." (Note: applies to main motion, limit debate, refer committee, fix time of next meeting, can be amended.)	No	Yes main motion, limit debate,	Yes	Majority

Motion (Second Required?)	Example	Interrupt Member Who Has the Floor	Chair Must Recognize	Debatable	Vote
(13) Main motion or question (Yes)	"I move we...."	No	Yes	Yes	Majority
Substitute motion	"I move as a substitute motion that we...." (Note: changes an entire sentence or paragraph; if adopted, it does away entirely with the original motion; it may be amended like any other motion.)				
(14) Rescind or Repeal (Yes)	"I move we repeal the motion that...." (Note: applies to main motions, appeals, and questions of privilege.)	No	Yes	Yes	Either 2/3 vote at one session or a majority vote in two successive sessions

Rise to a Point of Order   When a member believes the chairperson has made a mistake or a wrong decision, the member may rise to a point of order without waiting to be recognized by the chairperson. The member may even interrupt another member who has the floor. The chairperson then decides whether or not to accept the point of order.

Appeals   If any member is dissatisfied with the chairperson's decision, the member may rise and, without waiting to be recognized by the chairperson, appeal the decision to the assembly. This requires a second. The chairperson then states the reason for the decision and calls for a vote.

Out of Order   A motion is out of order when it is moved while a motion of higher precedence is pending. For example, after a motion is made to refer to committee, an amendment to the motion could not be considered. A person is out of order when speaking without being recognized by the chairperson. Remarks are out of order when they are insulting or not germane. The chairperson must explain the reason for the ruling.

Amendments   Amendments are designed to change the motion before it is finally voted upon. Sometimes amendments are intended to obstruct rather than facilitate business, or they may be well-meaning but absurd. Therefore, the chairperson may sometimes have to rule amendments out of order or help the member reformulate them.

Amendments can be made not only to change the main motion, but also to fix the time of the next meeting, to refer to committee, to postpone consideration to a certain day, and to the motion to limit debate. When amendments are made to these particular motions, they must be considered and voted upon before discussion of the motion to which they refer. Although in Table 4–2. amendments have low precedence, this is only for amendments to the main motion. Amendments to the other motions listed above take precedence in relation to the motion to which they refer. Hence, an amendment to fix the time of the next meeting must take precedence over all other motions.

An amendment made to another amendment has precedence over the original amendment. The first amendment is called the primary amendment; the second, the secondary amendment. For example, a motion is made to request a stop sign for a particular street corner. An amendment could be made to replace the stop sign with a caution light, an amendment to the amendment could be to replace the caution light with a stop light. The stop light would be discussed and voted upon first, then the caution light, then the stop sign. No more than two amendments are permitted, otherwise the deliberation becomes too complicated. If the two amendments are voted down by the assembly, then other amendments can be made. A member may alert the assembly of intentions to make an amendment if the two pending amendments are defeated.

Motion to Limit Debate   To prevent discussion from going on endlessly, a motion can be made to limit each speaker's time, to limit the number of speakers, to limit the overall time of debate, or to close debate at a set time and vote. These each require a two-thirds vote.

Motion to Table   A motion to lay on the table means to temporarily put aside one motion to consider another. A motion can then be made to take from the table either at the same or next meeting.

Withdrawal of a Motion   A motion may be withdrawn unless there is an objection by any member; in that case, withdrawal requires a majority vote.

Motion to Rescind (repeal)   Any member can move to rescind a motion. It requires a majority vote with previous notice or a two-thirds vote without notice. The motion to rescind reopens the whole question for discussion.

Substitute Motion   This is a motion of similar but different intent than the pending motion. Usually this involves changing an entire sentence or paragraph. If a substitute motion carries by majority vote, then the original main motion is now modified. The new substitute motion may be amended and voted upon in its entirety.

Unanimous Consent   Occasionally, suggestions are made which the chairperson determines do not require a vote by the assembly. For example, a request to close windows or a suggestion to make a slight correction in the wording of a motion could be accepted by the chairperson. The chairperson would say, "If there is no objection, then we will proceed with the discussion." Of course, an appeal could be made to challenge the chairperson's decision, in which case a formal vote would be put before the assembly.

Table 4–2 provides a list of the most commonly used parliamentary procedures.

PARLIASENSUS

The term *parliasensus* is not in the dictionary; it is a term coined to reflect the idea that meetings often combine parliamentary procedure and consensus. Generally, group decision making is informal and characterized by consensus, although a superficial form of parliamentary procedure is also used. Among the ingredients of parliasensus are the following:

1.   The chairperson encourages a free flow of ideas but, instead of remaining neutral, inserts personal opinions into the discussion. If the chairperson dominates the group, then discussion is likely to be stifled.

2.   Usually ideas evolve from an extended discussion. After the ideas begin to crystallize into a position, the chairperson entertains a motion.

3.   Amendments are made informally, e.g., "I suggest this modification. . . ."

4.   Group members speak to each other and interrupt with points or questions without being called upon by the chairperson.

5.   Sometimes votes are taken only after the group has appeared to have exhausted an idea; the chairperson senses when the group is ready for a vote.

In general, this hybrid approach works well for most organizations, particularly if the group is no larger than 15 to 20 persons. The natural inclination is to arrive at decisions through consensus, but the semblance of parliamentary procedure gives enough structure to expedite the group's business. Formal, though limited, parliamentary procedure is thus imposed upon informal discussion to control or expedite the traffic of ideas and actions. Most meetings could be facilitated if the major idea before the group could be made explicit as early in the discussion as possible.

RECORDING GROUP DISCUSSIONS

Because ideas can easily become lost in group discussions, it is wise to record them. During the course of the meeting large flip chart paper can be used. Following the meeting, either minutes or a group record can be prepared.

Writing down ideas that occur in the course of the meeting on flip chart paper (or newsprint easel pad) enables the group to keep track of the discussion. As each page is completed, it can be separated from the pad and hung up with tape. The advantage of this technique is that the group can (1) communicate many ideas at the same time; (2) visualize all the ideas at all times; (3) make changes in the wording of ideas; (4) easily determine gaps in, and overlap of, ideas; (5) focus, if the group wishes, on one idea at a time; and (6) prevent the same idea from being stated over and over again. These ideas recorded on the flip chart can be written up and transmitted to group members so they become part of the group memory.

Many groups have someone taking minutes as a way of preserving the ideas and actions agreed upon during the meeting. Then at the next meeting the chairperson insures that the minutes accurately reflect the essence of the session by providing an opportunity for corrections. Because the action of the group sometimes can be buried in the text, it is suggested that every group action be underlined for emphasis. Another way of highlighting actions taken by the group is to distinguish *discussion* from *action taken,* as shown below:

Discussion: Juvenile court staff expressed interest in developing a formal procedure process for mentally retarded offenders.

Action: Mental retardation staff agreed to prepare, in writing, procedures by April 15.

An alternative to minutes is the group record which is used when only one or two major topics are discussed.[6] It contains three sections:

(1)   the issue—how the group analyzed it and alternatives considered,
(2)   the decision of the group,
(3)   the tasks to be carried out, by whom, and within what time period.

Table 4–3 illustrates a group record format. The special advantage of this kind of recording is that it captures the essence of the meeting and pinpoints responsibilities for follow up, without requiring people to read extensive narrative.

Table 4-3. GROUP RECORD

NAME OF GROUP: Day Care Coalition   DATE: May 1

CHAIRPERSON: Nan Hare

PRESENT: Buce, Ander, Berg, Feran, Heim, Hustein

MEETING PURPOSE: To consider ways to pass legislation in the state assem-
                      bly on funding for day care for mentally and physically
                      handicapped children.

PROBLEM/ISSUE: Legislation on special needs day care is encountering
                      considerable resistance in the Human Resources Committee
                      of the House.

MAJOR POINTS
OF DISCUSSION: Major opposition appears to be those legislators who are
                      pressing to keep a lid on spending for human services.

                      General agreement was reached that committee members must
                      undertake a vigorous advocacy campaign between now and
                      June 5 when public hearings are held.

NEXT STEPS: Group to be divided into task forces.

Assignments	Responsible Person	By When
(1) Undertake letter writing campaign	Roz Buce	May 20
(2) Obtain editorial support of local papers	Alex Ander	May 25
(3) Have newspaper reporter write a human interest story	Rose N. Berg	May 28
(4) Have a busload of people appear before hearings	Joe Ferran	June 5
(5) Steering Committee to meet	Fred Heim	May 26

Chapter 5

GENERATING IDEAS THROUGH CREATIVE THINKING

In previous chapters problems that can be approached in a logical, step-by-step way were discussed. This logical method includes reviewing the problem, narrowing its definition, and examining its contributing factors. One author has described this commonly used approach as *vertical thinking:* planning is normally done sequentially as one proceeds step by step along a path.[1] Generally it makes good sense to tackle problems in such a rational fashion.

But sometimes the reasonable, rational, logical path leads nowhere, or organization members find themselves blocked. Many problems experienced in community organizations are not new; they have been around a long time and conventional solutions have not been adequate to affect them. The challenge is to view problems in a new way, thereby potentially arriving at new solutions. With creative thinking members hope to find new perspectives that may help them transcend stagnant approaches.[2]

To be sure, some people find it is easier to continue thinking in conventional ways and to go on doing things in the same manner as they did in the past, rather than considering what can be done differently. They complacently live with an apparent problem and are satisfied with the appearance, not necessarily the substance, of problem resolution. They are also satisfied with inbred ideas and with parochial thinking. Perhaps this complacent attitude that results in conventional ideas is understandable, for creative thinking is low-probability thinking. Creative ways of approaching problems require dealing with the unknown, the puzzling, the mysterious. And the chances of success are consequently limited.

Creative thinking is not confined to a few geniuses; anyone and any group is capable of being creative. It is true that some people have extraordinary talent that they use creatively. All of us, however, are capable of creative self-development, which can be manifested in anything we do.[3] When we prepare a meal differently, when we have a new insight, when we try a fresh approach at solving a problem, we are evidencing the creative process. In this chapter some of the basic attitudes and special techniques for encouraging creative problem solving will be described.

BASIC ATTITUDES TO ENCOURAGE CREATIVITY

Certain basic attitudes can greatly contribute to the creative process. One of these attitudes is dissatisfaction with the current state of affairs, with the status quo. Creative individuals function on the premise that nothing is fixed and anything can be doubted and challenged.[4] They question reasonable, rational approaches. They are also discontent with surface and superficial change, and they have a healthy skepticism about current answers, techniques, and approaches.

A second attitude contributing to creativity is the willingness to take risks. This is not easy, since most of us have been rewarded when we have succeeded and punished when we have failed. Past experiences have discouraged taking risks. When we produce or try to sell a creative idea, we are taking a risk of making a mistake. As Rollo May has observed, creative people experience a paradox. They must be fully committed to an idea, but at the same time live with the awareness that they may be wrong. Conviction and doubt can occur together. Consequently, it is realistic to be fearful of taking risks and of potentially being wrong.[5]

Certainly, being creative can result in taking a wrong step, but it may also set off ideas or produce an outlook which can lead to a solution that otherwise would not have occurred. Ideas that initially appear ridiculous may later stimulate sound ideas. Taking risks means putting oneself in the vulnerable position of being ridiculed and of experiencing doubt and uncertainty. It requires people who do not need to cling to the familiar, who are courageous, and who are accepting of their self-doubts.

A third creative attitude requires being willing and able to break out of the usual constraints operating in most problem situations. Often the solution is contained within predetermined boundaries. But these parameters could be either imaginary or self-induced, and the solution may be outside them.[6] For example, suppose a mental health agency is swamped with people requesting counseling. If a search for a solution requires being constrained by the current financial limitations, then the approach will be, "How can we live within our current state-financed budget, which means not hiring additional staff, and still provide services?" If, however, the budget constraint is put aside, then a solution may be explored through a different path: "How can we identify alternate sources of funding?" With this new line of thinking the agency and its supporters can now begin to explore other funding possibilities: raising money through charity drives, seeking a foundation grant, obtaining administrative waivers, or modifying the state budget bill. Hence, organizations always face the choice of living within both externally and self-imposed constraints or creatively finding ways to stretch the boundaries for possible solutions.

The fourth requisite for creativity is a willingness to be open to novel ideas without initially having any clear idea of where these ideas will be directed. Sometimes this is referred to as a *fishing expedition* where one throws out a line at several points before catching a good idea. At first, movement may be haphazard and then, in time, a pattern begins to form.[7] But until the pattern emerges and connections are made, the process may require creative people to pay a price of insecurity, hypersensitivity, defenselessness, and anxiety. They must be willing to tolerate ambiguity and uncertainty for a significant length of time and not seek closure or move to a solution too quickly. And they must be willing to pursue meaninglessness until they can force it to have meaning.[8]

In the course of such chaotic exploration, creativity is heightened by random intrusions of ideas and experiences, particularly from areas unrelated to the problem. Ways of carrying out conventional practices in one field become original and innovative when introduced in another.[9] Hence people searching for ideas seek experiences outside their own area to promote cross-fertilization. If, for example, an organization is concerned about improving the processing of client housing requests, members can become highly sensitized to other processing situations: airlines processing ticket holders, hospitals processing patients, supermarkets processing customers. Or if the organization is interested in promoting a human service tax levy increase to the public, its members will try to be open to other similar situations: TV commercials, political campaign strategies, use of polls, or mail order campaigns. During this period of fishing for ideas, some situations will, of course, prove more relevant than others.

To summarize, creative thinking requires several important attitudes: a dissatisfaction with the way things are which then stimulates a
search for new approaches, a willingness to take risks that results in
moving into uncharted waters, a desire to break away from the constraints of a problem and to stretch the boundaries to approach a
problem differently, and a willingness to be open to new ideas from
other fields and experiences. With these attitudes, creative problem
solving can result in thinking beyond the usual—thinking the unusual.

TECHNIQUES TO PROMOTE CREATIVE IDEAS

Two of the more effective techniques used in group processes to
foster creative thinking are brainstorming and nominal group technique.

Brainstorming

Brainstorming is a procedure that generates ideas and at the same
time suspends judgment and evaluation of them.[10] The group fosters
ideas through a process that initially limits censorship or criticism.
Judging the worth of ideas is deferred. The theory behind brainstorming is that if evaluation comes too early, then the number and quality of
formulated ideas will be limited. Group members should consider
using brainstorming when (1) conventional discussions are lacking in
fresh ideas or approaches; (2) individuals working separately need the
stimulation of other people's ideas; (3) a group has become so hypercri-
tical that ideas are being stifled; or (4) information needed for solving a
problem is scattered among different people. Brainstorming is not for
all problems; it works best for those that require idea finding rather
than judgment. The problem should lend itself to many alternative
solutions.

The group discussion format for brainstorming should be as follows:

1. Group members should have experience with or knowledge
    of the issue.
2. The size of the group should range from 6 to 15; beyond this
    size the group becomes too large for meaningful exchange.
3. The group leader should define the problem, stimulate
    ideas, prevent evaluative comments, keep the group on the
    subject, and end the discussion at the appropriate time
    (usually 15 to 30 minutes). A recorder should place all ideas
    on a board or on chart paper taped to the wall for easy
    viewing.

The ground rules for brainstorming are stated below:

1. Formulate a clearly stated and understood problem.
2. Defer all criticism and evaluation until a later time.
3. Stimulate as many ideas as possible—the more ideas gener-
    ated, the more likely original and fresh thinking will occur.
    "Crazy" ideas are encouraged. The group should be alerted
    to the likelihood that only a small percentage of the ideas will
    be finally accepted.
4. Encourage group members to build on others' ideas by im-
    proving or combining them in various ways.

Following the generating of ideas, a separate phase of idea evaluation should occur. The evaluation panel can consist of all of those
involved in the brainstroming session, some members and some
nonmembers of the brainstroming group, or a completely different
group of people. Those involved in the evaluation and selection of the
ideas should be people who will directly deal with the problem or will
be involved in implementing the ideas selected. Based on review, the
panel would rate ideas as immediately applicable, worthy of further
exploration, or not useful.

Nominal Group Technique (NGT)

The term *nominal group* means that it is a group in name only. The
major work effort occurs in the heads of individuals; those involved
have only minimal interaction. It can be used selectively when individual ideas can be merged into quality group decisions that are super-
ior to those made by each individual.[11] NGT is especially useful when
the group desires to do the following:

identify a list of problems, or
generate many solutions, or
establish priorities of either problems or solutions, and
insure that all members have opportunities to convey their ideas.

The reasons for constraining member interaction are based on the
following assumptions;

1. People are generally more comfortable in sharing only well-
    developed ideas, which means that potentially good but
    underdeveloped thoughts may not be transmitted in typical
    group discussions.
2. Every individual should be encouraged to take risks in pre-

senting ideas, but after the idea is presented it becomes the property of the group and not just of the individual presenting it.

3. Groups tend to be critical of ideas too quickly unless the ground rules foster an approach that every idea is worth considering.
4. Normally groups tend to focus prematurely on one idea without taking the time to examine a range of possibilities.
5. Members will more likely invest themselves in a later implementation process if they have had an opportunity to actively participate in an idea generating process.
6. More thoughtful and disciplined thinking is likely to occur in the group when members are required to think and write down their ideas before presenting them.

When the decision-making situation is complex and requires generating many ideas followed by the pooling of individual judgments, NGT should be considered. For routine meetings, where the focus is on information exchange and coordination or on one problem with limited solutions, other group methods, such as consensus or parliamentary procedure, are more appropriate.

The following procedures briefly summarize NGT:

Prior to the Discussion   Select groups of 6 to 10 members. Groups larger than 10 can be divided into subgroups. Although NGT can be conducted in larger groups (e.g., 15 to 20), this increases the complexity of the process, but it is still workable. Provide flip charts, since NGT meetings rely heavily on writing ideas in front of the group.

Orientation to Group Members   In emphasizing the importance of participation, the group leader explains the task or question under consideration as in the following illustrative remarks:

> Our mutual task is to generate a list of problem issues affecting the delivery of those day care services we want to work on this year.

> or

> Our task is to identify all the possible programs we can provide and then select the top three for our work agenda this year.

Silent Generation of Ideas in Writing   Group members are asked to write key ideas silently and independently. Their writing should be in short phrases. No discussion is permitted at this point except for very limited clarification of the process. Informal discussion, even among those who finish with the task early, is discouraged.

Round Robin Recording of Ideas   The group leader records all ideas on a flip chart. Each person around the table is asked for one idea at a time. This continues by going around the table several times until all ideas are recorded. The advantage of this approach is that each person is given the opportunity to express one or more ideas. By listing the entire array of ideas before discussion and voting, NGT insures that significant ideas will not be lost. Round robin listing will encourage a variety of ideas (similar to brainstorming). Also, with a long list, attention is on the ideas and not on those who initiated them.

Brief Discussion of Ideas   During the discussion phase, members have an opportunity to eliminate obvious duplications, clarify the meaning of ideas, and defend or argue against ideas. Preferably this is accomplished through serial discussion, i.e., taking one item at a time and asking for comments. NGT discourages lengthy debate on any one item since the purpose is to stimulate a variety of ideas, not to resolve differences of opinion. In this way all items are covered (although, some critics of this method may say, superficially). The NGT leader paces the group to avoid arguments and prevent an overemphasis of some ideas at the expense of others.

Preliminary Vote on Items of Importance   Suppose the group has generated 20 items. The group's task then is to arrive at a preliminary decision about four or five items the group considers most important. NGT requires that each member list those five items considered most important.

To reflect degrees of importance of each of the five items, NGT has evolved the following voting procedures:

Members are each given five 3 × 5 index cards.

They are asked to select the five (or some other number determined by the group) most important items and write one on each card.

In the upper right-hand corner of the card, members write the number that corresponds to the number on the flip chart to make recording easier (e.g., if item 13 on the chart is selected it would be so recorded on the card).

In the lower left-hand corner, members rank each item 5–1, with 5 being the highest priority.

The leader then collects the card, shuffles them to insure anonymity, and records the results on the chart which would look like Table 5–1.

Table 5–1 reveals that idea 6 is rated the highest; 13 next. As an alternative to writing their items on the five cards and then

Table 5-1.   <u>NOMINAL GROUP TECHNIQUE VOTE</u>

Item			Item		
1	-	3-2-3	11	-	1
2	-	2-3-3	12	-	
3	-	2	13	-	4-4-3
4	-		14	-	
5	-		15	-	1-1
6	-	5-4-5-5	16	-	
7	-		17	-	2-2-1-2
8	-		18	-	4-4
9	-		19	-	5-5-1-1-1
10	-	2-2-1-2	20	-	

collecting them for recording, an *olympic sports voting procedure,* which provides some anonymity but expedites the voting process, can be used. In this procedure each person is given three cards with the numbers 1, 2, or 3 written on them. As each item is called out by the leader, members hold up their cards (3 being the highest priority) and the tally is made on the master chart.

If anonymity is not essential, then an even simpler method for recording the vote can be used: Each person in the group selects five of the most important items and reads them off to the leader. These votes are recorded next to the 20 items and those that have the highest number of choices are selected. While this voting procedure is speedier and simpler than the others, it has the disadvantage of not reflecting the weighted preferences of the participants.

Discussion of Preliminary Vote   The vote is then discussed to examine inconsistent voting patterns (e.g., 5–5–1–1–1) and provide an opportunity to rediscuss items which are perceived as having too many or too few votes. This offers the chance for members to clarify their positions and assures that the split vote really reflects differences in judgment, not unequal information or misunderstanding. Discussion is not intended to pressure members to change their votes.

Final Vote   A final vote is taken to obtain closure to the meeting. At this point the group may need to make some arbitrary decisions. Should it select only the top three items or the top five? Should it select only those that have ratings of 4s and 5s? The group must set its own final ground rules for selection.

Aggregation of Several Nominal Groups   If several nominal groups are functioning at the same time on the same topic, then their separate votes need to be placed on a master list for final discussion and priority voting for the entire group.

The underlying approach of NGT is that through extensive individual participation many ideas will be generated, and through a group voting process the list can be narrowed to a few that will be acceptable. As with brainstorming, the initial priority list will undoubtedly require further evaluation and analysis. Creative ideas may later prove to be too difficult to implement or they may be superseded by new events. Hence, the results of NGT should be subject to further careful analysis.

ENCOURAGING NEW AND DIFFERENT IDEAS

In both brainstorming and nominal group technique people are encouraged to express ideas spontaneously. Ideas emerge and judgments about their worth are deferred. But sometimes a group is faced with a problem situation in which ideas do not flow easily; people feel they are at a dead end and they need stimulation to trigger creative thinking. Under these circumstances, several approaches—using analogies, employing a checklist, and reframing the issue—can be considered to promote novel ideas.

Simulating Novelty Through Analogies

Using analogies can help a group to view a problem in a new way. By making a comparison of a problem situation with something else that is in some way like it (and in other ways quite unlike it), one comes to see the problem from a different perspective. Through the use of analogies, familiar situations become strange because they are temporarily distorted.[12]

Personal analogies require empathy, i.e., putting oneself in the other person's place. The question to be asked is, "How would I react if I encountered a problem experienced by others?" By identifying oneself with a hypothetical person in a given situation, one is in a better position to understand how that person would feel and act.[13] Consider the following example: You want to convince resistive legislators to increase grants to ADC recipients. If you were in their shoes, what tactics and appeals would be most convincing? Among your answers might be receiving appeals from welfare constituents, from businesspersons whose businesses might be affected, and from concerned middle-class constituents.

Direct analogies involve the comparison of a particular situation with similar, but not exactly the same, situations. Previously, some examples of this approach were given in the discussion on being receptive to novel ideas, such as the idea that airline passenger processing is like client processing. Frequently analogous ideas occur to people spontaneously, but sometimes a group may wish to promote analogous thinking by asking members to consider comparable situations in other settings.[14]

If, for example, a group is considering how it could get more people involved in working on a community problem, members would be asked to think of a situation similar in nature. Someone might suggest looking at insects. Then members would be asked, "What insects do we see working together?" There might then be a discussion on how bees or ants work cooperatively with some further contemplation on what makes this possible, followed by an exploration of how this could be accomplished with people.

Or if a community organization is concerned with disharmony between two ethnic groups, the organization would be asked to consider what other situation is comparable from which solutions might be drawn. One of several responses could be to compare the situation with a sports game (e.g., football or basketball in which opposing sides live within clearly defined rules). Are there other ideas that can be drawn upon from the sports world that are applicable? Or can analogous examples be drawn from cooking, machine functioning, gardening, the seasons? These analogies may seem farfetched and may not in themselves lead to a solution, but they are mind stretching and offer new perspectives. Thus, group members stray momentarily from the problem, develop one or more analogies that serve to expand their thinking, and then seek to make a connection—to find relevance between the analogy and the problem with which they are grappling.

Using a Checklist to Stimulate Novelty

Another method designed to generate ideas when the group is running out of ideas is to make a checklist. For example, a group has developed some preliminary ideas but is still dissatisfied. So, to expand the group's thinking, the following list of questions (with verbs designed to trigger thinking *italicized*) could serve as a stimulus to more and different ideas:[15]

(1) Can the idea be *copied?*
     What else is like this?
     Are other communities doing this?
     Has something like this been done before?

(2) How can the idea be *modified?*
Should a new twist be tried?
Should the format be changed?

(3) Can the idea be *expanded?*
What can be added?
What can be done more frequently?
Can we multiply it?

(4) Can this idea be *reduced?*
Can elements be substracted, condensed, made shorter, streamlined, or split up?

(5) What could be *substituted* for the idea?
Who else could pursue it?
In what other place could it be conducted?
What other approaches could be considered?

(6) Can the idea be *rearranged?*
Can components be interchanged?
Can the sequence be altered?
Can the pace be modified?

(7) Can the idea be *reversed?*
Can roles be reversed?
Can negative aspects be turned into positive ones?

(8) Can ideas be *combined?*
Can units be combined?
Can purposes be united?

The following examples illustrate how the *italicized* verbs above trigger creative approaches:

Problem: An organization wants to provide a group home for mentally retarded offenders in a middle-income, potentially highly resistant community.

Question: How can people in the community become involved in the project so as to soften their resistance?

Trigger Verb: *Magnify.* What are the ways to involve a variety of new people in the issue?

Potential Solutions:
(1) Involve high school students in an essay contest.
(2) Conduct a community carnival sponsored by the Veterans of Foreign Wars, Teamster's Union, and the local Chamber of Commerce.
(3) Involve grandparents in giving presentations to local groups about the mentally retarded offenders.
(4) Involve PTAs in a community bake sale.

Trigger Verb: *Reduce.* What are the ways to involve a small, select group of leaders?

Potential Solutions:	Arrange for high-status businesspersons to have dinner with the mayor and selected councilmembers.
Problem:	A group wants to help adolescents who are failing in school.
Question:	How can the group help these youngsters develop greater motivation?
Trigger Verb:	*Reversal.* How can these youngsters shift from passive to active participants in their educational process?
Potential Solution:	Have the adolescents become teachers of younger students.
Problem:	A group wants to find financial support for a battered women's home, but local community funding appears impossible to obtain.
Question:	Are there sources of funds which have not been tapped?
Trigger Verb:	*Modify.* How can an existing source of funds be used, with a slightly new twist, to justify expenditures for a battered women's home?
Potential Solution:	Just as license plate funds are used to fund highways, advocate that marriage license fees should be increased by a nominal amount to support battered women's homes throughout the state.

Thus, the checklist of ideas can be used to trigger novel ideas.

Reframing the Issue to Stimulate Novelty

Previously we described a willingness to break out of the usual way of doing things as one of the important ingredients conducive to creativity. The technique of reframing the issue is useful in stimulating new ways of dealing with a problem situation.[16] By going through the exercise of reframing the question, the group inevitably must be prepared to challenge the underlying premise of the current question or point of view under consideration. Some examples of the reframing process are listed below:

Original Question:	How can we recruit more foster parents for the long waiting list of foster children?
Potential Answers:	Conduct an annual foster parent recruitment campaign.
Reframed Question:	How can we reduce the number of foster children on waiting lists?
Potential Answers:	Work more intensively with natural parents to reduce the need for foster care.

Original Question: How can we get employees to become more productive?

Potential Answers: Increase pay; improve working conditions; give bonuses.

Reframed Question: How can we make work more interesting?

Potential Answers: Rotate jobs; reorient jobs around group decision making.

Original Question: How can we obtain more money for speedier ambulances?

Potential Answers: Special charity drives; work for a tax levy for ambulances.

Reframed Question: How can we prevent more accidents from occurring at the railroad crossing?

Potential Answers: Pass a law requiring a safety light.

Original Question: How can we obtain more medical services for people who need them?

Potential Answers: Obtain more Medicare, Medicaid.

Reframed Question: How can we provide health services geared to the prevention of illness?

Potential Answers: Retrain medical personnel; encourage consumers to keep their own health records; offer special health education courses to people.

Original Question: How can we keep teenagers from stealing automobiles?

Potential Answers: Provide more social activities, basketball courts, and other recreation.

Reframed Question: How can we prevent automobiles from being stolen?

Potential Answers: Educate people to remove their distributor caps at night.

As can be seen from the above examples, the reframed question changes the fundamental premise. It requires looking at the issue in a new light, a different way of perceiving the problem. The result: a new set of solutions to be considered.

These different approaches to stimulating creative ideas can, of course, be combined by the group. For example, when brainstorming the group could decide to promote additional ideas with analogies. Or the group could agree to reframe the issue to provoke a different list of ideas. What makes creativity possible is not the rigid adherence to any one technique but the attitude of evoking heretofore unexplored ideas.

Two Cautions

Two cautions should be mentioned. First, organizations in search of ways to solve intractable human problems should not overvalue creative approaches, as helpful as they may be. Organization members should not expect tremendous breakthroughs from one or two sessions using analogies. For such difficult problems as teenage pregnancy, inner city unemployment, and inadequate housing, tremendous odds work against significant resolution. Even efforts to deal with less demanding problems require considerable trial and error. Hard work and a willingness to persevere after hitting dead ends will need to accompany creative thinking. Second, although initially innovative ideas are stimulated by holding back critical judgment, eventually the ideas must be subject to critical review to be certain that they are in fact feasible and that they do not produce too great negative side effects. The next two chapters propose ways to test ideas through strengthening the reasoning process and through subjecting ideas to critical questioning.

Chapter 6

AVOIDING TRAPS OF THE PROBLEM-SOLVING PROCESS

As members of the group attempt to define a problem, set objectives, and consider alternative action plans, they must constantly be on guard against problem-solving traps—some obvious, but many other subtle and seductive—that can affect their thinking. These traps often give the illusion of dealing with problems, but for unwary problem solvers they can lead to dead ends or pseudosolutions. The proposed solutions are specious—they appear sound, plausible, and convincing, but upon closer scrutiny or with experience they are found not to be genuine answers to the problem. Groups should be wary of the problem-solving traps that follow.

NON SEQUITUR THINKING

Trap 1: *Considering solutions based on assumptions that do not necessarily lead logically to the solution.* In the field of logic, this kind of reasoning is known as *non sequitur,* meaning, "it does not follow."[1]

Proposed solutions should be based ideally on logical connections. When these logical connections are missing, when conclusions are based on false or missing premises, then non sequitur thinking occurs, as reflected in the following statements:

If we add day care centers, then women in the lower economic classes will be able to find employment.

If we conduct better sex education classes in the high school, then we can reduce teenage pregnancy.

If we provide house repair workshops in low-income neighborhoods, then we can drastically reduce housing deterioration.

If we raise welfare grants, then we will be able to prevent family breakups.

The common element in all of these statements is that they leap from an assumption to a solution, without having sufficient basis for doing so. In each instance it does not necessarily follow that the solution proposed will automatically resolve the problem.

Because there is always the danger that proposed solutions or programs may be based on invalid premises, it is important for an organization to make clear what the underlying assumptions are that have led it to consider a particular course of action. By making these premises explicit and by critically examining them, the group is in a better position to arrive at more sound solutions. Does it truly follow that giving poor families increased financial grants will prevent family deterioration? The underlying assumption is that by raising grants marital tension will diminish. But could an alternative premise be that increasing grants might cause more separations as unhappy spouses are able to afford to live separately?

Similarly, does it automatically follow that more day care centers will result in more women working, that sex education classes will reduce teenage pregnancy, that housing workshops will prevent deterioration? This can be non sequitur thinking unless the groups make explicit the premises upon which they are basing their programs and show how the proposed solution logically follows from these premises.

CIRCULAR REASONING

Trap 2: *Considering solutions based on circular reasoning.* Sometimes this is referred to as, *begging the question.* In this kind of thinking, a statement or premise is assumed to be true without needing additional proof. Arguing in a circle means that we assume to be true what has yet to be proven.[2] In effect, the proposer of the solution argues, "We should do X plan because we should do it"—without offering a fuller, noncircular explanation. Consider the following circular position: Counseling should obviously be provided by agency X because the problems of the target population can only be dealt with by agency X. The statement assumes that the point is already proven (agency X is the only one to deal with the target population's problems), and the agency hopes to convince others on the basis of this circular reasoning. Any statement that contains such phrases as "It is obvious that . . .", or, "Everyone agrees that . . ." should be watched with suspicion.

Oversimplification

Trap 3: *Oversimplifying cause-effect relationships in analyzing complex situations.* As was discussed in the chapter on problem definition, most problem situations are complex. Because of this we must avoid looking for simple explanations when we may be dealing with a reality that involves many factors contributing to a problem, as well as many factors that could affect resolutions. In this light we are reminded of Menkin's cogent observation, "For every problem there is a simple, easy solution—that is wrong."[3]

One form of oversimplifying cause-effect relationships is known by the Latin phrase *post hoc ergo propter hoc,* meaning "after this, therefore, because of this." In this kind of thinking an assumption is made that because one event followed another, the former was the cause of the latter: Because event A preceded event B, event A was the cause of event B. But in attributing A as the cause of B we may be jumping from a premise which at best creates a probability that A is the cause of B to a conclusion which is treated as a certainty.[4]

An example of this type of thinking is reflected in the following statement: "When we sent a letter last time to the Streets Commissioner complaining of delays in rubbish pickup, we received an immediate response. Therefore, let's send another letter about inadequate street lighting." Although the letter may have hastened rubbish pick up, other factors particular to the situation—the mayor's running for reelection, the availability of federal funds for extra workers, the absence of demands from other neighborhood groups—may have had as much or more of an influence. The organization should therefore not assume that because event B (rubbish pick up) followed event A (letter) that A was the cause.

Another form of oversimplifying the cause-effect relationship is to ignore a chain of cause-effect relationships in which effects can themselves cause other effects. A chain of cause-effect relationships could be diagrammed as shown in Figure 6–1.[5]

Mounting inflationary costs with no accompanying increase in outside funding is a primary cause which forces the agency to increase client costs and reduce agency staff. The effect is to reduce the actual number of clients served. Actually, the cause-effect chain need not stop here. Because of the reduction in clients served it is possible the agency would experience a later reduction in funds. To isolate one simple cause contributing to one single effect is an oversimplification that denies how an effect can itself become a cause at another point in time.

Figure 6-1.   CAUSE-EFFECT CHAIN

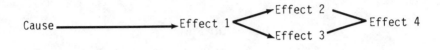

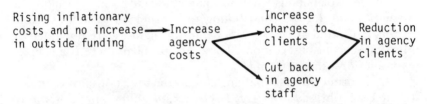

To deal with only one point in the chain may not suffice in dealing with a problem. Because the problem-solving process often involves a chain of cause-effects, members of community organizations must be prepared to trace a general problem through the chain. They must also be prepared to look beyond the obvious and manifest problems (e.g., unemployment, poor housing, or delinquency) to the less observable, latent problems that are likely to affect the problem.

Oversimplification can also occur when the group focuses on only one cause, ignoring other concomitant causes.[6] For example, a group determines that the city's lack of aggressive leadership is contributing to a decline in the number of central city businesses, thus leading to the decline in the financial base of the city. But other factors may play as significant a role in the economic condition of the community, as diagrammed in Figure 6-2.

When we uncritically accept one explanation or one proposed solution we tend to ignore other explanations. We jump to a conclusion without subjecting it to other, competing ideas or contributing factors, thereby limiting other possible approaches. In this example, a community might concentrate on only one factor—election of a mayor— but ignore other contributing factors.

Finally, oversimplification can take the form of ignoring counteracting causes.[7] The consequence of this denial is that the group will not be able to anticipate properly why a particular course of action may prove to be futile. Suppose, for example, that a group wishes to reduce teenage unemployment by developing a job training program. As long as school dropout rates remain high, it is likely that the pool of unemployed teenagers will continually be replenished no matter how effective the training program. Figure 6-3. reflects the counteracting causes.

Figure 6-2.   IGNORING CONTRIBUTING FACTORS

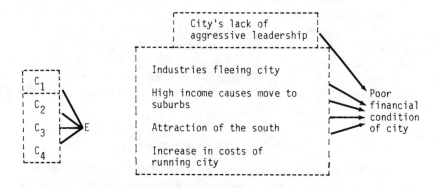

It is imperative that the group seek to understand that no matter how desirable a potential solution may appear, other factors may be operating that could neutralize or even sabotage it.

Thus, the trap of oversimplification is always present in considering both causes of problems and their solutions. Often a group is faced with simultaneous causes and effects that would be diagramed like Figure 6–4.[8]

The group may have to consider one cause-effect relationship at a time, but it must be aware that it is the cumulation of multiple causes having an impact on several effects that contribute to the overall

Figure 6-3.   IGNORING COUNTERACTING CAUSES

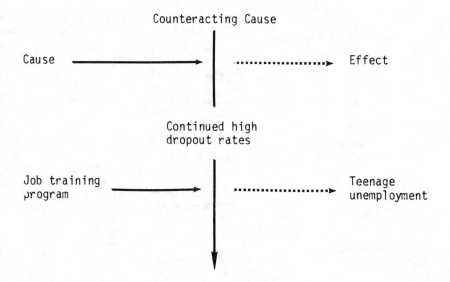

problem. In the example above, for a group to work only on reading materials without also focusing on parent and teacher attitudes would not likely result in improving student performance.

It is important that community groups be aware of and guard against this natural tendency for people to look for simple explanations to difficult problems. They must continually seek to understand and deal with the complexities of problem situations. Then, though they may select one aspect of a problem to work on, they should be prepared to shift to another aspect should they find their proposed solution does not adequately deal with the problem.

ANALOGIES TO PROVE SOLUTIONS

Trap 4: *Using analoguous thinking uncritically to justify proposed solutions.* As was discussed in Chap. 5 on generating ideas, reasoning by analogy consists of making a comparison between two similar situations and implying that what is true in one case is true in the other. Because A resembles B in some ways (X and Y), it may be assumed that if A has the property of Z, then B will also have Z. To be used effectively, analogies must be confined to the relevant characteristics of A and B.[9] But how can we be certain that specific similarities between A and B are relevant to the property Z?

For example, suppose one argued that because a state income tax benefitting the poor was passed in one state, such a tax increase could succeed in another state. Is the analogy valid? Only by determining that the states had common and relevant characteristics and circumstances can we be confident that this analogous thinking is valid.

Figure 6-4.   SIMULTANEOUS CAUSES AND EFFECTS

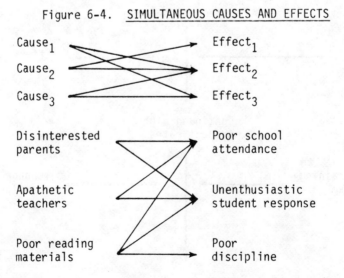

One way of dealing with analogous thinking is to identify the essence of a given analogy. We need to determine whether or not certain similar characteristics are relevant to the possession of some further characteristics. Our reasoning would be that the two states have significant common characteristics:

> Both are located in the Northeast and have heavy manufacturing industries.
>
> Both have a sizeable portion of urban and rural poor people.

State B has enacted a major income tax to benefit the poor. Therefore we conclude that state A could enact such legislation.

But if on further exploration it is learned that the governor of state B was highly committed to tax legislation and that the legislation was passed 2 years ago (before a "taxpayers' revolt"), then we might conclude that the circumstances facing the two states are not identical in all aspects.

The advantage, then, of an analogy is that it can establish a beginning idea for worthwhile exploration. This would be particularly true for literal analogies, i.e., where one is comparing cases in the same classification. The comparison of states is a literal analogy. On the other hand, figurative analogies, i.e., comparing cases in different classifications, while helpful for illustrating a point, do not represent in themselves conclusive proof. For example, comparing an income tax increase with taking aspirin may not be sufficiently valid if one is making the point that too much of a remedy may not help and can even be harmful. Figurative analogies can have an impact on discussion, but, in themselves, they are not a sufficient basis on which to draw conclusions.

The following questions should be used as tests for reasoning by analogy:

1. *Are there significant and relevant resemblances?* In the example of the two states, we would want to see if they had similar size urban populations and industrial composition.
2. *Are the points of resemblance critical to the comparison?* One would have to look beyond the general resemblances of the two states to reexamine their respective tax laws and fiscal policies.
3. *Are the points of difference noncritical?* This will depend frequently on the context within which the comparison is made. Apparent minor differences may become major ones, depending upon the issue involved. In the comparison of the two states, the fact that both have a sizeable suburban population may or may not be significant, depending on the voting patterns of suburbanites.

4. *Is the analogical reasoning cumulative?* An analogy is enhanced
if it can be shown that more than one comparison may be
advanced. Thus, if it could be shown that not only state B,
but also other states in the Northeast region passed similar
tax increases that benefited the poor, and these states resem-
ble state A, then this argument would be strengthened.

Thus, while analogies can be useful in generating ideas, they can
be used only with caution in proving the validity of a position.

GRANDIOSE SOLUTIONS

Trap 5: *Promising grandiose solutions.* Programs are continually
proposed that offer the possibility of solving some aspects of a problem, but not necessarily all aspects, despite the rhetoric of their proponents. Consider the following: (1) Tax abatement, designed to induce
companies to build in the city rather than the suburbs, is touted as a way
of reducing inner city unemployment. Tax abatement may make the
city more competitive, may add to the tax base (if companies do build
offices in the downtown area) and may improve the general economic
climate. But if the work force is drawn largely from suburban areas, tax
abatement is likely to have little impact on inner city unemployment.
(2) Restructuring county government, by electing a county executive,
might increase county government accountability to the electorate, but
would not necessarily result in improvement in such city services as
police and fire protection, rubbish pick up, and dog warden services.

Most proponents tend to oversell the results of their proposal or at
least to convey the impression that the proposal will make an impact on
all aspects of a community problem.[10] Sometimes this is not done
intentionally; proposals often describe in elaborate detail unmet needs
and leave unanswered precisely how the proposal will have an impact
on these unmet needs. Both the proponents and the audience rely on
wishful thinking that the solution will be a panacea. Then after the plan
is adopted, despair occurs because the proposal was unable to live up to
all the stated expectations and implicit hopes. Wise members of groups
considering proposed solutions will ask, "What exactly will the program do, and what exactly won't it do?"

LIMITING THE PROBLEM SOLUTION

Trap 6: *Limiting the scope of the problem solution.* Groups tend to
focus on that part of the problem that they have identified as being part
of their universe and ignoring that which is considered outside of it.
Unfortunately, many problems persist either because solutions require
multifaceted approaches involving different people at different levels

within an organization or because they require different organizations to mesh their efforts. If only one unit (whether internal to the organization or external to it) does its part, but the others do not do theirs, then the problem may appear from one perspective to be resolved when in reality it has not been. Note the following examples:

The director of a human services agency sees that recruitment of foster homes has been a problem. The solution: hire one staff member to actively recruit foster parents by speaking to church and civic groups and arranging for public media coverage. For 2 months 50 new potential foster parents make phone inquiries. But the department does not provide for extra secretaries to handle paper work, develop a brochure to mail out to prospective parents, or establish follow-up procedures. Consequently, several hundred inquiries are received, but not adequately followed up.

A community committee working with the common pleas court has surveyed availability of group home slots for mentally retarded offenders. But the committee is unable to arrange for adequate backup services: job training, counseling, volunteer pal program. The former offenders get into trouble again. As a result, group homes became reluctant to accept additional mentally retarded offenders.

Both examples illustrate the trap of thinking a solution is at hand when actually it is not because all the pieces are not in place. The scope of the problem resolution has been too narrowly focused on the most obvious and manifest needs (e.g., need for a foster home recruiter and need for mentally retarded offender group home slots). But the solving of one part of the problem can usually give rise to different sets of organizational or interorganizational difficulties. These need to be anticipated or the solution becomes unraveled. Because one unit tends to focus only on its part of the problem resolution, mechanisms need to be developed, e.g., task forces composed of various units or an ombudsman who can ease the bottlenecks through the system. In the examples given above, the human services agency staff from various units (public information, intake, foster care) should have meshed their efforts before recruitment occurred so that all those that needed to be involved would be ready when the first phone call was received. Similarly, those working to obtain group homes would, of necessity, concern themselves with seeing that backup community support services were provided so that those placed in the group homes had the best possible chance of making a successful adjustment.

PALLIATIVES

Trap 7: *Reducing the pain of the problem without actually solving it.* The term *palliative* is used to describe any action that lessens the pain or severity of a problem without curing it. Sometimes this is referred to as a *band-aid approach* to solving problems. The danger of a palliative is that though it may temporarily alleviate the impact of a problem (like a pain killer that deadens the pain of arthritis), it does not prevent the problem from returning with the same or renewed intensity. Furthermore, by softening the effects of the problem, it may reduce the investment necessary to grapple with the core issue.

Despite these dangers, palliatives are not uncommon recourses for dealing with community and human service problems. The likely explanation is that concerned professionals and community leaders resort to partial solutions because they are within reach, or because they have not defined the problem properly.

To be sure, they may operate under what they perceive to be realistic constraints. They do not want to take on the impossible dream, for, as one author put it, "While (they) pursue the unattainable (they) make impossible the realizable."[11] They want to avoid a vain search for solutions that do not exist because then they will face the inevitable despair and futility of not finding answers. Moreover, they see searching for utopian answers as detracting from achievable (if meager) objectives. They hope, therefore, to gain some satisfaction that at least something is being done and that half solutions are better than none. So they work on changing a problem in a limited fashion. Consider the following palliatives:

> Welfare recipients annually receive grants that are far below acceptable minimum standards of decency. Unable to secure substantial increases in payments, action groups resort to collecting and distributing canned goods and clothing to poor people. But with inflation the welfare poor continue to exist at below a subsistance level.
>
> Mentally ill persons are detained in the workhouse illegally beyond the time stipulated by law for a minor crime they have committed. Through a law suit and political pressure the state is forced to release the criminally ill. But no provision is made for them to be hospitalized and receive proper mental health treatment in their communities.
>
> An assumption is made that inner city teenagers are unemployed because they lack information. A program is designed to increase their awareness of the job market. But they still remain unemployed in large numbers because jobs are unavailable.

These examples are palliatives because, though in each instance some improvement has occurred, these improvements do not remedy basic conditions: the welfare poor receive more food and clothing, but because of inflation they are not better off; the mentally ill are no longer detained illegally, but they still receive no treatment; inner city teenagers have more information, but they still lack jobs.

It is tempting to become cynical about these proposed remedies, for in all three of these instances the basic underlying problem remains unchanged. The French have a saying to describe the appearance, without the substance, of change: *Plus, ca change, plus c'est la meme chose*—the more it changes, the more it is the same. Though change appears to take place, in reality nothing is really altered. The trap to be aware of, then, is that of being misled that a proposed course of action will solve a problem when, at best, it can alleviate it in only the most limited way.

DENIAL OF NONRATIONAL PROBLEM SOLVING

Trap 8: *Denial of the nonrational problem-solving process.* We assume sound and systematic reasoning can play a major role in the problem-solving process. Indeed, much of this book is devoted to systematic examination of a problem and implementation techniques for problem resolution. But it would be a grave mistake to deny the existence of irrational or nonrational factors in problem solving. Few community problems are ever dealt with in a purely rational mode, with all participants rising above their self-interests and altruistically considering the best interest of the community. This is because people bring with them all the conditions of the human psyche: loyalties or animosities toward people, concerns about personal and organizational survival, a need to enhance their own power, a need for self-aggrandizement, or mistrust and jealousy.

So members who consider rational decisions without regard for the underlying feelings of participants may think they have arrived at a proper solution only to discover that nonrational factors can contribute to the undoing of the best of plans. Group members must always be mindful of the politics of any given situation: who has influence over whom, whose self-interests are at stake, how the enhancement of one member or group or organization will be perceived. Organizations, after all, are not abstractions; they are collections of people and the needs of these people must be understood. Thus, problem solving will often occur on both a rational, analytic level and on an emotional, less rational level.

These eight traps—solutions based on inadequate premises, circular reasoning, oversimplification of issues, analogous reasoning used uncritically to prove a position, developing grandiose conclusions, delimiting problem solution, resorting to palliatives, and denial of nonrational factors—constitute major obstacles to true problem solving. Knowing about these traps does not, of course, guarantee positive results, but it does identify major pitfalls to avoid. With these cautions in mind, groups can be in a better position to examine alternative action plans.

Chapter 7

DEVELOPING ALTERNATIVE ACTION PLANS

Previously the importance of developing a number of alternatives and eventually selecting one as the action plan was discussed. Selecting a single course of action from among two or more alternatives requires anticipating uncertain future events that might affect the course of action, as well as consequences and reactions that might flow from the action taken by the organization.

CONTINGENCY ANALYSIS

Events are defined as situations that could occur regardless of the alternatives selected. Consequences are defined as results that directly flow from the alternative selected. Because of the unpredictability of events and because every alternative is likely to have both positive and negative consequences, each course of action must be carefully weighed. Contingency analysis is a systematic way of anticipating both events and consequences and then deciding on how to proceed. It involves making purposeful guesses about an uncertain future by asking "What if . . .?" questions.

Anticipating Events Through Decision Trees

Selecting from among several alternatives is risky because events affecting these alternatives are not absolutely predictable. Group members cannot know for sure the extent to which events will take place and so they must make guesses. They want to be able to foresee events and estimate the risk involved to either consider actions that will reduce anticipated risks or select different alternatives if the risks are perceived to be too great.

Most groups consider the likelihood of an event occuring, as illustrated in these remarks:

> What are the odds of the vote passing a legislative hearing after we write letters?
>
> How likely are we to get an increase in requests for service if we conduct a special outreach program?

One approach used to map out events is a decision tree which provides a visual display of a decision that is about to be made, the events that could take place, and the different results that might occur following the different events. It can serve to translate abstract thinking into a logical picture by showing how different potential events can affect alternatives. By calculating the probability of an event happening, the group is then influenced about whether or not to embark on an alternative plan.[1]

It is possible, even likely, that there will be different opinions about the probability of an event occuring, particularly when the group has had little previous experience in a given situation. Of course, a degree of error can exist in estimating the probability that an event will occur. That is why such calculation should be based as much as possible on knowledgeable people's assessments. The preparation of a decision tree should therefore be seen as a tool to help people make informed guesses about events that could affect their selection of alternative courses of action.

The following steps are used for making a decision tree when events are unpredictable:[2]

(1) Identify two or more alternative decisions designed to solve a problem and achieve an objective.

Example: A community committee is considering a housing development of 50 units for disabled but ambulatory persons. One alternative is to limit the housing to persons over 65; another alternative decision is to set aside 40% of the units for disabled, middle-aged adults.

(2)   Identify certain crucial *events* likely to affect the alternatives. These events are likely to be affected by chance or by circumstances not controlled by the organization.

Example: A major *event* affecting the project is the extent to which both older and middle-aged disabled adults are likely to request the units. This event will occur regardless of which alternative is selected.

(3)   Calculate the probability of the event occuring from 0 to 100%.

Example: In the case of the housing units, the committee estimates that there is a 40% chance that those under 65 will have a high request rate as compared to a 70% chance of those over the age of 65.

(4)   Indicate the anticipated consequences from each *event*.

Example: If the committee chooses to have part of the housing units available to middle-aged, disabled adults, one result could be that the building would not be filled.

(5)   Consider *alternative action plans* that would be necessary if consequences were to occur.

Example: In the event that few requests were received, with the consequence that the building was not filled, then the organization would need to either conduct a special publicity campaign, develop alternative building usage, or close part of the building.

(6)   Diagram the situation the organization is faced with by means of a decision tree. The task is to determine which alternative course of action is appropriate to take in light of the prediction of the event and its potential consequences and special demands on the organization (see Figure 7–1).

(7)   If other events are anticipated that can have a bearing on the alternatives, these should each be separately identified with other decision trees and the same procedures repeated. In the housing development illustration, a calculation can be made about the likelihood of receiving funding for one approach as compared to another. Or a calculation of the neighborhood reaction to each alternative approach could be considered. Each of these could be diagrammed.

Figure 7-1. UTILIZATION ISSUE

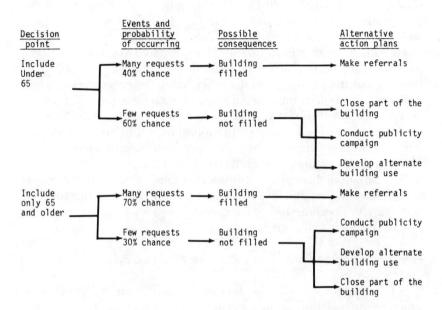

Taken together these anticipated and distinctively separate but crucial events will influence the selection of one alternative approach over another. Thus, the group is in a better position to consider several different events simultaneously rather than on a piecemeal basis. Another decision tree related to the issue of funding is illustrated in Figure 7–2.

In narrative form, each of the different scenarios or possibilities

Figure 7-2. FUNDING ISSUE

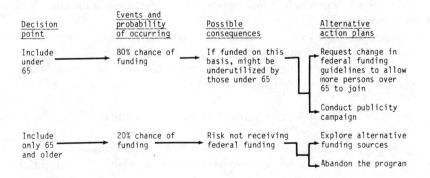

might be something like this: If the organization were to decide to build a facility to include those under 65, there is an 80% chance of funding as compared to 20% if it builds only for those over 65. If the group selects the former route, it risks a 40% chance of having the building filled, as compared to 70%. And in the event that the building was not filled, the organization should be prepared to conduct a special publicity campaign to fill the building, find an alternative use for it, or close part of the building. On the other hand, the organization might decide that it would rather prepare plans for a building only for people over age 65, in which case it risks not receiving federal funds. Now the group must determine which event (utilization or funding) will be most crucial in influencing its decision about which plan to select.

The special value of decision trees is that the group is required to walk a situation through, to consider seriously one or more events before selecting an action plan. Ideas put on paper in the form of decision trees become less elusive as the group focuses on potential events and their consequences.

Preparing Standing Contingency Plans for Projected Events

The previous discussion focused primarily on the process by which an organization, by considering events, would select one alternative plan over another. In addition to reflecting anticipated events, the decision trees also identified possible consequences (building being filled or not) and potential courses of action (e.g., conduct publicity campaign). When an organization attempts to determine in advance what it will do when certain events occur, this is called contingency planning. Preplanning or standing contingency planning is especially important when there is insufficient time between events occurring and the need to take action. For example, suppose a neighborhood group is planning a large community outdoor event. If it rains, the group will not have time to move the event indoors unless it has planned for this eventuality in advance. Only by means of a standing contingency plan would it be in a position to take action immediately in the event of rain.

Suppose, for example, an organization wants to support a bill to modify methods of raising taxes. It has decided that it will take different actions depending on the kind of situations that might occur. Standing contingency planning could take the following forms:[3]

(1)   If event A occurs, do X: If a legislative bill is brought up in committee hearings, then be prepared to testify.
(2)   If B and C occur, do Y: If both labor and business support the bill, then be prepared to form a coalition to campaign actively for it.

(3)   If only B but not C occurs, do V: If labor supports the bill but business does not, then be prepared to limit efforts to letter writing to legislators.

(4)   If only C but not B occurs, do W: If business supports the bill but the press does not, then do not support the bill.

(5)   If anticipated event A does not occur, do Z or T: If the House turns down the bill, then be prepared to actively campaign for its passage in the Senate (or be prepared to fight for it in the next legislative session). If anticipated funding does not materialize, then prepare a proposal for a special government grant. If no additional funds are available, cut staff across the board by 10%.

Note that this last kind of contingency planning is referred to as having a *fallback position* and is useful to have when implementation of the originally preferred action plan proves to be impossible.

The advantages of developing a standing contingency plan are that it reduces the need for continuous decision making and provides a consistent and timely response to predictable situations. Its disadvantage is that an organization might automatically implement the contingency plan even when all the nuances of a situation have not been explored. Some groups tend to rely unduly on a standing plan even when conditions warrant new or different responses. With this caution in mind, contingency planning is a useful way of an organization's anticipating "what if . . ." situations.

Contingency Planning Based on an Assessment of Advantages and Disadvantages

Almost every alternative under consideration will have advantages and disadvantages associated with it. Each alternative has to be assessed not only in relation to its own set of trade-offs ("Do the advantages outweigh the disadvantages?"), but also in relation to other alternatives ("Are there more advantages to this alternative as compared with other alternatives, and are there less disadvantages?"). A program could conceivably have great advantages, but relative to other options it may have drawbacks that would warrant its being rejected. A group should try to select an alternative that insures the likelihood of achieving its objectives and limits negative effects.

The reason for identifying the possible negative side effects of an action plan before implementation is to provide time in the planning process to do the following:

(1)   reject the plan and abandon the project because the risks are greater than the rewards;

(2) substitute an alternative plan—second best, perhaps, but potentially less damaging;

(3) accept the plan, knowing that negative effects will have to be taken into consideration.

In analyzing positive and negative consequences of a proposed action, several aspects should be kept in mind:

Value Judgments Affect Perceptions of Consequences.   Different groups or constituencies will evaluate different alternatives in different ways. They will especially be influenced by what they perceive to be their self-interest regarding how the proposed alternatives will affect them. What may be beneficial for one party may be inconsequential or detrimental for another. Therefore, group members should ask, "Who benefits and who does not from the action—and why?"

Proposed Remedies Sometimes Create Negative Side Effects.   Sometimes a remedy directed at solving one problem bears the fruit of other, different problems. In medicine the word *iatrogenic,* meaning medically caused illness, reflects this concept. (Example: For some people aspirin may reduce the pain of arthritis but can contribute to bleeding ulcers). No word exists to describe the frequent negative side effects of remedial community efforts, although the term *do-gooder* is sometimes used in a pejorative way to connote a person who, intending to perform a beneficial act, instead produces ineffectual or harmful results. An example of negative side effects is the recent national and state practice of discharging mentally ill persons from mental institutions. These deinstitutionalization programs have helped many people to make positive adjustments, but they have also placed special burdens on many former patients who have not been able to manage outside of a protective environment. They also present overwhelming challenges to local communities for special services. Hence, it is important to anticipate what possible negative side effects are likely to result from a proposed action plan.

Anticipate the Worst That Can Happen.   Many organizations have a tendency to oversell one alternative, thereby overlooking possible inherent flaws in the plan. Social reformers and politicians are notorious for making exaggerated claims to convince the public of their programs. All of us have developed blindspots in our zeal to sell an action plan. To compensate for this tendency, it is sometimes useful to ask the question, "What is the worst that could happen if this approach is undertaken?" This is sometimes referred to as *the worst case scenario.* The answers to this question should produce ideas about how to either deal with the negative consequences or how to select other, perhaps less damaging, alternatives.

Suggested Format for Analyzing Advantages and Disadvantages.   For each action plan list all advantages and all disadvantages.

Example: A consumer advocacy organization that has received special foundation funding for two years is now meeting for the purpose of deciding whether, after a year and a half of being in operation, it should continue to exist autonomously or become part of another ongoing organization. In discussion, group members list the following advantages and disadvantages of such a merger:

Advantages of becoming part of another organization
(1)   Continued funding assured
(2)   Coordination of services in the larger agency
(3)   Availability of the larger agency's resources, includilng public information, duplicating machines, etc.

Disadvantages of becoming part of another organization
(1)   Possible undue influence
(2)   Constraints on advocacy role
(3)   Lower visability of the consumer action program
(4)   Possibility of lower priority in the larger agency

Inherent in almost all decisions and proposed courses of action are trade-offs. By making these trade-offs explicit, through a conscious listing of advantages and disadvantages of each action, the group can avoid later surprises and shocks. Before the group embarks on a course of action it would ask such probing questions as the following:

(1)   Do the potential short-term advantages (disadvantages) outweigh the long-term ones?
(2)   Will embarking on this action plan detract from other efforts of the organization?
(3)   Will the benefits experienced by some people (in and out of the organization) be offset by the liabilities felt by others?

After deliberating about the trade-offs the group is in a better position to make a thoughtful decision.

APPLYING CRITICAL QUESTIONS TO A POTENTIAL ACTION PLAN

As the organization begins to identify a potential plan of action, it is important to ask a series of critical questions that will aid in determining the feasibility of the final selection process. Figure 7–3 displays six critical questions.[4] The figure provides a means of comparing alternative action plans with each other. The following should be considered:

Figure 7-3. CRITICAL QUESTIONS

Alternative Plans	How successful likely to be based on experience elsewhere? (High/Med/Low)	How feasible based on availability of resources? (High/Med/Low)	How appropriate in relation to the basic style of the organization? (High/Med/Low)	Extent alternative deals with scope of the problem? (High/Med/Low)	How efficient is alternative in relation to potential accomplishments? (High/Med/Low)	Negative side effects or new demands? (High/Med/Low)
Alternative A — New facility	X	X	X	X	X	X
Alternative B — Use existing facilities		X	X	X	X	X
Alternative C — Create group homes	X	X	X	X	X	X

116

(1)   Based on a review of experience elsewhere, how successful is this alternative likely to be? How is this particular problem being tackled by other communities? What conditions operate in these communities to suggest success (or failure)? By examining what others are doing or have done, the organization can capitalize on successes and avoid pitfalls.

(2)   What resources are available? Among the resources to be considered are the following: personnel, money, time, equipment and facilities, knowledge and skill, political influence, energy and commitment. Each alternative should be considered in light of the questions, "Does it require more resources than are available, given certain priorities? If so, is there a good chance of developing needed resources to carry out a particular action plan?"

(3)   Is the action plan in keeping with the purpose and style of the organization? If the organization relies on good will to effect coordination of various elements, is a strategy of confrontation appropriate?

(4)   Does the action plan deal adequately with the *scope* of the problem? If 300 people need a special kind of service, but the action plan will only provide enough service units to meet the needs of 60 people, will the organization be satisfied with this limited scope?

(5)   How efficient is the action plan? How do the costs of this action plan compare with the costs of other plans, and how do the costs relate to the potential benefits?

(6)   What negative side effects or new demands could occur from the action plan?

Example: Suppose that children's treatment institutions would be willing to consider accepting adolescent mentally retarded offenders, thereby reducing the need to inappropriately house them at the juvenile detention home. Could the new set of demands placed on the children's institutions be handled, including providing vocational education, increasing staff supervision (which would require obtaining additional funding), and dealing with possible problems with peers in the institutions?

Taking the example of the mentally retarded offender, suppose a community organization has decided to explore various alternatives. Although its analysis would undoubtedly be quite extensive, for purposes of this discussion, the alternatives under consideration would be as follows:

Alternative A: Request that the county commissioners seek voter approval for a $2 million facility for mentally retarded offenders.

Alternative B: Request an existing children's institution to reserve 30 juvenile mentally retarded offender spaces.

Alternative C: Create three group homes that would house mentally retarded offenders. Provide necessary support services.

Figure 7–3 illustrates how an organization might consider these alternatives. By looking at this figure, alternatives can be summarized and visually compared in anticipation of making difficult decisions.

FORCE FIELD ANALYSIS

Force Field Analysis (FFA)[5] is another general problem-solving approach that can assist in analyzing the feasibility of alternative action plans under consideration.

The major focus of FFA is to identify the forces that promote the action plan (driving forces) and those forces that serve as restraints (restraining forces). If these forces offset each other, then no movement occurs and the status quo remains. The action plan can be implemented if the helping or driving forces can be increased or the restraining forces can be decreased. One caution: If the group is considering an increase in the driving forces, it should be aware that this could, in turn, increase restraining forces—the backlash effect. For this reason, it is often better to try to concentrate on reducing restraining forces. Figures 7–4 and 7–5 show how the driving and restraining forces can be illustrated.

Figure 7-4.   FORCE FIELD ANALYSIS

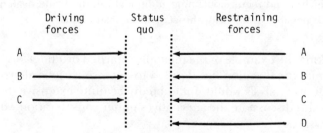

Figure 7-5. FORCE FIELD ANALYSIS APPLICATION

Example: A Women's Managerial Promotion Program Committee is interested
in identifying driving and restraining forces affecting women
in managerial positions.

```
┌─────────────────────────────┐        ┌──────────────────────────────┐
│ Current problem:            │        │ Objective:  To add 20        │
│ Women are underrepresented  │        │ women to management positions│
│ in managerial positions     │        │ in 5 target business         │
│                             │        │ organizations                │
└─────────────────────────────┘        └──────────────────────────────┘
```

STATUS QUO

DRIVING FORCES   RESTRAINING FORCES

                                          Resistance by some people
                                          to women in management
                                          positions

                                          ◄─────────────────────────

Recent pressure from women's
groups for management
positions

          ─────────────────────►

                                          Insufficient training and
                                          experience for potential
                                          women managers

                                          ◄─────────────────────────

More women graduates with
law and business degrees

          ─────────────────────►

                                          Women not connected to
                                          informal business network

                                          ◄─────────────────────────

Desire of businesses to
demonstrate their receptivity
to women's equity issues

          ─────────────────────►

After listing the driving and restraining forces, several questions
can be asked to deepen the analysis of the situation and help pinpoint
those forces on which to concentrate. Through this analysis an organization can come closer to selecting an alternative action plan:

(1)   Over which of the driving forces do we have an influence?

Example: Can the organization demonstrate to businesspeople
that women would be more likely to buy their products if they were
aware of women being in managerial positions?

(2)   Over which of the restraining forces do we have influence?

Example: Can the organization develop special managerial
training programs for women?

(3)   What new driving forces could be generated?

Example: Can the organization threaten a law suit or conduct a
study showing the disproportionate number of women in lower
level jobs?

As with any tool, FFA can be developed in as much detail as the
group deems necessary. For issues that are highly complex, the group
may want to undertake an in-depth FFA. For simpler situations, it may
be enough for the group to develop a limited FFA framework and
move quickly into the implementation process.

OBTAINING ACCEPTANCE OF THE ACTION PLAN

The hope for change is inherent in the problem-solving process.
The reason for working on a problem is to improve the way things are.
But change is invariably resisted. Sometimes this resistance is healthy
and desirable since, as was discussed previously, change in a condition
can bring with it negative side effects or detrimental consequences. Not
all change will always benefit all people.

From the perspective of a group wanting to produce change,
resistance must be taken into account. If not, the best analytic problem
definition, the most coherent set of objectives, and the most creative
planning ideas will go nowhere.

Although it is difficult to formulate universal guidelines that can
apply to all situations where a group has settled on an action plan and
must convince others to accept it, some general guidelines follow.

Involve those who will be implementing the action plan in its creation. This
guideline is based on the assumption that people who have an investment in a plan they helped to shape will be more willing to carry it out.
They feel a sense of ownership and commitment to seeing it through.[6]
This is why a committee to study a problem should include those who
will be involved in implementing recommendations. If, because of time
constraints or other reasons, the implementors or approvers of the

action plan cannot be involved, the next best thing is to keep them apprised on a continuous basis. No surprises.

When an action plan calls for changes involving considerable risk and dealing with unanticipated, future events, build in go/no-go points. This approach will permit investing resources in incremental steps. The group could review progress before it makes a longer range commitment. Action plan advocates can gain acceptance by assuring group members and the organization's leadership (who may tend to be more cautious and conservative) that if the action plan does not work out as planned, the organization can abort the project and consider other ventures.[7]

By determining at various stages whether or not to continue to proceed, the group avoids risking resources to a long-term project that may not prove feasible. For example, a community organization may decide it wants to establish a special program for school dropouts. Before embarking on the project, it might establish a 3-month study process to determine whether (1) the local school system is interested in cooperating in the venture, (2) local or state funding could be made available, and (3) a sample of youngsters not in school would be interested in the program. If these three basic conditions could not be met at the end of the time period, a no-go decision would be made. If, after the initial 3-month period, tentative funding is provided for a building, but not for operating costs, then a second go/no-go decision period of 3 months might be established to determine whether operating funds can be secured. If not, then a decision not to proceed can again be made. In this way a long-term commitment and investment in high-risk ventures can be based on the extent to which fundamental conditions can be met.

Because nothing succeeds like success, action plan advocates should consider proposals that have a high chance of achieving results. Building upon achievements which foster a sense of confidence, action plan advocates can become emboldened to propose more radical actions.[8] In addition, action plan advocates should be wary of proposing a plan which, if it fails, may make it much more difficult to try again. This is why frequently an organization may undertake a pilot project: it will try out an idea to determine pitfalls before embarking on a large-scale program.

Advocates of an action plan must think of themselves as salespeople. Advocates are selling an idea. They cannot complacently assume that because they are enthusiastic about the plan, other key persons will be easily convinced. Resistances of others will have to be understood and dealt with. Just as in the business world, where good salespeople develop a point of sale, so, too, one must be developed in selling human service and community programs. The advantages of the program must be clearly spelled out—who will benefit and how. At the same time, the disadvantages and potential concerns must be anticipated: Whose vested interest, status, or power is threatened by the proposed change? A good strategy includes analyzing how objections might be prevented or neutralized. Hence, by understanding fully the nature of the resistances, advocates can prepare convincing proposals.

Anticipate controversial situations. When proposals or programs are controversial and the organization is composed of a broad cross section of the community, then those proposing the plan must anticipate likely reactions and how they will respond to them. It is never too early to begin asking how the organization will deal with controversial questions both internally and with other organizations.

Because resistance to change is sometimes based on lack of complete understanding of the proposal and how it can be carried out, the advocates of the action plan should do the following:

(1) Work out details of the plan with special attention as to how it can be implemented. If, for example, the proposal is going to cost money, the proponents should determine how much and from what sources it can be derived.

(2) Prepare visual aids—charts, graphs, and other materials —to present to people needing to be convinced.

(3) Spell out the action steps that will be required to implement the plan.

These guidelines may not be all inclusive because, as noted earlier, every situation is unique and will require its own special kind of preparation. Regardless of the situation, however, it is important to conduct a mental trial run of how the group expects significant others, not directly involved in the initial development of the action plan, to react. Doing this kind of homework will eventually increase the likelihood of acceptance.

Chapter 8

COLLABORATING AND NEGOTIATING WITH OTHER ORGANIZATIONS

Many groups concerned with community problems have a tendency to operate in a highly independent, autonomous manner. This is because organizations generally want to control their own decision-making process, develop a sense of identity among their members, and convey to the world their particular efforts and accomplishments. The need for autonomy and identity is so profound that many community organizations pursue their goals without relating to other organizations.[1] They avoid interaction to preserve their independence, reduce the risk of possible loss of support or resources, or keep from paying a price for entangling with other groups. They think they can achieve their own limited goals without having to relate to others.

Despite this strong tendency to be independent, organizations that work on complex community problems find it necessary, even essential, to deal with other organizations. Two major approaches concerning the interaction between organizations can be identified: collaboration and negotiation. A collaborative approach requires organizations to identify unity and agreement between diverse groups, to harmonize ways of working together. A negotiating approach usually is based on different organizations pursuing their own interests. An organization knows what it wants and attempts to influence others who control decisions or resources through rational persuasion, coercion, or other strategies to be discussed later. This chapter will highlight significant aspects of the collaboration and negotiation approaches in dealing with problems.

THE NEED FOR COLLABORATION

It is sometimes assumed that organizational collaboration is the most desirable way to affect community issues. In reality, however, cooperation between organizations is not necessarily a preferred way of relating; under some circumstances tasks and efforts are better accomplished by a single, unencumbered organization.

By having to join with others, some organizations find their original goals displaced by an overemphasis on cooperation and coordination.[2] Other organizations may not be as intensively concerned with an issue, and the resulting coordinated effort is bland and ineffectual. A strongly partisan welfare rights organization, for example, may find that by joining with other community groups its aggressive advocacy becomes diluted. Or a child advocacy organization may decide not to participate in a coordinated community effort to improve foster care to preserve its advocacy "gad fly" role vis-à-vis human services agencies. If the danger exists that, by combining with others, an organization will reduce its effectiveness in accomplishing its goals, then avoiding collaborative attempts may be appropriate.

There are, however, compelling reasons why organizations collaborate. As has been discussed earlier, many community problems, such as unemployment, inadequate housing, and delinquency, are both complex and interrelated. Often organizations become highly specialized and concentrate on a given aspect of a problem. But as specialization has increased, so too has the need for interaction among organizations. Establishing an employment program, for example, requires more than setting up training programs—health services, transportation, day care, counseling, and housing services all become necessary components. Hence, while many organizations strongly desire to preserve a high degree of decision-making authority and power, the complexity of problems and the need for funds, skills, staff, community support, and other resources may compel them to interact collaboratively with other community groups.

FACTORS INFLUENCING ORGANIZATIONAL COLLABORATION

Collaboration occurs when one or more organizations perceive that their own goals can be achieved most effectively and efficiently with the assistance and the resources of others.[3] Their goals can be similar, as when various organizations in a community decide to work together to reduce crime in a neighborhood. Or the goals can be complementary, as when one agency decides to serve clients it ordinarily would not serve because it will be paid by another agency for doing so.[4] Sometimes goals can even be dissimilar, as "strange bedfellow" organizations harmonize their efforts to achieve their respective goals. Of course, if goals are too divergent, collaboration may not occur.

Collaborative efforts between organizations are also likely to be enhanced when sufficient resources exist to reduce competition or when organizations can work out agreements to divide resources. Sometimes organizations are willing to make transfers to other organizations without an expectation of having something returned of equal value. More frequently organizations participate in a cooperative undertaking with the expectation of receiving a return. An exchange occurs because those participating anticipate benefits.

Resources that organizations exchange can be tangible, involving funds, facilities, personnel, clients, information, and services, or they can be intangible, involving prestige and goodwill. Sometimes the exchange is immediately reciprocal: organization A agrees to serve the clients of organization B in exchange for funding. Sometimes the exchange is initially unilateral: organization A agrees to assist organization B on child welfare legislation in anticipation of organization B assisting organization A in passing a human services levy the following year, though this expectation may not be explicitly stated. Organizations thus often weigh anticipated costs of the exchange against potential benfits.[5]

Other factors influencing collaboration among organizations include whether (1) the respective national organizations or funding bodies are encouraging it; (2) all participating organizations have clear expectations of the performance and products of their efforts; (3) a way of dealing with potential conflicts exists; (4) the organizations have distinctive and complementary roles in relation to the same target population or they clearly serve different populations; (5) good feedback is provided to the participating bodies; (6) prestige of all groups is enhanced; and (7) influence is shared.[6] Perhaps the most intangible factor, yet one that is most indispensible, is that members of respective organizations basically trust that others will live up to their commitments. This trust is most likely to grow over time as relationships are established. As organizations have opportunities for successfully conducting joint programs, there is greater willingness to accept new forms of interdependence. A health center, for example, may be willing to accept clients from a senior citizen center if previously the two organizations had participated in collaborative programming. Table 8–1. summarizes the conditions that facilitate or impede organizational collaboration.

Table 8-1.   FACTORS INFLUENCING ORGANIZATIONAL COLLABORATION

	Facilitating Conditions	Impeding Conditions
Goals	Simultaneously maximize their goals	One organization maximizes its goals at the expense of others
	Similar goals/complementary goals	Divergent goals
Resources	Resources are sufficient for organizations to benefit or agreement on how resources are to be divided up	Competition over scarce resources
		Perception that costs of the exchange exceed benefits
	Reciprocity in exchange of resources	
Role of higher authority	State or national organization encourages local coordination	State or national organization sets up procedures and funding arrangements that discourage local coordination
Expectations of performance	Clear expectations of performance and products	Ambiguity about performance and products
Conflict resolution	Mechanism developed for dealing with conflict	No procedures for resolving differences
Domain of activities and target population	Complementary roles and different roles in relation to target populations	Perception of encroachment on activities and target population
Feedback	Essential information available to all participating organizations	Limited or no exchange of essential information
Prestige	All parties feel their prestige enhanced	Perception that prestige is reduced in favor of other participating organizations
Influence	Perception that each can preserve its autonomy	Perception that one organization will have undue influence over others
	Influence is mutual	
Trust	High degree of trust	Low degree of trust

STRUCTURE

The structure developed as a result of the need for collaboration can vary, depending on the desired ends. Where the situation requires autonomous agencies to retain a high degree of independence while linking temporarily on a specific issue, the collaborative process is limited. A special crisis, e.g., a hurricane, may require organizations to temporarily mesh their programs, but once the crisis recedes (and in the absence of provisions for an ongoing structure) organizational relationships will likely vanish, as autonomous groups return to their independent ways.[7]

Sometimes organizations with different goals will work together informally through a loose *coalition* on a temporary basis. Coalitions emerge from the joining of two or more parties who discover they have more to gain by collaboration on a given issue or activity than by pursuing independent courses of action. As soon as the issue is resolved or the activity is completed, the coalition is dissolved. Organizations may also establish a formal ongoing relationship through a *federation*. Each organization is self-directing, neither entirely dependent upon nor completely responsible to the federated body.[8] Organizations within the federation remain primarily accountable to themselves and only in a limited way to the federation. Usually actions proposed by a federation must be approved by the constituency groups. Since one of the major purposes of the federation is to harmonize and integrate different groups, controversial issues that might cause a breakup are often avoided.[9]

Organizations may also form a *consortium,* a formal partnership to undertake joint activities or programs. The following are ways two or more organizations can coordinate their efforts:[10]

Joint Planning
   Planning coordinated delivery of services
   Information sharing of resources or policies
   Joint evaluation of program effectiveness
Administrative Services
   Central record keeping on clients seen in more than one organization
   Centralized purchasing and use of equipment
   Joint advertising
   Joint fund raising
Service Coordination
   Joint outreach of clients
   Common intake, diagnosis
   Formal referral patterns
   Follow-up with clients receiving common services
   Combined transportation
   Combined case conferences on families seen by different organizations
   Service management to coordinate services by different agencies

Personnel Coordination

Co-location of staff in a commonly shared facility

Outstationing of staff by one organization in that of another

Lend-lease of staff from one organization to function under the administration of another organization for a specified time

Staff teams composed of staffs from different organizations working on a common objective

Compacts involving formal agreements, though no funds are exchanged

Financial Coordination

Joint funding of a common project

Purchase of service involving a formal agreement of one organization to provide a specified service in exchange of funds

Through these kinds of linkages organizations can leverage their own resources to accomplish their goals. By joining with others in this synergistic manner, the sum of the parts can contribute to a more powerful and effective effort than if the organizations were to go their separate ways.

Of course, as noted earlier, not all situations respond to collaborative efforts between organizations. In fact, many community situations require organizations to campaign for a redistribution of resources or change in power relationships. The next section will discuss this negotiating process.

THE NEED FOR NEGOTIATION

In trying to solve pressing problems, community organizations often find it necessary to negotiate with other parties. These negotiations take various forms: community groups advocate with legislators to pass a budget bill, meet with county or city officials to provide special funds for a project, appear before a United Way budget panel or mental health board to request an increase in allocations, discuss with resistive community groups an endorsement of a public policy, request government officials to alter agency policies, or persuade employees to change their hiring procedures.

The common element in all these examples is that the community organization attempts to hold discussions with those who evidence varying degrees of resistance, in the hope of ultimately arriving at an agreement.[11] This is the essence and the end point of the negotiating process. In this context a *negotiant* is anyone whom the community organization is trying to influence. A negotiant can be undecided, neutral, or hostile. An *opponent* is a hostile negotiant who, at least for the moment, actively resists the advocate's position.

In successful negotiations both parties ideally perceive that they have given up something of limited value to gain something of major value. The goal of negotiators is to achieve as strong a position for their organization as they can, or at least to minimize the potential loss for their weaker organization when negotiating with stronger opponents.[12] Often, one party may actually gain more than the other; there may not be an equal exchange. But even in less than ideal negotiations, both negotiating parties must feel that some of their needs are satisfied, that something was gained from the process. If the members of one side suffer a humiliating defeat, this leaves open the possibility of their wanting to return some day to even the score. If one side feels it must make a great sacrifice, with minimal gain, it has no stake in making the agreement a stable one and may be provoked into laying plans for future retaliation.[13]

PREPARING FOR THE NEGOTIATING PROCESS

Clarifying Objectives

Before the negotiating process begins, the community organization must have a clear understanding of what it intends to accomplish, both in the short run and the long run. Little is to be gained if a community organization wins a short-run gain that could jeopardize its long-term interests. For example, a community organization committed to improving the educational experience of its children will weigh carefully whether to use possible pressure tactics to force teachers to provide tutoring. If these tactics serve to so antagonize the faculty that they go through the motions of complying but reduce their involvement with students in other ways, then, to repeat an old cliche, "the battle may be won but the war is lost." Before negotiating commences, therefore, the community organization must clarify its goals and objectives. It must ask how the negotiations will serve to advance its short- and long-term interests.[14]

Setting the Agenda

Part of the preparation of negotiations will also involve establishing an agenda for discussion. The agenda reflects both the power of the two parties and the importance of issues. It is the first step in which both the community organization and the other parties' expectations, attitudes, and values are formally identified. Agendas can be used to clarify or hide motives. They can keep negotiations on track or permit digressions. And they can contain issues that are meaningful to both parties or can serve as a smoke screen for latent problems.[15]

Obtaining Information on the Issue

Knowledge is power. The more information a community organization has available, the more likely it will be able to present its case forcefully and with conviction.[16] One way of obtaining the data is through gathering it systematically. If an organization is concerned with low-paying jobs for women, it must research how many women are in menial jobs. If an organization is concerned that minorities are not represented in administrative positions in proportion to their numbers, then it must document its case. Data can be obtained from census material, county court house records, community or national studies, or through specially designed research.

Sometimes data cannot be collected, in which case a community organization may need to rely on less systematic procedures. For example, if a community organization were concerned with the redlining practice of banks (drawing a red boundary line on a map to indicate where mortgage loans will not be given), then volunteers might need to make informal inquiries in the neighborhood or with real estate companies to determine where people were denied loans.

Sometimes knowledge is gathered informally from employees who work for the institution being challenged. For example, if a community organization were concerned with decisions regarding a city's community development fund, a well-planted informant could provide it with advance information. Informants serve as one of the best sources of inside information, and their identity should always be protected.

Knowledgeable experts are another source of information. Attorneys, accountants, economists, and businesspersons can provide both information and insights on issues. These experts can be particularly valuable when dealing with technical matters.

Preparing The Case

Although logic and reason alone will not sway decision makers whose self-interests are at stake, an essential minimal requirement of negotiations is preparing a sound case. Arguments supporting a position must include a good definition of the problem, a clear statement of what ought to be changed, and a proposed solution for what could be done.

As discussed in the first chapter, problems should be delineated as precisely as possible. Terms must be defined (e.g., sexism) and then concrete application to a particular situation shown (e.g., "sexism exists in both attitudes and behavior of top management"). Since the natural tendency for most organizations and communities is to resist change, the burden of proof falls to advocates to document that something is wrong with the status quo.[17] It is essential to present facts and figures that substantiate the organization's position.

In defining the need, considerable thought should be given to framing the issue in a way which is easiest for the negotiants to agree. For example, in an effort to raise welfare grants, a community organization would try to arouse positive sentiment by concentrating on the benefits to children.

Providing a Solution: Two Viewpoints

There is a difference of opinion about the extent to which a community organization should develop methods for solving the problem as part of the preparation of its position. Some would argue that a detailed proposed solution impresses the negotiants and will go a long way to moving them to accept the community organization's position.[18] Advocates appearing before county commissioners to obtain more day care funding, for example, would show precisely where funding could be located in the budget. By offering a concrete, feasible solution, the group helps decision makers to justify their position. But there may be tactical reasons for *not* proposing a solution. If the community organization becomes involved with locating additional revenues or changing legal mandates, then it may be detoured into unfamiliar territory.[19] So another approach often taken, especially by neighborhood groups, is manifested in the expression, "We have identified the problem— now *you* find the solution." This approach could, of course, turn a negotiant into an adversary.

Obtaining Information on People

A community organization must also be keenly aware of the people with whom it will be negotiating. What do members of the other side believe is important? How have they responded to similar situations in the past? With what organizations are they affiliated? Whose opinions do they respect? How are they likely to respond to pressure tactics? In dealing with middle management administrators, it is always useful to know to whom they report and under what rules they operate.[20]

Anticipating Response of Opponents

In addition to developing general background information about negotiants, it is necessary to anticipate their reaction to the particular proposal and to develop a response and alternatives to their potential reactions. In this regard, negotiation is like a chess game in which one needs to consider not only one's next move, but also the opponent's response to that move and one's subsequent responses, and so forth. This approach requires mentally working through the possible scenarios (as was previously described in Chap. 7 on contingency planning).

In anticipating possible responses of the negotiant, it is particularly useful to consider what might have special value or appeal to the other side's self-interest, such as enhancing its prestige or stature if the proposal were adopted. In addition, the community organization will want to anticipate how it will respond if objections are raised. What responses can be prepared in advance if the other party says that it does not have sufficient staff or funds to implement the proposal, or that there is insufficient support for the proposal, or that the opposition is too strong? Through this kind of anticipation, the community organization can avoid being caught off guard in negotiations.

Often opponents will agree that a change is needed, but then argue that the proposed solution is worse than the problem. One way of dealing with these resistances is for the community group to prepare the opponent's case as it prepares its own.[21] The advocacy organization raises as many harsh objections and questions as it can about its proposal and then develops its response to them.

> Example: A community organization is concerned with an extremely difficult issue: how to develop more group homes for recently released mentally ill patients. It has decided to concentrate on five suburban areas that have heretofore resisted group homes. The organization has embarked on a campaign to convince the legislators from each municipality to modify their zoning laws. Below are listed some of the anticipated objections to change as they might be expressed by the legislators and how the organization tends to deal with them.

Objections	*Responses*
(1) "Property values will decline."	(1) "Our research of other communities where there are group homes shows homes have maintained their values in proportion to rising inflation."

(2)   "Why should we change zoning that would open up group homes? Residents would not be from our communities."

(3)   "Our constituents will be hostile if they learn we have altered zoning."

(4)   "Current zoning laws are adequate, why change?"

(5)   "If we change our zoning, then group homes will be attracted to our community."

(2)   "We can document that each year approximately 120 to 250 people from your communities need special living arrangements, until they are able to move out on their own."

(3)   "In other communities across the country where group homes have been installed, the initial reaction is fear, but this usually gives way to confidence that neighborhoods will function normally. In addition, we can identify key community leaders who will support your efforts."

(4)   "If you do not change your zoning laws, you may experience what has happened in other communities: the possible concentration of group homes in less desirable neighborhoods. Our proposal provides a formula that insures that homes will not be located closer than one-half mile to each other."

(5)   "We are working with four other continguous communities; all have expressed similar concerns. They have agreed to sign a joint pledge that if four out of the five agree to our proposal, they will introduce legislation into the communities."

Through the exercise of listing all the anticipated resistances, the community organization can begin to prepare its case.

Developing a Fall-Back Position

Some community organizations have a tendency to express their concerns through moral self-righteousness. Indeed, their profound sense of indignation and sincere commitment to their cause greatly contributes to their power at the negotiating table. But since the negotiation process will often involve compromises, the community organization needs to think out in advance what it is willing to compromise on—what its fall-back position is. At the same time, the community organization needs to determine what its minimal, bottom-line requirements are. Hence, it must be clear on what it is, and is not, willing to compromise.

Communicating with Constituents

Because there always exists the danger that the negotiating team could take a position different from the group it represents, it is crucial that reporting procedures and mechanisms for decisions be worked out in advance.[22] Such procedures could include periodic meetings where group consensus process or votes would take place either with the entire membership or a body representing the membership.

BEING WATCHFUL ABOUT NEGOTIATING MANEUVERS

The negotiating process often fosters situations in which parties try to outmaneuver each other. These maneuvers or gambits (in chess, a gambit is an opening in which a pawn is sacrificed to get an advantage in position) are intended to manipulate the negotiating situation to special advantage of one party over the other. By being aware of the most common maneuvers that could be attempted by the opposition, community organizations can be in a better position to deal with the negotiating process.

Using the Pressure of Timing

There are two ways that time can be used as a maneuver: stalling or pressuring deadlines. Opponents who stall do so with the intent of preventing quick resolution of the issue in exchange for the expectation of gaining more in the future.[23] They deliberately decide to extend negotiations over a long period of time in the anticipation that they can hold out longer than their opposition. An example of this would be a landlord who deliberately delays negotiations in the hopes that the renters will be unable to sustain the consequences of a long rent strike.

Sometimes the opposition will use the pressure of time to precipitate action. The urgency of a deadline for legislative bills or year-end funding decisions can push both parties to compromise.

Slicing

This maneuver (sometimes called *slicing the salami*) is designed to get the community organization to agree to a relatively innocuous position, with the intent of obtaining more (and then more) later.[24] The small concession made at one point opens the door for larger concessions later. The remedy is to gain assurances in advance that a minor concession will not lead to others.

Fait Accompli

A *fait accompli* (accomplished fact) is a surprise maneuver by the opposition to take action that produces a result so as to make any negotiations meaningless.[25] For example, community groups are invited to a mental health hearing to discuss potential models for psychiatric emergency services, when a decision has already been made. Or, at a state budget hearing, community groups are invited to present their views only to discover that the budget has already been established. In both instances, the hearings are a charade. To remedy potential fait accompli situations, it is desirable to determine in advance whether a decision already has been made. Negotiations should make explicit that decision making would be open to options. If it appears that the decision has already been made and therefore the negotiations are a sham, then negotiants have to be challenged or an appeal made to a higher authority.

Limited Authority

In this maneuver, negotiants are able to influence the community organization to make concessions, but when they in turn are asked to make concessions, they plead the need to check with a higher authority. They are unable to make final decisions, and they are subject to veto. To prevent this from happening, it is important to clarify in advance the extent of the authority of the opponent.[26] If necessary, community organization members may need to go directly to the higher authority under which the negotiants' team is operating, such as the director of an agency, the governor, or a board of trustees.

Cooptation

Sometimes opponents bring into the decision-making process outspoken and antagonistic community organization members with the intent of softening their position.[27] When those advocates who formerly took a strong position are invited into the decision-making process of those they once attacked, the advocates tend to lighten their demands. An example of this would be a school board that requests that vociferous community leaders serve on an advisory committee. Although being invited to participate in the decision process may offer opportunities for influence, the chief danger is that such participation may be illusory.

Quid Pro Quo

The Latin term *quid pro quo* (something for something) describes how each party makes a concession in exchange for the other party's concession. While the quid pro quo process is a common part of negotiations, two aspects require special vigilence: First, the opponent could concede relatively minor points with the expectation that the community organization will concede on major items. Second, the opponent may make significant concessions but then propose to offset these with other actions, thus nullifying the original concessions. The negotiants deliberately make an enticing offer, an inducement that is difficult to refuse. It is like the grocery store that attracts customers with "loss leader" items that sell below normal market costs, but makes up the loss by charging customers regular or higher than normal prices on other items. An example of this would be a funding body agreeing to pay for a special request, but then reducing funds in another part of the community organization's budget.

Pleading Powerlessness

Public officials sometimes plead that they are powerless to act on a request. For example, state mental health officials may claim that their facilities are incapable of dealing with persons who are both mentally ill and retarded. But then state retardation officials claim the same thing. Both want the other administration to deal with dually diagnosed people, with the result that neither does.

Public officials often claim that they have no control over funding. Obviously, funding organizations do not have monies to fund all requests. They have to make priority decisions. But when they say they have no power to provide funds for a particular community organization's request, what they really mean is that they have made a decision (based on past or current commitments) to give priority to other funding requests.

Ambiguity

Ambiguity is often used as a way of facilitating the negotiation process to come to a resolution on a difficult or complex issue. At times, negotiants may purposefully use ambiguous words as a possible basis for reopening discussions later if they are not satisfied with the results of the negotiations. Vague words or escape clauses are purposefully written to permit self-serving interpretations later. If the ambiguity leaves basic issues unresolved, they could flare up again.

Escalation

Some negotiants purposefully appear to work out agreements with the intent of introducing last minute requests. Although the community organization thinks it has reached an agreement, suddenly, as time appears to be running out, it is faced with new and different demands. It then has the difficult choice of accepting the new demands or renegotiating.[28]

Final Offer

At times, the opponent may make a take-it-or-leave-it offer. This is likely to occur when opponents feel that the preponderance of power is in their hands. Negotiations can then result in an impasse, capitulation, or an open fight.

Stonewall

As the name indicates, the purpose of this maneuver is to place an obstacle in the way of the discussion so that important issues are not fully discussed. An opponent will ignore or deny that a problem exists, as illustrated by school officials who say that children are as well educated as any in the county or state. Employment services administrators may claim that services are quite adequate for finding people jobs, despite unemployment figures being to the contrary. This approach is introduced to prevent negotiations from occurring.

Diversion

An opponent may attempt to shift the issue away from the original concern.[29] For example, a community organization may want to discuss how unresponsive and inefficient staff is, but the negotiant will shift the discussion to the lack of adequate staff.

Another form of diversion occurs when, faced with mounting community criticism, some institutions create a community relations unit to work with advocacy groups to reduce tension and improve perceptions. A police department will create a community relations division; private industry, a community affairs unit to improve communication. A community organization has to determine whether the new unit is a sincere effort to alter institutional practices or a means of diverting the discussions from focusing on its immediate concerns.

Repudiation

At times an agreement may appear to have been consummated when the opponents retract or repudiate their positions. Because this is an ever-present danger, it is wise to make agreements public. Witnesses should be present. To avoid repudiation, it is helpful for both parties to sign drafts of agreements.[30] If repudiation does occur, the community organization may have, as its only recourse, the publicizing of the bad faith of its opponents.

STRENGTHENING THE NEGOTIATING POWER OF COMMUNITY ORGANIZATIONS

In many respects, the negotiations involving community organizations are similar to those used by salespeople, lawyers, labor and management, and others concerned with working out agreements. But in two major respects the negotiation process differs. First, many community organizations do not always have within their capacity the power to gain access to decision makers. As a consequence, they feel frustrated and compelled to develop special techniques for reaching those in power. Just as a potential card player with only $10 cannot gain access to a poker table when the minimum stakes are $100, so community groups lacking power frequently find themselves locked out of the negotiation process. Hence, community organizations invest heavily in trying to develop power that allows them to sit at the table.

Second, even if they are fortunate enough to gain access, community organizations often deal with public officials who do not have a profound investment in working out a particular issue at the bargaining table. Certainly many public officials have a high degree of integrity and commitment to improving the lives of people for whom they bear responsibility. Legislators want to pass laws that improve their community, public administrators want to improve procedures. But unlike legal negotiators involved in a law suit or labor and management

negotiators working on a wage dispute, public official negotiants usually are beset with demands from many pressure groups, and they do not
have a clarity about the outcomes they want to see occur. Furthermore,
unlike legal negotiants, public official negotiants are not required to
meet or negotiate. They are prone to respond to political pressures
beyond the particular issue under discussion. This is why the "squeaky
wheel" syndrome more often than not works. Those clamoring the
loudest, those able to exert the most pressure are listened to. Because
of the lack of clarity about what public officials themselves want and
because of their vulnerability to extraneous influences, community
organizations must pay close attention to what is important to the other
side as they participate in the negotiating process.

To gain access to negotiations and enhance their bargaining positions, community organizations use a variety of approaches: supporting survival needs, demonstrating public support and sympathy, forming alliances, conducting behind-the-scenes discussions, targeting
pressure points, threatening, and waging campaigns.

Supporting Survival Needs

Helping politicians with their campaign, supporting a local department to gain state or federal appropriations, assisting in a fund
raising campaign, supporting public officials in their budget requests—these are some of the favors that are undertaken in the hopes
that someday favors may be returned. Some of the community's business is conducted on the basis of favors rendered, chits owed.

Demonstrating Public Support and Sympathy

Community organizations can use a variety of approaches to show
that the position they espouse has widespread community support:

holding mass rallies,

conducting letter writing campaigns,

circulating petitions,

increasing membership.

These indicators of public support can particularly influence public
officials who know how to count votes.

One effective organization conducted a campaign to raise public
assistance grants. Among their techniques were the following: (1)
arranging for a press conference to announce the campaign; (2) organizing petitions to be signed by inner city merchants; (3) conducting a

letter writing campaign to legislators throughout the state; (4) obtaining editorial support; (5) arranging for bus loads of people to converge on the state capitol; (6) presenting testimony to legislative hearings; and (7) organizing leading citizens to contact their legislators. The culmination of these campaign tactics resulted in increasing the grants to a cause that normally is not supported by the general public.[31] Legislators will, in private discussions, express how impressed they are with organizing efforts of community organizations.[32] In general, strong organizational efforts can have a profound effect on the negotiation process.

Forming Alliances

As a general rule, the broader the base of support, the more power can be exerted in the negotiating process. This is why community organizations frequently form alliances. Such alliances can be composed of organizations whose members have similar values, or they may have little in common except the particular issue that draws them together. Alliances can be fragile and often only temporary arrangements, unless there are compelling reasons to form them. All parties must feel they will gain more by joining together than they could by going their separate ways. And the rewards of the alliance, e.g., substantial increase in funding for all parties or the passage of major legislation, have to be sufficiently meaningful to warrant an interdependent arrangement.[33]

A breakdown in an alliance is always a possibility if organizations feel their internal decision-making process is preempted, if the decision process becomes too cumbersome, if groups, though agreeing over ultimate ends, strongly disagree over means, or if some see that other groups are benefiting to their detriment.

If member organizations can develop trust in each other and agreement on strategy can occur, alliances can be powerful instruments in the negotiating process. More groups mean more votes, more money, or more public sentiment. Legislators, fund raisers, and administrators are all greatly impressed when they see the size and variety of support of an alliance.

Conducting Behind-the-Scenes Discussions

While organizing alliances plays a significant part in influencing negotiants, it is not always necessary, or desirable, to make an issue a public one to gain the support of certain key decision makers. In most political and institutional situations, certain people bear major responsibility for what happens. In the State Assembly, the Speaker of the House or the President of the Senate wield tremendous power. If, through behind-the-scenes discussions, they become convinced about a certain legislative matter, then the odds will favor its passage. Depending on the particular issue, other key people can include the governor, the president of the county commissioners, the police chief, the executive director of the local United Way, the director of a human services department, to name a few. Each of these persons has friends, people to whom they owe favors and people whose opinions they respect. Through quiet discussions with these "gatekeepers" the key decision makers can be convinced to carry out a course of action promoted by the community organization. In fact, these key leaders sometimes become the crusaders of the cause, and the initiating community organization may have to be satisfied with little credit even though their position is implemented.

Targeting Pressure Points

Community organizations develop strategies that pinpoint pressure points as a prelude to negotiations. They select targets that are vulnerable to the special kinds of pressure a community organization can bring to bear.[34] If a group is concerned about neighborhood housing rehabilitation, it is likely to select savings and loan associations to challenge rather than commercial banks because, for the most part, savings and loans are located in the neighborhoods. If a community group is concerned about a particular legislative bill, it will identify key constituents of the legislators to act as influencing agents. If a group wants to influence a voluntary funding decision, it will involve spokespeople who are themselves large contributors to the voluntary fund. If a group wants to influence the state director of a human service agency, it will locate a legislator who has been influential in the department's budget to make the initial contact with the state director.

Similarly, timing of the pressure is important. A community group concerned with legislation needs to be aware that the time to obtain support is 6 months to 1 year before the expected vote in the assembly. The time to put pressure on the mayor is during the campaign. The time to pressure local officials is during a levy. These are the times when negotiants are more vulnerable.

Hence, opportunities for influencing the negotiation process are affected by the targets chosen, the people selected to do the influencing, and the timing.

Threatening

By its very nature, negotiation often involves a degree of threat. The fact that rewards can be withheld or punishment inflicted constitutes a threat. The main question confronting the negotiation process is not whether threats will be used as a tactic, but whether there are benefits to using them as a tactic.[35] The answer to the question depends on several considerations:

(1)   Is the threat compatible with the overall strategy of the community organization? For example, if the group feels it will require the goodwill and cooperation of the other side once the negotiations are concluded, it may not want to rely heavily on threat as a tactic.

(2)   Does the community organization have the power to inflict significant punishment without experiencing substantial retaliation? There is an old saying, "If you shoot at the king, aim for the heart." A slightly wounded adversary can become a vicious enemy. A threat could result in the opponent's mounting a counterattack.

(3)   Is the threat believable? If not, and it is seen as a bluff, the community group's position may be weakened. Some actions may need to accompany the threat: a threat of a lawsuit is more believable when it is known that legal counsel has been hired. The threat of losing votes at the next election becomes more believable when opposition candidates are being considered.

(4)   Is the threat scaled to the situation? In the heat of emotional negotiations, community groups sometimes threaten more punishment than the situation warrants or they may have actually intended. If they feel they must follow through to make their position creditable, they may be embarking on self-destructive actions.

(5)   Is the threat from the organization likely to produce results when the negotiant weighs it against other considerations? For example, a community organization threatens to withdraw its support of the mayor if better street lighting is not provided. The organization should speculate whether its demands carry sufficient weight when compared with other, possibly more influential, organizations making similar demands.

Waging Campaigns Against Persons or Institutions

When other approaches seem to fail, when a community organization feels frustrated, or when it senses that it is removed from the normal community decision-making process, it may, as a last resort, attempt to open conflict and confrontation. This approach is intended to prevent opponents from continuing to function as usual or to neutralize their power, in the hope of moving them toward some acceptable reconciliation.[36]

The poor, the elderly, minority groups, women, and others who normally have little power will organize themselves to challenge decision makers and institutions. They seek to change existing status relationships through a variety of campaigns, as follows:

Conducting Public Demonstrations.   One objective of these public demonstrations is to draw the attention of the usually apathetic public to the plight of those who feel powerless. The second objective is to disrupt business as usual: handicapped people sitting on the floor of the welfare office to demand special grants, or elderly people shouting at the mayor for lack of services, or neighborhood people picketing at their landlord's suburban home—these demonstrations cannot be ignored. Or, if they are ignored, then it is at the risk of appearing cold and unresponsive. A third objective of demonstrations is to goad the opposition into taking arbitrary and oppressive actions. As a result of the opponents' overreaction, the underdog community organization gains sympathy from those who might otherwise be neutral or uninvolved in the issue. Sit-ins by civil rights and antiwar activists produced this effect in the 1960s and 1970s.

Negative Publicity.   Sometimes a community organization uses the public media to embarrass the opposition. For example, women will organize to nominate the worst boss of the year award and announce this through the newspapers. Or a child advocacy organization may use the newspapers to describe the inefficiency of a state's human services department. The intent of these public attacks is to put pressure on individuals or community institutions in the hope that they will eagerly seek resolutions.

Taking Legal Action.   Filing a lawsuit can serve as an embarrassment to institutions and persons that pride themselves on working for the betterment of the community. Lawsuits are also intended to have the courts force the opposition to work out an agreement.

Risks in Waging an Open Campaign

The results of open fighting can either be effective or detrimental, depending on a number of unpredictable circumstances. Under some circumstances disruptive demonstrations can produce positive change, but under other circumstances they can polarize a community and produce ill will rather than sympathetic support. A tactic that has worked well to produce change in one community at a particular point in time may not necessarily be effective in another community at a different point in time.[37] Because of this unpredictability, waging an open campaign may or may not lead parties to the negotiation table.

Some community groups consider the gamble worth taking even if they may not succeed, for at least they have dramatized the issue and perhaps raised the consciousness of the community for a more positive response at a later time. But even if the community oganization is successful, it would be aware of certain inherent risks of open fighting.

One of these risks is that fighting fosters a seige mentality by those who are under attack. Just as those pioneers who trekked across the plains had to be prepared to circle their wagons in the event of attack, modern public officials may tend to develop an attitude that constantly puts them on the defensive. Having been frequently attacked in the past, they are not receptive to the challenges of a community organization, even if the criticisms are intended to be constructive. A climate of mistrust and suspicion prevails. To the attacked administrator, funder, or legislator, the best defense is an offense. And often public officials and administrators will tend to protect and support each other, for if one is for the moment vulnerable to attack, then others reason the same situation could affect them. Negotiations proceed unsatisfactorily when both parties invest energy in stubbornly adhering to their positions.

The second risk to the community organization is that because it is identified as the attacker, it becomes unacceptable as a participant in the subsequent negotiating process. Consequently, though it may have served a useful purpose in laying the groundwork for negotiations, because of its militancy, it may find itself excluded from working out specific agreements.

The third risk in open fighting is that attitudes in the community organization itself may serve as a deterrent to negotiations. Rather than seeing fighting as a means to an end, some members of the group will enjoy the fight as an end in itself. Often the anger that has energized the organization can evaporate when conciliation takes place through negotiations. Winning the fight can paradoxically reduce member involvement in, and commitment to, the organization. Knowing that this can happen, leaders of the organization may tend at times to want to perpetuate the fight to keep a hold on their members.

Hence, open fighting can have such negative consequences as causing the other side to become defensively unbending, excluding the advocate from the bargaining table, and creating a climate within the community organization itself of perpetuating the fight.

WORKING OUT A STALEMATE

Assuming that both sides (1) have come to a bargaining table more or less as equals and capable of influencing each other, (2) want sincerely to work out an agreement, and (3) are sophisticated about manipulation techniques, how, then, can negotiations be conducted creatively and constructively? And how can impasses be overcome?

Developing a willingness by both sides to compromise is one major way to overcome a stalemate. Each side is asked to reduce its demands or to raise its offers. Sometimes one side will make a greater compromise than the other because, based on its assessment of the situation and its own power position, it determines that it has achieved as much as possible. Sometimes a community organization compensates for its lack of power with an intensity of commitment and sheer will. This explains why a well-organized group that is emotionally aroused and highly vocal can wear down a more rational, but less invested, administrator or city official. Sometimes the parties are so exhausted from the protracted, marathon discussions that they seek a resolution by splitting the differences: "We will concede on this point, if you will concede on that point." It should be noted that because both sides usually anticipate the likelihood of compromises, they will initially put forth their maximum position.[38] When they feel the time is right, they bring forth their fall-back positions. The most acceptable compromises are ones in which both sides emerge from the negotiations with at least some of their needs satisfied.

Another approach to breaking an impasse is through a special inducement or offer.[39] For example, it may become clear in dealing with an overworked and overextended public institution that it cannot take on another program because it already has so many other demands it cannot fill. Special inducements, such as finding volunteer staff or providing training or assistance in proposal preparation, could result in its considering the project.

Diffusing an emotionally charged atmosphere is another approach to dealing with a stalemate. Defensive responses will be evoked when both parties are accusatory, judgmental, and so highly competitive that they are constantly looking for ways to win or "zing" their opponents (this is called the *gotcha!* attitude). What are some of the ways that help shift from a highly competitive climate to a more trusting one?

One way is to require that each side state its position completely and without interruption except for questions of clarification. This procedure permits each side to fully air its position while the other side listens.[40] Another technique is for each side to reiterate in summary form the position of the other side so that it is clear that each side fully understands the other's position. A third procedure is to make explicit the ground rules that no depreciating remarks are to be made in the discussions. Each side's position can be challenged and clarified but no insults are allowed.[41] A further technique is to concentrate on the

points of agreement, putting aside until later areas of major conten-
tion. By achieving some limited success (and, hopefully, trust) the two
parties may be in a better position later to deal with the more divisive
issues. A fifth approach is to have one side soften its position tentatively
and in an exploratory manner: "We will consider lowering our demands if you will alter yours." This approach could soften the hard line
position on both sides.

Finally, stalemates can be broken if the style of the negotiation is
changed from a win/lose stance to a position in which each side actively
explores creative alternatives.[42] Both sides would adopt the attitude
that for any given problem, there may be a variety of solutions possible,
which can be mutually explored to determine advantages to both.
Instead of each side trying to conquer the other, each would try to
experiment with ideas and take a provisional attitude about its own
proposal. Both parties would avoid being locked into a position.

To facilitate this exploratory approach, both sides would join
together in determining the facts. Then they would attempt to seek a
variety of alternatives. Members from both sides would be engaged in
putting forth suggestions so that there would be a broad participation
in considering the final solution. Through this give-and-take process,
resolution may be reached in the negotiations.

Chapter 9

DEVELOPING ACTION PLANNING CHARTS

The special advantage of action planning charts is that they show at a glance exactly how an organization intends to carry out its decisions. The visual display further reveals how the organization is implementing its activities and tasks. Six different kinds of action planning charts will be discussed in this chapter. They are presented in summary form in Table 9–1.

ASSIGNMENTS CHART

When it is important to identify the people who will carry out specific responsibilities, an assignments chart can be useful.[1] Table 9–2 displays how an organization can pinpoint assignments and identify team leaders, participants, and those who might carry out consultative, supervisory, and final approval roles.

DEVELOPING ACTIVITY AND TASK SCHEDULES

Following its decision about an action plan, an organization will normally want to develop a detailed schedule of activities and tasks.[2] This is particularly important if the plan calls for following a schedule

Table 9-1. SUMMARY OF ACTION PLANNING CHARTS

CHART	APPLICATION(S)	PREPARATION REQUIRED
ASSIGNMENTS CHART	Displays specific responsibilities of major units in the organization	Specific assignments and roles have been determined
GANTT CHART	Shows major activities and tasks in relation to time frame	Objectives have been determined Activities and tasks have been identified either through reverse order or forward sequence planning
PERT CHART	Shows interrelationships between activities and tasks Shows estimated time of all work necessary to reach objectives Useful for nonrecurring events	Same as GANTT
NARRATIVE NETWORK CHART	Shows estimated time in relation to calendar dates Visually displays activites on chart	Same as PERT and GANTT
PROJECT DEVELOPMENT FLOW CHART	Shows sequencing of activities, decision points, and revision points of an organizational or community process	Objectives have been determined Revision points have been identified
ALTERNATIVE CHOICE CHART	Orderly sequence of questions and instructions for solving a problem Routine decision making on client flow or whether clients qualify for program	Objectives have been determined Series of questions with (or without) instructions leading to alternative, pre-determined outcomes have been developed

that will require several months of effort. As a first step in scheduling, the organization needs to identify a detailed list of activities and tasks.

Major Activities/Specific Tasks

Major Activities are the most important efforts required to achieve one or more objectives within a specified time period. Major activities include the following elements:

Table 9-2.   ASSIGNMENTS CHART

ASSIGNMENTS	TEAM LEADER	PARTICIPANTS	CONSULTANTS	SUPERVISORS	APPROVERS
Prepare manual	Levo	Rinds/Timwal	Sherson	Craf/Binski	McMarlay
Prepare newsletter	Rinds	Levo/Johnson	Sherson	Craf	McMarlay
Recruitment campaign	Craf	Levo/Rinds/ Johnson			McMarlay

They are essential for achieving an objective.

They should result in one single identifiable product, such as a report, a meeting, or a major assignment completed.

They can occur either in sequence or simultaneously with other activities.

Tasks are specific jobs required to accomplish a major activity. Feeding into a major activity, these tasks can usually be achieved in a time span of a few days or weeks. Individuals or units of the organization are generally assigned these tasks. Although the spelling out of tasks can sometimes be time consuming and tedious, preparing for completion of major activities in this way can more readily insure that the proper actions will be implemented. If there appears later to be a lack of progress in achieving a major activity, then the specific tasks around which the breakdown occurred can be pinpointed.

Techniques for Developing Tasks

Two approaches can be considered in specifying tasks: (1) reverse order and (2) forward sequence planning.

Reverse Order Planning.   In reverse order planning the group begins with the final result to be achieved and identifies the tasks that feed into activities by reviewing, "What must we do just before reaching our final result, and then what needs to be done before that, and before that, and so forth?" until it arrives at the beginning point.[3] For example, to organize a speakers' bureau, the following tasks might be considered in a process of reverse order:

Promote speaking engagements (last task)

Train speakers (fourth task)

Prepare speakers' kits (third task)

Recruit volunteers (second task)

Plan training sessions (first task)

Forward Sequence Planning. In forward sequence planning the group begins with what it considers to be the appropriate first set of tasks and then asks, "What should we do next, and what after that, and so forth?" until the end result is reached.[4] Whether the group uses the reverse order or forward planning approach, it is important to consider what preparation will be necessary to complete each task. For example, to prepare speakers' kits will require developing written materials, writing out instructions, including forms to be completed, and so on. Hence, for each task it is possible to identify subtasks, if this level of detail is desired.

In actual decision-making situations, groups will combine reverse order with forward sequence planning. That is, typically members of the group will consider by what date they want to achieve a particular result and then consider all the tasks that they need to undertake prior to that deadline. If the predominate mode is reverse order planning, the group will find it useful to employ forward sequence planning as a double checking device (and vice versa) to see if any task has been omitted.

To illustrate how activities can be scheduled, assume that professional staff and volunteer leaders have determined that their community needs to recruit 30 new foster parents within a 9-month period. To achieve this objective, a steering committee has been organized consisting of representatives from the human services department (H.S. Dept.), a special task force of foster parents and concerned citizens (task force), and a public relations (PR) firm willing to donate its services to the foster parent recruitment campaign. The steering committee is responsible for developing the sequence of activities and tasks and determining the timetable for major accomplishments.

The steering committee has determined that several major activities must be undertaken in the period beginning in April and ending with a recognition dinner in December. These activities include the following:

developing a plan and structure to carry out the recruitment campaign,

preparing and distributing public relations materials,

preparing a foster care manual that clarifies roles and responsibilities of new foster parents, organizing a speakers' bureau,

conducting orientation sessions for new foster parents,

providing a recognition dinner.

Under each major activity, the steering committee also identifies a series of tasks that must be accomplished, as shown in Table 9–3.

In reality no group would come up with such a clean looking chart as shown in Table 9–3 following a first round of discussions. Whether forward sequencing or reverse order planning were used, a review of the list of tasks would reveal the need to omit some tasks because they were too demanding, reschedule tasks to prevent overload, or add tasks initially omitted. Even when the task list appears to be in final form, the organization should be prepared for further refinements based on new knowledge and circumstances.

DISPLAYING ACTIVITIES AND TASKS

After a group prepares a detailed list of activities and tasks and it wishes to display a timetable to visually check its actual progress and accomplishments against its projections, it can use two major devices: the GANTT chart (named for its founder) and network charts.

GANTT Chart

The GANTT chart (timeline chart) is comprehensible, easy to prepare, and requires a minimum amount of time to construct.[5] Note that in Figure 9–1 the major activities and tasks correspond to those listed earlier in the activities and tasks chart, Table 9–3. The lines related to each task graphically show beginning and end points. By reading the chart from top to bottom, it is possible to determine which activities and tasks are expected to occur within a particular time period. A review of the GANTT chart shown in Figure 9–1 shows, for example, that during the months of July and August public relations, speakers' bureau, and foster manual tasks will be undertaken. People will therefore need to be available during these months to carry out assignments. As will be shown later in Chapter 11, Figure 11–2, the GANTT chart can be used to monitor whether tasks are being accomplished on schedule.

The main limitation of the GANTT chart is that it does not link significant tasks under one activity with those of another activity.

Table 9-3. LIST OF TASKS

		Who's Responsible	Estimated Time (Weeks)	Estimated Dates
Major Activity:	Develop a plan and structure	Steering Committee		
Tasks:	Appoint task force	Steering Committee	2	4/1-4/15
	Interview foster care agencies, parents, and H.S. Dept. staff	H.S. Dept.	2	4/15-4/30
	Formulate foster care plan	Steering Committee	2	5/1-5/15
Major Activity:	Prepare public relations materials	H.S. Dept.		
Tasks:	Identify profile of unserved children	H.S. Dept./ Task Force	2	5/15-5/30
	Identify profile of potential foster parents	H.S. Dept./ Task Force	2	5/15-5/30
	Prepare PR campaign strategy	H.S. Dept./ Task Force/ PR Firm	4	6/1-6/30
	Prepare bus posters	PR Firm	6	7/1-8/15
	Prepare radio tapes	PR Firm	6	7/1-8/15
	Transmit to new foster parents in orientation sessions	H.S. Dept.	2	11/15-11/30
Major Activity:	Organize speakers' bureau	H.S. Dept.		
Tasks:	Plan speakers' bureau	H.S. Dept.	2	7/15-7/31
	Recruit volunteers and staff	H.S. Dept.	6	8/1-9/15
	Prepare speakers' kits	H.S. Dept.	2	9/15-9/30
	Train speakers	H.S. Dept./ Task Force/	2	10/1-10/15
	Distribute PR materials	PR Firm	4	9/15-10/15
	Promote speaking engagements	H.S. Dept.	2	10/15-10/31
	Conduct speaking engagements	H.S. Dept./ Task Force	4	11/1-11/30

Table 9-3 (cont'd.)

		Who's Responsible	Estimated Time (Weeks)	Estimated Dates
	Prepare TV ads	PR Firm	6	7/1-8/15
	Prepare written materials for speakers' kits	PR Firm	10	7/1-9/15
	Contact public media	PR Firm	4	8/15-9/15
	Submit materials to media	PR Firm	6	9/15-10/31
Major Activity:	Prepare a foster care manual	H.S. Dept., assisted by Task Force		
Tasks:	Appoint committee and staff	H.S. Dept.	4	6/1-6/30
	Prepare outline	H.S. Dept.	4	7/1-7/31
	Prepare drafts	H.S. Dept.	4	8/1-8/31
	Obtain H.S. Dept. staff reactions	H.S. Dept./ Task Force	2	9/1-9/15
	Obtain foster parents' reactions	H.S. Dept./ Task Force	4	9/1-9/30
	Revise drafts	H.S. Dept.	4	10/1-10/31
	Arrange for printing	H.S. Dept.	2	11/1-11/15
Major Activity:	Process applicants	H.S. Dept.		
Tasks:	Plan processing procedures	H.S. Dept.	2	9/1-9/15
	Orient staff	H.S. Dept.	2	9/15-9/30
	Prepare phone instructions	H.S. Dept.	2	10/1-10/15
	Prepare follow up materials	H.S. Dept.	2	10/1-10/15
	Conduct screening interviews	H.S. Dept.	4	10/15-11/15
	Conduct group orientation sessions	H.S. Dept.	2	11/15-11/30
Major Activity:	Provide Recognition Dinner	Task Force/ H.S. Dept.		
Tasks:	Obtain commitment for funding	Task Force	2	10/1-10/15
	Reserve room	Task Force/ H.S. Dept.	2	10/15-10/31
	Obtain caterer	Task Force	2	10/15-10/31
	Send out invitations	Task Force	2	11/1-11/15
	Plan dinner program	Task Force	4	11/15-12/15

Figure 9-1. <u>GANTT CHART</u>

<u>Objective</u>: To recruit an additional 100 foster parents by the end of the year.

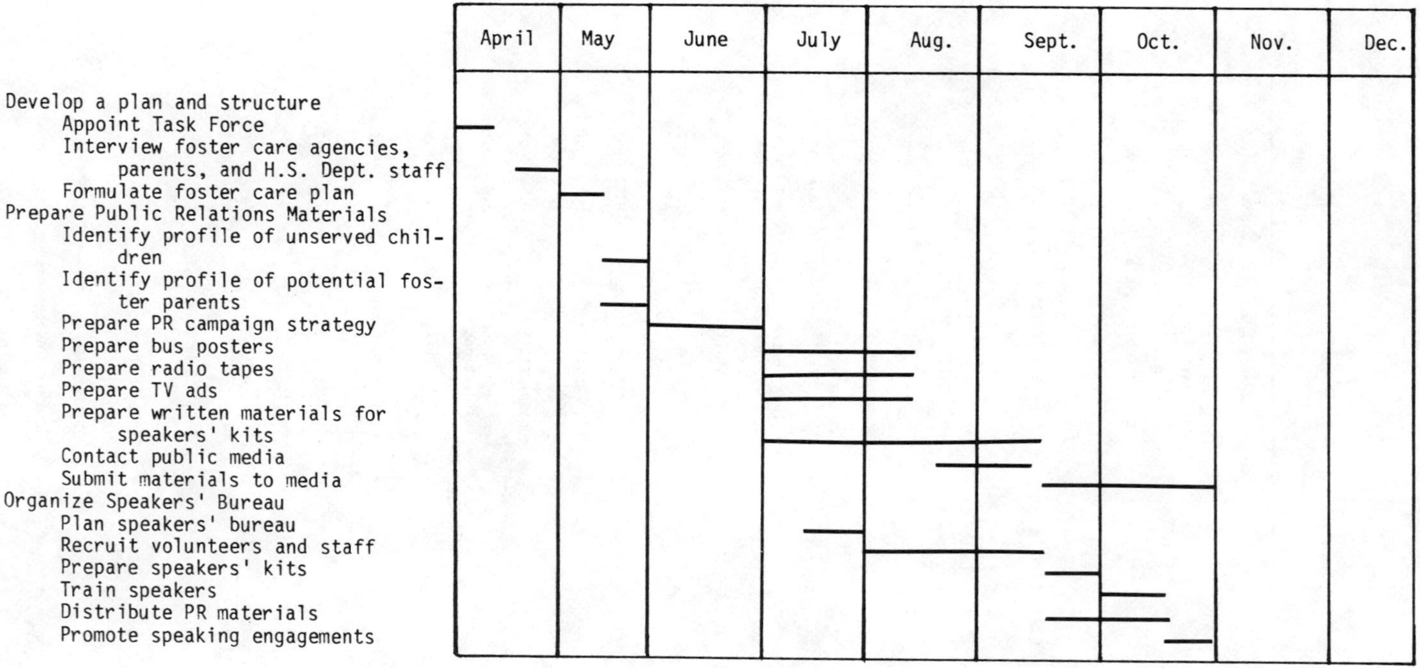

	April	May	June	July	Aug.	Sept.	Oct.	Nov.	Dec.
Develop a plan and structure									
Appoint Task Force	▬								
Interview foster care agencies, parents, and H.S. Dept. staff		▬							
Formulate foster care plan		▬							
Prepare Public Relations Materials									
Identify profile of unserved children		▬							
Identify profile of potential foster parents			▬						
Prepare PR campaign strategy			▬						
Prepare bus posters				▬					
Prepare radio tapes				▬					
Prepare TV ads				▬					
Prepare written materials for speakers' kits				▬▬▬					
Contact public media					▬				
Submit materials to media						▬▬▬			
Organize Speakers' Bureau									
Plan speakers' bureau				▬					
Recruit volunteers and staff					▬▬				
Prepare speakers' kits						▬			
Train speakers							▬		
Distribute PR materials						▬			
Promote speaking engagements							▬		

Figure 9-1 (cont'd.)

	April	May	June	July	Aug.	Sept.	Oct.	Nov.	Dec.
Process applicants									
Plan processing procedures									
Orient staff									
Prepare phone instructions									
Prepare follow up materials									
Conduct screening interviews									
Conduct group orientation sessions									
Prepare Foster Care Manual									
Appoint committee and staff									
Prepare outline									
Prepare drafts									
Obtain H.S. Dept. reactions									
Obtain foster parents' reactions									
Revise draft									
Arrange for printing									
Transmit to new foster parents in orientation sessions									
Provide Recognition Dinner									
Obtain funding commitment									
Reserve room									
Obtain caterer									
Send invitations									
Plan dinner program									

155

Network Charts: PERT and Narrative

A network chart has the advantage of disciplining the group to consider the interrelationships of tasks to each other. It visually displays not only how tasks feed into a major activity, but also how they connect with other activities at a particular point in time. It is useful when dealing with nonrecurring events and when there is pressure to complete a project or a major activity in the shortest possible time. A network chart can be displayed in one of two ways: (1) program and evaluation review technique (PERT) charts (Fig. 9–2.) or (2) narrative network charts (Fig. 9–3.)

PERT Chart   When the interrelationships of tasks and their timing are crucial, then the PERT chart is a useful tool. As shown in Figure 9–2 a PERT chart can accomplish the following:

identify specific tasks,

estimate the time necessary for completion of activities and the entire project,

coordinate these tasks, so that the project is viewed as an integrated whole,

communicate visually the tasks needing to be accomplished.

If the primary purpose of a PERT chart is to provide a visual display for an audience, then the major activities or a few tasks can be shown. More commonly PERT and narrative network charts would be developed for displaying numerous tasks that must be interrelated, as shown in Figures 9–2 and 9–3. Note that both the PERT and narrative network charts illustrated in Figures 9–2 and 9–3 contain identical tasks previously listed in Table 9–3 and Figure 9–1. This was done to show the reader alternative ways of presenting the same material.

The procedures for displaying a PERT chart are as follows:

(1)   Determine the objective of a project and set a deadline.
(2)   List all the tasks that are required to achieve each major activity. Use both the reverse order and forward sequence planning to compile the list. Next to each task place a number indicating the sequence and also estimate the time for completion of the particular task. This could be listed as follows:

Activity: Prepare and distribute foster care manual

Tasks	Order	Time Estimate
Appoint committee and staff of foster care manual	1	2 weeks
Prepare outline	2	4 weeks
Prepare drafts	3	4 weeks
Obtain H.S. Dept. reactions	4	2 weeks
Obtain foster care association reactions to drafts	5	4 weeks
Revise drafts	6	4 weeks
Arrange for printing	7	2 weeks
Transmit to foster parents	8	2 weeks

(3)   As illustrated in Figure 9–2 the actual performing of tasks (expressed as a verb) will be displayed in the form of arrows (→).

(4)   The accomplishment of tasks are known as *events* and are shown as a number within a circle, such as ③⑦ .

(5)   Each task starts with a leader event and ends with a follower event. Example: ㉙ → ㉚ Event ㉙ is the leader event and event ㉚ is the follower event. The line represents the task necessary to advance the project from event ㉙ to event ㉚ and is called task 29–30 (appoint committee and staff).

(6)   Each major activity within a project starts with a single (first) event and ends with a single (last) event. Events occurring after the first event and before the last event are known as in-between events.

(7)   A milestone is an outstanding event; milestones indicate the beginning or ending of a major activity of the project. The symbol for a milestone is a circle enclosed in a square: [⑤] .

(8)   Sometimes a dotted arrow (- - - - - - →) is inserted to clarify a task pattern. It is called a dummy task because it requires neither time nor personnel. It is used to show that one task may follow another in time, but is not dependent on it. Also it indicates that a specified event cannot occur until another event has taken place. Usually it involves the completion of one activity or task and the start of another even though the two are not directly related. For example, in Figure 9–2, a dotted arrow occurs between ④ and ㉙ to show that the manual preparation begins several weeks after the initial plans for the project are formulated.

Figure 9-2. PERT CHART

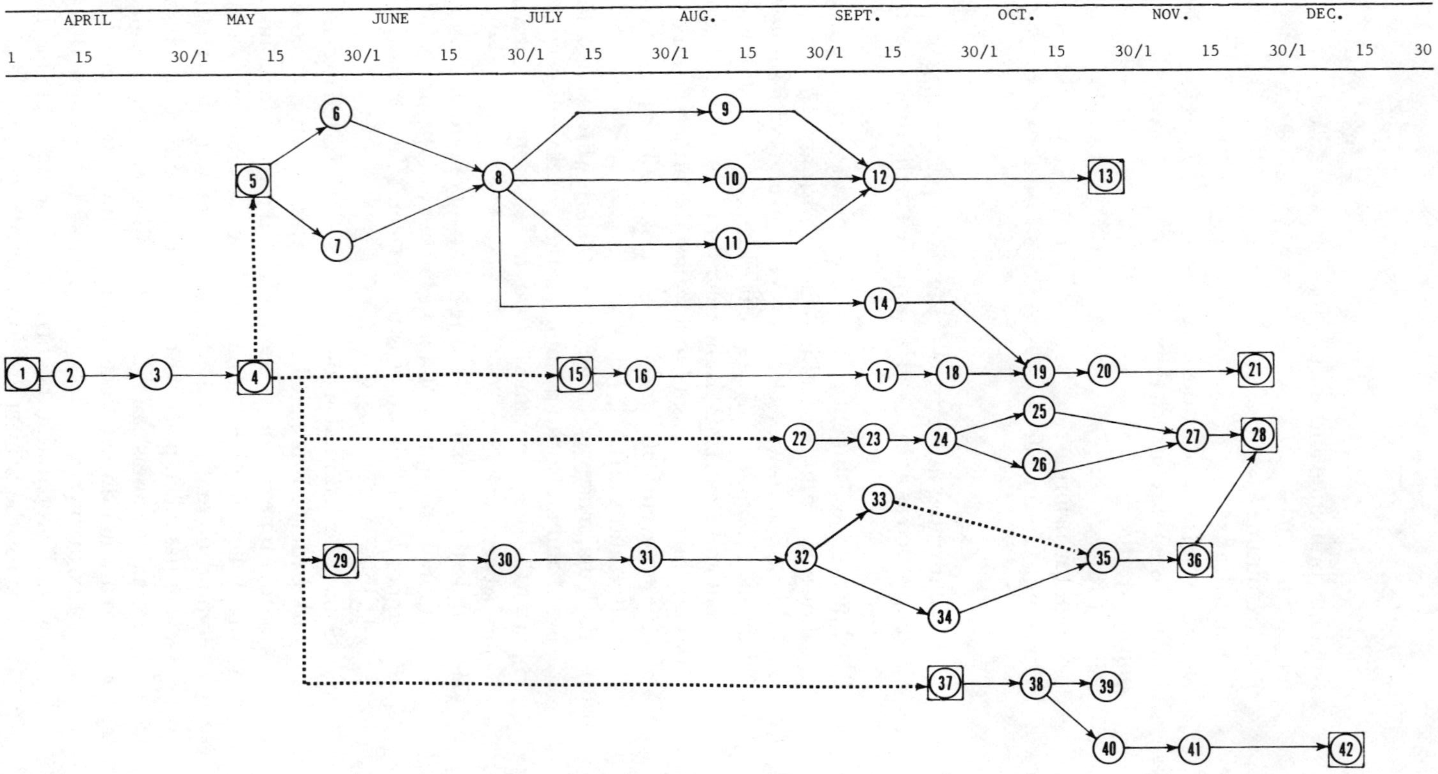

KEY TO PERT CHART

1 - 2	Appoint Task Force
2 - 3	Interview Staff, Agencies, Parents
3 - 4	Formulate Plan
4 - 5	Begin Profile
5 - 6	Identify Unserved Children
5 - 7	Identify Foster Parents
7 - 8	Prepare PR Campaign
8 - 9	Prepare Posters
8 - 10	Prepare Radio Tapes
8 - 11	Prepare TV Ads
10 - 12	Conduct Public Media Campaign
12 - 13	Submit Materials to Media
8 - 14	Prepare Written Materials for Speaker's Kit
4 - 15	Begin Speakers' Bureau
15 - 16	Plan Speakers' Bureau
16 - 17	Recruit Volunteers and Staff
17 - 18	Prepare Speakers' Kit
18 - 19	Train Speakers
14 - 19	Distribute PR Materials
19 - 20	Promote Speaking Engagements
20 - 21	Conduct Speaking Engagements
4 - 22	Begin Processing Procedures
22 - 23	Plan Procedures
23 - 24	Orient Staff
24 - 25	Prepare Phone Instructions
24 - 26	Prepare Follow-up Materials
26 - 27	Conduct Screening Interviews
27 - 28	Conduct Orientation Sessions
4 - 29	Begin FC Manual Preparation
29 - 30	Appoint Committee Staff
30 - 31	Prepare Outline
31 - 32	Prepare Drafts
32 - 33	Obtain Staff Reaction
32 - 34	Obtain Foster Parents Reactions
34 - 35	Revise Drafts
35 - 36	Arrange Printing
36 - 28	Submit Manual to Orientation Sessions
4 - 37	Begin FC Dinner Preparation
37 - 38	Obtain Funding
38 - 39	Reserve Room
38 - 40	Obtain Caterer
40 - 41	Send Invitations
41 - 42	Plan Dinner

(9)   Thus far, we have described events that occur in sequence; one must be completed before another can begin: ① → ② → ③. An event can be followed, however, by two or more tasks that can occur simultaneously and independently of each other. Usually, simultaneous tasks occur when two or more persons or groups are involved.

Tasks: 31–32 Prepare drafts
         32–33 Obtain H.S. Dept. staff reactions
         32–34 Obtain foster parents' reactions

(10)   If two or more lines lead to an event circle, this means that the event cannot occur until all tasks that end at that event are completed:

Thus before a PR campaign strategy can commence ⑧, it is necessary to develop a profile of both unserved children ⑥ and of potential foster parents ⑦.

(11)   Referring again to the list of tasks in Table 9–3, note that the amount of time required to complete each event is estimated. The estimated time (hours, days, weeks, months, years) is based on whatever measure is appropriate for the project. In the foster care project it was determined that weeks were the best measurement of time. Sometimes PERT charts are constructed to reflect estimated times above each arrow. This is done to permit determining the earliest expected time by which each activity would be completed, to calculate when the entire project would be finished. In the foster care manual activity for example, the estimated times would be shown in this manner:

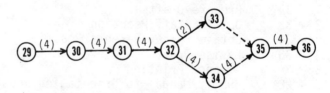

(12)   In this example the minimal amount of time to complete the foster care manual will be 24 weeks, which is determined by totaling the estimated times of the longest path from beginning to end: 29–30–31–32–34–35–36. (Note that 32–33–35 is omitted in the sequence.) In the example of the foster care manual, it is anticipated that while staff reaction to a draft will take only 2 weeks, processing the drafts through foster parents will require a total of 4 weeks before the

writing of the final version can begin. The longest path to completing the activity is referred to as the *critical path,* for it represents the earliest expected completion of the activity. It is critical because any delays would require more time than originally planned and the entire project would be delayed.

(13)   If it is important to decrease the critical path (longest) time, then ways must be found to expedite the completion of tasks. In the foster care project example, the H.S. Dept. could have several units review the drafts of the manual simultaneously to shorten the total review time. Tasks could therefore be expedited by diverting staff from other parts of the organization to meet with foster parents about the manual. On the other hand, if it is necessary to add more tasks or if more time than originally planned is needed to accomplish tasks, the critical path time would have to be increased. If halfway through the preparation of the manual it appears that it will require 30 weeks to complete, instead of 24 as projected, more resources or staff would be required to complete it on time. If this is not possible, then other choices include extending the time frame of the activity, which in turn may affect the completion of the entire project, or discarding some tasks.

(14)   It is possible, on the other hand, that the project would experience slack time in the completion of some events. In the foster care manual activity, slack time occurs in the H.S. Dept. review task. If the staff were to take 3 weeks to review the manual instead of 2 weeks as projected, this would not slow down the completion of the manual. Also, if the review of drafts by the foster parents were to take 3 weeks instead of 4, then the project would experience slack time, which may permit the personnel in this activity to devote time to another activity, such as assisting with the speakers' bureau. (It should be noted that in some instances it may not be possible to make shifts in personnel because those with slack time may not have skills that can be transferred to other activities.) Since it is anticipated that most community organization personnel wanting to prepare PERT charts have preestablished target dates for achieving their objectives, we have modified the PERT Chart in Figure 9–2. Note that the times are omitted above the arrows; the critical path procedure has been substituted with months displayed at the top of the chart for easy identification of the time points for each event.[6]

(15)   Note the interrelationship of tasks under different activi-

ties. For example, (14) → (19) reflects that the materials prepared by the PR firm will be provided in the speakers' kits. Similarly (36) → (28) shows that the foster care manual will be available in time for the orientation program for foster parents.

Narrative Network Chart.   Like the PERT chart, the narrative network chart shows the relationship between tasks, but it is easier to read because the task is written over each line. The timeline, with beginning and ending points in circles, is indicated above the description of activities as shown in Figure 9–3. The advantage of this network chart is that the interrelationships of tasks are visually shown within designated time periods, without having to refer to a key, as is necessary with a PERT chart. Figure 9–3. illustrates in part the foster care enhancement and recruitment project.

Advantages and Cautions About Network Charts

The chief value of timeline charts is that they illustrate the projected sequence of activities which can be monitored during actual implementation. Every task is anticipated at a given point or range in time. Everyone involved in a project knows precisely when tasks are to begin and when they are to be completed. Each person sees how the accomplishment of an assignment bears on other people's work. Both GANTT and network charts visually display which tasks can occur simultaneously and which must be conducted in sequence. And at any given point in time it is clear what demands on personnel will be required.

The GANTT chart is simpler to construct and read, though both PERT and the network charts have the advantage of showing more precisely the relationship among tasks. Since most long-term projects require continuous updating, the GANTT chart is frequently chosen in preference to PERT because it is easy to revise. PERT is infrequently used in social planning projects where precise timing of events is not easily predicted, or in projects involving an uncomplicated sequence of tasks. Network charts are more likely to be used when it is important to identify critical tasks in implementing projects. If these tasks are not carried out in proper sequence, then the entire project could be delayed or even aborted.

One other caution about using GANTT or network charts as scheduling tools: achievement of work efforts does not necessarily mean that the work is of high quality. A group may feel euphoric about completing its tasks even though the quality of the work suffers. Just as concrete in a building may be poured on schedule, but the quality may

Figure 9-3. NARRATIVE NETWORK CHART

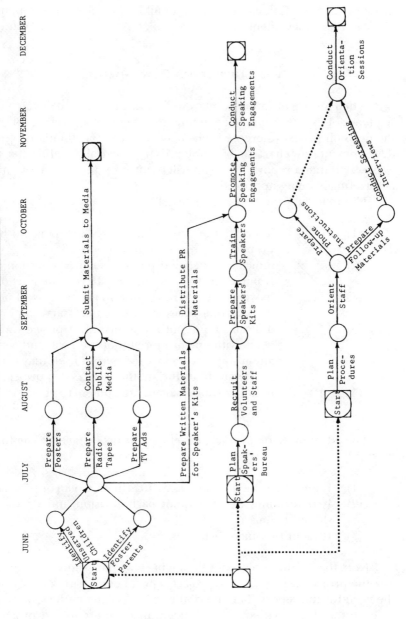

be so poor that the foundation later cracks, so work projects may be accomplished on time only for the group to discover later that they are inadequate. Each task can either be a building block or a stumbling block to the achievement of objectives.

Project Development Flow Charts

When an organization is interested in displaying visually (1) the sequence of events from the beginning to the end of a project and (2) the decision points where revisions may be necessary, then a project development flow chart can be employed. It is especially useful when it is expected that a report or project will require a number of revisions before finally being approved.

The following symbols may be used:

(1)   ☐   indicates the processing of work: reports to be prepared or research to be done.

(2)   ◇   indicates a decision point. Usually a question is framed for a yes/no answer. If yes, then action moves on to the next point in the process; if no, then further revisions will be necessary.

(3)   ▱   indicates input/output points. Most projects will begin with one or more inputs and will end with an output. Frequently the output itself may constitute an input for another process or project.

(4)   ▽   indicates submission of a document to a group for review.

The advantages of a project development flow chart are the following:

(1)   It identifies the steps necessary to achieve a plan or project.
(2)   It determines at what point each revision and decision should be made.
(3)   It identifies major activities.

Note that in the project development flow chart shown in Figure 9–4 the projected plan for the project report begins with identifying the need for the report. The rest of the chart anticipates the sequence of events with special consideration given to points in the process where changes and revisions may need to be made. These points include the following:

(1) If the committee rejects the charge given to it, then either it has to be rewritten or different members selected.

(2) If the committee elects not to accept some or all of its task force reports, then the reports will have to be redone.

(3) If citizens' groups, agencies, and experts react critically to the committee's report, then it will have to be revised.

(4) If the board of trustees does not find the report acceptable, then it will have to be redrafted by the committee.

By building in these various decision points, those setting up the project can anticipate where the project might experience delays and where critical reactions might be encountered.

Since the project development flow chart is a projection of efforts and decisions, it should be revised as circumstances warrant. A projected 6-month project, for example, might take 4 or 8 months, depending upon reactions to it.

ALTERNATIVE CHOICE CHARTS

The purpose of the alternative choice chart is to develop a set of procedures leading to desired results. It is usually applied to structured situations where the objectives are clear and predictable. It uses a series of yes/no questions proceeding from a general situation to specific outcomes. And it structures the decision process by identifying specific, relevant factors that must be considered.[7]

To use this chart, one should do the following:

(1) obtain all the information necessary to make relevant decisions;

(2) develop questions which identify specific alternatives, preferably no more than two or three;

(3) prepare the chart for a specific audience that already has some familiarity with the problem.

The alternative choice chart method should be used when it is possible to develop a chain of questions leading to precise and finite outcomes. It is particularly useful when routine decisions are involved in answering such questions as, "Does a person qualify for a particular service? Does a projected program meet certain legislative requirements?"

The alternative choice chart shown in Figure 9–5 reflects a routine set of decisions and instructions in processing potentially mentally ill

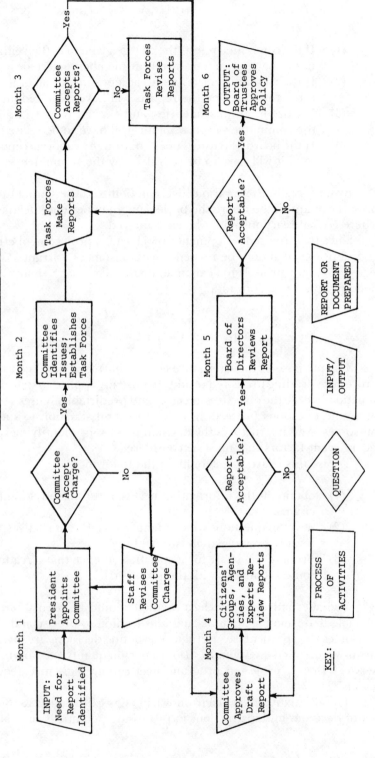

Figure 9-4. PROJECT DEVELOPMENT FLOW CHART

166

Figure 9-5. ALTERNATIVE CHOICE FLOW CHART

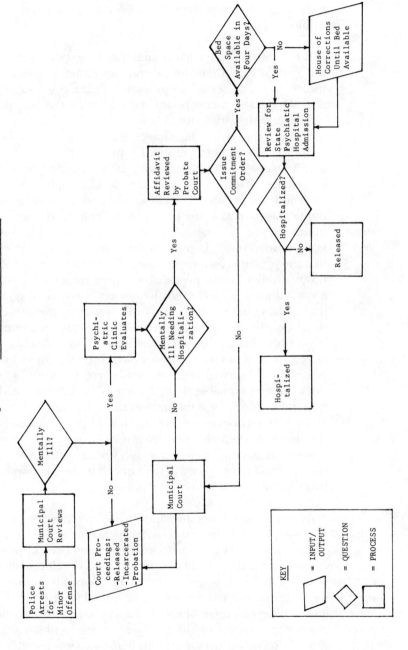

minor offenders (misdemeanants) through both the criminal justice and mental health systems.

Note in the example given the various decision points requiring alternative choices:

(1) If the municipal court determines that an arrested person is not mentally ill, then the person can either be released, incarcerated, or placed on probation. If the court suspects that the person might be mentally ill, then the person is referred to the psychiatric clinic.

(2) The municipal court determines the person's disposition, including release, incarceration, or probation, based in part on the clinic's recommendation. If the psychiatric clinic determines that the person is mentally ill, then two courses of action are possible: the clinic could recommend to the municipal court that the person could be referred to community resources (mental health center, alcoholism halfway house, nursing home). Or the clinic could rcommend that the probate court review the affidavit to order possible hospitalization. If the probate court determines not to issue a commitment order, then the person is returned to the municipal court for disposition. If, however, the probate court decides upon hospitalization, it can issue a commitment order on the basis that bed space is available.

(3) If bed space is not available in 4 days, then the mentally ill person would be sent to the house of corrections until a bed does become available. If bed space is available, then the hospital would review the person for admission.

(4) If the hospital does not determine that the person should be hospitalized, then the person would be released. If the hospital determines that the person would be hospitalized, then this will happen and at the same time the court waives jurisdiction over the case.

The alternative choice chart attempts to identify various choice points and pathways. Variations of this chart can be used in a variety of settings and situations: referral of clients to different services, depending on their needs and the availability of services; development of pathways foster children can take (e.g., permanent custody, return to natural parents, adoption); determination of eligibility of clients for welfare grants; and development of instructions to state mental health and retardation departments of their respective responsibilities for dealing with dual diagnosed persons. In each instance it is possible to develop a complete chain of questions leading to precise outcomes. Alternative choice charts have the special advantage of being clear cut and efficient, thus permitting people to concentrate on more complex decision making.

SUMMARY

In summary, the following can be said about the action planning charts:

An assigments chart defines specific responsibility of persons or units of the organization.

A GANTT chart graphically displays major activities and tasks in relation to a specific time frame.

PERT and network narrative charts also display major activities and tasks. In complex projects they can graphically show inter-relationships.

A project development flow chart shows the sequencing of activities, decision points, and potential revision points of an organization or community process.

An alternative choice chart describes the sequencing of questions and instructions for decisions.

Chapter 10

OBTAINING FUNDS FOR PROBLEM SOLVING PROJECTS

After members of a community organization select a problem they want to change, they frequently will consider developing a special program or project. They will probably be interested in learning how they can acquire new funding resources to implement their ideas. They then will want to explore potential funding and consider preparing a proposal. If you are likely to be involved in preparing a proposal, then this chapter can help guide you through the process of obtaining resources for problem-solving projects.

CAUTIONS ABOUT SEEKING FUNDS

Before rushing into writing a proposal it is important to assess whether this is what you really want to do. For the process is hard work and the competition is keen. Regardless of whether you are applying to a foundation, corporation, or a government agency, there will always be many more requests for funds than there are funds available. A good proposal—one that convinces a funder that you should be funded instead of others—will be exceedingly challenging to prepare. Here are some questions you may need to consider before you invest in the process.[1]

First, will the effort of preparing and negotiating the proposal require a disproportionate amount of time and effort? You will likely spend many hours attending committee meetings, writing drafts for review, and taking trips to funders—time that is diverted from other important assignments. The benefits of obtaining a grant, when compared with how precious time could otherwise be spent, just may not be sufficiently worthwhile to warrant your embarking on the money chase.

Second, is the projected program realistically within the capability of the agency? Sufficient skilled staff may not exist or the technology for producing major success with certain intractable problems may not be available. In their zeal to obtain new funds, some community organizations promise to deliver the undeliverable. Government funders involved in delinquency reduction, for example, might request that projects reduce delinquency by an unusually large percentage. Contracting to achieve such unrealistic expectations guarantees failure. Similarly, the time frame for funding may not be conducive to the accomplishment of agency objectives. If, for example, funding is limited to 1 year and a substantial part of that year would have to be devoted to "tooling-up," i.e., hiring staff and developing publicity to attract program users, then surely the agency must be cautious about its ability to make any impact upon the problem. Hence, an agency may be enticed by the prospects of additional funding to perform worthwhile services, but in the long run may overcommit itself and then succeed only in acquiring a poor reputation. As a result of this loss of credibility, the agency jeopardizes its chances for subsequent funding. Before undertaking a proposal it is therefore important to assess realistically the agency's capability of meeting the expectations of funders.

Third, will the funders' demands affect agency autonomy and internal operations? The lure of funds has its price in the form of conditions and restrictions: limitations on client eligibility, constraints on the manner in which clients will be served, qualifications required of staff, prescribed methods of reporting agency activities, review of internal agency records, fiscal accounting review, and the restraints on being able to criticize governmental bodies. Hence, there is always the potential for conflict between the funder's need for control (particularly government) and the organization's requirement for autonomy. Certainly, demands made upon agencies can have positive as well as negative impact upon agency operations. But these conditions must be carefully weighed before a proposal is submitted.

Fourth, what are the possible consequences of the program being discontinued after a designated time period? Frequently funds are offered either on a time-limited basis or they are assured only on a year-to-year basis. What are the potential effects on staff and, more importantly, on clients if the project cannot continue to receive funds? It is not enough "to hope for the best," a phrase that often obscures the problem that staff preparing proposals have absolutely no idea about how the project will be continued once funding is discontinued. An assessment must be made of the prospects for continuing the program, or the consequences of its discontinuance, before the proposal is submitted.

Finally, are there negative consequences regarding the extent and method of financial reimbursement? Certainly, equity would require that payments be commensurate with the nature and quality of services rendered and that reimbursements should amount to the actual expenses of the organization. In some instances, however, funding may be based not on actual or anticipated costs, but upon some arbitrary and even antiquated formula that results in the organization's having to subsidize the cost of the program. It is desirable to determine what the experience is locally or in other parts of the country regarding the adequacy of cost reimbursement for similar projects.

Cash flow is another problem related to reimbursement. You should anticipate that there could be a time delay between the submission of the first invoice and the receipt of funds that could strap the organization. Unless financial reserves exist, paying staff on time can become a major problem. It is essential, therefore, to be fully aware of whether the payment procedure will impose a significant hardship on the organization.

These cautions and considerations have been presented so that they can be balanced against the irresistible enticement of gaining additional funding for needed projects. The clear message: know what you are getting into when you consider applying for funds.

SEARCHING FOR THE FUNDING SOURCES

Assuming that you are aware of the pitfalls of obtaining funds and that nevertheless you are determined to secure special funding to deal with a problem, how do you go about searching for funding sources? Your first line of inquiry is to determine whether you think funding can best be obtained from the voluntary sector—corporations and foundations—or from the governmental sector. Private sector funding may give you considerable freedom to develop your own project, but then you may not be able to receive as much funding as you need. The government sector may provide you with a sizable grant, but then you will have to abide by specific conditions of the grant and you may experience more competition.

Identifying Private-Sector Funding Sources

Because there are hundreds of foundations that exist in any large or even moderate-sized urban community, you must go through a process of elimination to determine which ones are right for you. To avoid a time-consuming, scattered, and often futile approach, it is best to identify initially a core of foundations that match your interests. Through research you can pinpoint those foundations whose patterns of giving over the past several years reflect an interest in your problem area.

The best approach to learning about community, private, and corporate foundations is to write to the Foundation Center, 888 Seventh Avenue, New York, New York 10106. The Center will send you a publications catalogue that describes major sources of information about foundations. These sources, which include summary statements of each foundation's requirements, are available to you through purchase or through the facilities of the Center in New York or its offices in Washington, D.C., Cleveland, or San Francisco. The Center also has a cooperating network of 90 library reference collections in all 50 states, Mexico, and Puerto Rico. (Write to the Center for a complete address list.)

Among major publications and computer services of the Foundation Center are the following:

> *Foundation Directory* lists the country's major foundations which distribute $100,000 or more annually or have assets of $1 million or more. The data is arranged by state and is indexed by fields of interest, geography, and foundation representatives. In many instances it also describes whether to approach initially a foundation by phone, brief letter, or proposal. It can be ordered from the Foundation Center.
>
> *Foundation Grants Index* is an annual publication (or subscription on a bimonthly basis) that lists grants of $5,000 or more reported during the year covering about 400 foundations. Each grant is identified by amount, name of recipient, location, date of grant, and grant description. (Write to the Foundation Center.)
>
> *Foundation Center National Data Book* provides material on thousands of smaller functions not listed in the Foundation Directory. It is useful for identifying smaller foundations in a given geographic area. Though no subjects are listed, it provides the address, the name of the principal officer, the assets,

and the amount of grants made. (Write to the Foundation Center.)

Comsearch Printouts offers inexpensively prepared computer printouts on about 70 of the most commonly used subject categories of grant making (e.g., mental health, the aged, the handicapped, women, blacks, citizen participation, community development, social services, child welfare, youth programs). Also, geographic printouts are available on selected states. For a nominal fee, grant records will identify the foundation, recipient, amount, date, and activity funded. (Write to the Foundation Center.)

Foundation Fundamentals is an excellent guide for grant seekers that presents information on how to research the particular foundation for your organization. It is available from the Foundation Center at a modest price.

The Foundation Center has other services, including customized information through a computer service, and *Source Book Profiles,* a bimonthly service that analyzes approximately 1,000 of the largest foundations.

Approaching Foundations for Funding

Assuming you have identified a list of foundations whose interests, based on past grants, appear to match your concerns, the next step is to determine how to make the approach. Although there is no universal rule—each foundation has its own preference and style of operating—in general, small, private foundations require a brief (two to five pages) letter telling who you are, what your concern is, what you propose to do, and how much funding you seek. A letter to small private foundations suffices because they rarely have fulltime staff, they have limited funds, and their scope is limited; they can therefore readily indicate whether the proposal is within their area of interest.[2]

This same procedure can be used when approaching company-sponsored foundations. These foundations are also listed in materials available in the 90 library reference collections mentioned earlier. In addition to sending a letter, it is important to make a personal contact with the person responsible for the corporate foundation (sometimes the president of the company, sometimes a person in public relations, and sometimes a specially designated program officer). Often those requests for funding that show how employees can benefit (e.g., an alcoholism program) have a special advantage. In addition to providing grants, corporations can provide other valuable resources, including the expertise of their personnel, gifts from their inventory, company facilities, and released time of employees.[3]

Your approach with a community foundation is somewhat different from that which you would use with a private foundation. A community foundation has such a broad charge—it has to be concerned with the charitable needs of the local community in which it resides—that almost anything fits within that charge. Because community foundations are primarily concerned with local needs, mailing requests for funding throughout the country is probably a waste of time. One director of a large community foundation advises against wasting time on writing a letter; instead, submit a proposal and then arrange to come in to discuss it.[4] If, however, you have questions or doubts, talk with the program officer before investing considerable time and energy on a proposal. Meeting with staff is crucial because, although not everything they recommend to the board of the foundation passes, their opinions and recommendations are highly regarded.

The sequence of the foundation search process involves these major steps:

(1) Through the *Foundation Directory, Comsearch Printout, Grants Index,* and other specialized directories (including, in some instances, state foundation directories) identify foundations that make grants in subject areas similar to yours.

(2) Research the foundations you have identified by checking the following: source book profiles; published annual reports of the foundations; tax returns of foundations. (Note: Private foundations are required to file annual tax returns that include the names of organizations receiving grants and the dollars awarded. The Foundation Centers' regional collections have these tax returns on microfiche.[5])

Having done this homework you can now concentrate your funding requests on those foundations most likely to be receptive to your proposal.

Identifying and Approaching Government Sources

Tracking governmental funds can be even more challenging than searching for foundation grants. The stakes are bigger, but then so are the restrictions. To be chosen over your many competitors, you will have to conduct careful research, have tremendous perseverance, and be lucky. Here are some steps that will help you get through the bureaucratic maze.[6]

Step 1: Become generally knowledgeable about government programs, agencies, and activities in your general area. One way to do this is to call your Federal Information Center, which has recently been established in selected cities across the country to serve as a referral agent for federal programs. Suppose you hear about a newly funded mental health program and want to find out more details. By calling the toll free number of the office nearest you, you can learn the name of the specific agency, and the name and phone number of the program officer. For a free brochure on Federal Information Centers, write to Consumer Information, Pueblo, Colorado 81009, No. 245D.

Step 2: The federal government prints sources of information which can alert you to available program grants. One of the most significant of these is the *Federal Register,* published each weekday. For those interested in a variety of grant possibilities and those interested in responding speedily to what can often be short deadlines, it should be read daily. The "Highlights" section in the front lists major topics. The "Notices" section describes grant availability. Announcements are made of rules governing programs, so that even though money is not immediately available, you gain some idea of what grants are likely to be funded later. It is available at most major public or university libraries, or write to Superintendent of Documents, U.S. Government Printing Office, Washington, D.C. 20402 for subscription information.

The Catalog of Federal Domestic Assistance, published annually, is the most comprehensive source of government grant programs. It provides detailed information on how to apply, who is eligible, and deadlines. The financial section describes money available for the past and current year and indicates the pattern of grant giving. Because it is not absolutely current—changes may have occurred since it went to print—check with the appropriate program officer for up-to-date information. Many libraries have the catalog available or write to the Superintendent of Documents.

A Federal Assistance Program Retrieval System is available to provide all the information available in the Catalog. For an information packet, write to the Federal Program Information Branch, Office of Management and Budget, 726 Jackson Place, N.W., Washington, D.C. 20503.

The Commerce Business Daily lists all potential contracts. Unlike grants, which give grantees more latitude over the use of funds, contracts require activities specified in advance by funders. The federal agency determines the type of program, format of activity, expected outcome, costs, and length of time. Write to the Superintendent of Documents.

In addition to these regular sources, every federal agency will periodically announce funds available for specific projects. Called *Requests for Proposal* (RFP), these announcements provide detailed guidelines. It is useful to call the appropriate federal agency to get on the mailing list for an application packet.

The best way to keep up with trends and potential funding possibilities is to read at least one newsletter in your speciality area. Most
community organizations subscribe or have access to newsletters that
describe pending legislation, appropriations bills, and new regulations.
Many national organizations provide newsletters to alert their constituents of funding opportunities.

Step 3:   Based on readings and general contacts with officials, you
should be able to determine what is being funded. Your next step,
then, is to make alterations in the framing of your original issue or
problem area to fit government priorities. To obtain federal funding,
you must conform to the federal requirements, rather than expect that
the federal government will make changes to meet your particular
needs. Federal agency priorities, as published in the *Federal Register,*
usually include the specific population to be served, the deadline for
application, and the type of proposal document to be submitted. Suppose, for example, you are concerned with delinquency in your community and you learn of grants that are available for delinquents who
are also retarded. Your choice is whether or not to develop a program
for this specific population or pass it up.

Step 4:   If you have accepted the reality of conforming to federal
guidelines for a particular grant, it is advisable to call the program
officer responsible for the grant in your regional office or in Washington through a name and number supplied by the Federal Information
Center or listed in the *Federal Register.* The program officer will be able
to provide you with selection criteria for the project and an application
packet for the grant program, which includes forms, rules and regulations, and guidelines. If the program officer cannot supply you with
this year's selection criteria because of delays, then ask for the last
year's. Selection criteria are extremely important because they indicate
on what basis the proposal will be judged by impartial readers. Since,
generally, the procedure is for proposal reviewers to subtract points
when a proposal does not measure up to the selection criteria, your
proposal will want to be as responsive to these as possible.

Step 5:   To the extent possible, you will want to find out, through
phone or personal contact with the program officer, about details of
the grant: how many programs are likely to be funded, the average
grant award, the availability of new money this year, the background of
proposal reviewers, and information on similar projects. With this
information you now have guidelines for preparing the proposal.

Writing the Proposal

Proposal formats may vary depending on the requirements of funders. Government proposals use a highly structured format. Proposals for foundations are not usually as structured, but generally all will want to know what you intend to accomplish and how you propose doing so. Some funders may prefer that the proposal be organized so that the problem is discussed first. This is followed by a description of the group. Others may prefer the reverse order. Some prefer a summary statement in the front of the proposal; others may prefer it at the end of the narrative. Whatever the format used, it should flow so that there is a natural connection from one section to the next. Hence, consider the following format proposed here as a guide, to be modified if it makes sense for you to do so:

Summary Statement
Statement of Need
Goals and Objectives
Program Components: Activities and Tasks
Monitoring and Evaluation
Capability of the Organization
Budget

Summary Statement

Normally a summary statement should appear first because readers need a general description to orient them to the project and to prepare them for the details that are to follow. The summary should be less than one page and contain the following elements:

what the need is,
what will be accomplished,
who you are and why you are qualified,
what activities you will perform,
what it will cost,
how long it will take.[7]

The summary should be prepared after the full proposal is written.

Statement of Need

The purpose of this section is to define precisely what condition your organization wants to change. Your primary purpose could focus on the conditions of people in your community that would likely appeal to a local foundation. Or your purpose could be to examine and deal with a particular problem or issue which would have implications beyond your own community.[8] For example, you might want to demonstrate how a variety of teenage pregnancy programs can be more effectively coordinated. Because this focus could have impact on other communities and might advance the "state of the art," it would more likely appeal to large national foundations and to federal agencies. But it generally requires more research, more rigor, and more money than a proposal that concentrates primarily on improving local conditions.

Although the *statement of need* is presented before the section on *goals and objectives* of the proposal, it should be written with objectives clearly in mind. Frequently, a proposal devotes considerable space to a major problem, but then tends to ignore the objectives when describing what the organization actually intends to accomplish. The final outcome of the proposal may be to convey a right answer to a different problem. Because there must be a clear consistency between needs and objectives, it might even be desirable to write the latter section first.[9] This would be necessary especially if the prospective funder has specified what the proposal should accomplish, which is usually the case with federal agency grants.

The statement of need should cover many of the ideas covered previously in Chapter 1. If appropriate, it should specify who the target population is, what specific problem will be addressed, where the problem is located, what its origin is, and why it continues to exist. If the problem is multifaceted, then all the significant aspects would need to be identified. For example, a problem statement about out-of-school, unemployed, adolescent delinquents living in poverty would need to describe their educational lags and their need for income.

If possible, the theoretical basis for the problem should also be discussed. It is not enough, for example, to say that the problem is the lack of the service you intend to provide. As discussed in Chap. 6, one of the major traps in proposal writing is circular reasoning. It is not sufficient to say that adolescent delinquents lack counseling, which you will provide; a full explanation of *why* this is a problem requiring special counseling is needed.

To demonstrate your grasp of the problem, it would be desirable to provide prospective funders with data from a variety of sources: national studies and their local applications, testimony from congressional records, local surveys, or quotes from local authorities. Unless funders request this detailed information in the narrative, do not inundate them with pages of statistics; summarize the data and place detailed, statistical tables in an appendix.[10]

Because many problems are chronic, the statement of need should convey why there is a special urgency to seek funding now. What new crisis has arisen? For example, are the kinds of crimes being committed by adolescents more serious than before? Are more adolescent girls now committing crimes than in the past? Does new state legislation put a special burden to deal with delinquency on the local community? Are local institutions more prepared now than before to deal with delinquency? Describing special circumstances lends weight to the importance of funding the project.

Where feasible, it is recommended that the prospective community constituency or client group be involved in defining the problem. This is obviously desirable if the proposal is related to community improvement, for the clients are in the best position to comment on what their special needs are. Even those who normally do not participate, e.g., mentally retarded offenders or recently released mentally ill patients, can be consulted. Evidence of their participation in the problem-defining process further conveys a depth of understanding.

Goals and Objectives

To review the discussion in Chapter 2 of setting objectives, consider the following example: A community organization has become concerned with the growth of juvenile delinquency in its community. After investigation and discussion with court officials, youth workers, and teenagers themselves, the group decides to establish an alternative education program for out-of-school delinquent youth. Specifically, it is concerned that a certain group of youngsters tends to commit crimes repeatedly because they are unable to find jobs and because they lack education—all of which makes them feel they will never succeed in obtaining more than the most menial jobs. Furthermore, organization members are concerned that even though they may be successful with a small group of youngsters on a pilot basis, long-term community benefits will occur only if the board of education incorporates the program as part of normal schooling.

Based on the definition (see Chap. 2) that goals are lofty ideals of what the organization would like to see happen, the goal statement would be written, "to reduce the rate of delinquency in the community."

As Chapter 2 describes, objectives are relevant to the achievement of the goal, are within reach, are tangible and measurable, and can be accomplished within a specified time period.[11] The overall *organizational objective* would be written: "To reduce by 70% during the next program year the rate of recidivism (re-arrests) for the 200 program participants who have previously participated in robbery, burglary, and assault."

Specific *impact objectives* would be written as follows:

(1) to place 50% of the youth enrolled in the vocational training program in full- or part-time jobs within 18 months;

(2) to increase educational attainment of the 200 entering students, 80% will complete at least one full semester and 60% will complete 1 full year of school;

(3) to obtain a commitment from the board of education and the youth commission to incorporate the program, by the end of the third year, into the regular school program.

The advantage of each of these objectives is that they alert the funders to expect a clear-cut outcome from the project. Stating the objectives in quantifiable terms disciplines the preparers of the proposal to identify only that which the agency can reasonably achieve, not what it would ideally like to achieve. Refer to Chapter 2 for a more complete discussion of setting objectives. The same principles in establishing objectives for organizational purposes apply in a proposal for outside funders.

Program Components: Activities and Tasks

This section of the proposal states how the organization intends to accomplish its objectives. To convey the logic and continuity of the project, the proposal should describe, in relation to each objective, *what* you will do, *who* will do it, and *when* you are going to do it. Chapter 9 discussed in depth the formulating of activities and tasks through the process of reverse order and forward planning approaches. Note that Table 3, in Chapter 9 identifies in the foster care project the objectives, the major activities related to each objective, the tasks that must be carried out to achieve each activity, the units responsible, and the time period for each task. In similar fashion, the alternative education project proposal would relate activities and tasks to each of its major impact objectives.

For example, under the category of employment, the following information might be conveyed:

Activity: To hold 10 employment workshops
   Tasks: (1) Visit three worksites
         (2) Provide job readiness exercise: interviewing techniques; grooming tips; filling out application blanks
         (3) Provide information on job market
Responsible person: Employment counselor
Time period: First 2 months

This same process would be repeated for the other two objectives of increasing educational attainment and obtaining a commitment to incorporate the project into the regular school program. By spelling out this kind of detail you convey to the prospective funder that you have a well-thought out, logical proposal.

It is usually helpful to show the relationship of activities and tasks to objectives on a chart similar to Table 9–3 because this format provides the reader with a capsule view of what you are describing in the narrative. In addition to a chart, you may wish to describe in more detail how the program would actually function. When relevant, you would state in the narrative, for example, how the proposed work program has been successfully used elsewhere, how it will relate to existing programs in the community, and what current resources of the organization will be used.

This actual determining of activities and tasks will typically involve some group processes, because usually knowledge is not concentrated in one person and a consensus may need to emerge if organizational members are to be involved in implementing the proposal. Chapter 5 describes brainstorming and nominal group technique that can be used to arrive at a consensus about what methods the organization should undertake to carry out its objectives. But the actual proposal writing itself cannot be accomplished through a committee process; one or two people have to take primary responsibility. The group can then react to a draft and their suggestions can be incorporated in a later version.

After the group has generated a wide range of possible activities through general discussion, brainstorming, or nominal group technique, it will then want to develop criteria for selecting those it wants to use in the project. Chapter 7 describes some of the more typical criteria that can be considered:

How successful is the plan likely to be?

How feasible is it?

How appropriate is it in relation to the basic style of the organization?

Does it adequately deal with the scope of the problem?

How efficient is it in relation to potential accomplishments?

Are there any negative side effects?

These criteria are suggestions; each organization must tailor criteria that are relevant to its situation. For example, if it is important that the proposed plan of action meet with the approval of other selected groups in the community, then this criterion would be added to the list. It is imperative that the group establish criteria against which proposed program components can be assessed.

Time Charts: If the proposal contains a long list of activities and tasks, the funders will usually like to see in chart form the sequence of events. The GANTT chart shown in Chapter 9 (Fig. 9–1) will provide such an overview, as it highlights what needs to be accomplished in specified time periods.

Monitoring and Evaluation

Monitoring is the process of assessing whether, and to what extent, a course of action is being carried out as planned. As will be discussed in Chapter 11, monitoring questions include: (1) Were the activities and tasks implemented as intended? (2) Were resources adequate to do the job? (3) Were actual costs in line with anticipated expenditures? and (4) Were tasks accomplished on time? In the example of the alternative education project, a monitoring approach would determine whether the 10 employment workshops were carried out as planned, with the staff as projected, under the projected budget, and within the time frame anticipated.

Evaluation is the process of examining the extent to which an organization has achieved its stated objectives and the extent to which the accomplishment of these objectives can be attributed to the program. Evaluation is essential in all problem-solving proposals because it forces the proposal writer to examine the clarity of objectives, the ease with which they can be measured, and the possibility of their being achieved. To be effective, evaluation must be part of the planning process from the beginning. Moreover, as will be discussed in Chapter 11, provision of evaluation conveys to funders that you either know what you are doing or will have information on which corrective action can be based.

Whether evaluation should be conducted within the organization or by an outsider is open to debate. The disadvantage of its being conducted from within is that it can detract from the program efforts, and it is less creditable to the funder. Evaluation conducted by an outsider is more creditable, but also more costly, and both the organization and the funders have to weigh the value of such costs.[12]

If the objective statements are clear and measurable, then the evaluation process becomes that much easier. In Chapter 2 in Table 2–1, as each objective was written, a measurement indicator was also identified. Following through with the illustration of the hypothetical alternative education project, information would be collected on (1) the number of youths compared to total enrolled who advanced one semester or more; (2) the number of youths compared to the total who found part- or full-time jobs; and (3) the commitment of the board of education and the youth commission to incorporate the program as part of the regular education.

Although the guide as shown in Table 10–1 may not actually be written into the proposal in this form, by filling in the spaces you will have a logical format on which to base your proposal.

Capability of the Organization

Funders want to know how capable the organization is of implementing the project. Because they must be sold on your competency to accomplish what you say you will achieve, give them every possible reason to consider you creditable. Describe briefly how and why the organization was formed, the prior and current activities, the support you receive from other organizations, and your significant accomplishments. Most important, provide evidence of your involvement and competency in the area in which you are requesting funds. This is especially important if you are unknown to the funders. Finally, indicate what financial or other resources you can draw on. For example, letters of commitment (not just endorsement) by other agencies are impressive.[13]

Because the proposal itself must be concise, you may want to make reference in this section to the competency of staff, but in the appendix list positions which show titles, qualifications, to whom they are accountable, salary levels, and their responsibilities.

Funders appreciate knowing that the board of trustees under which you function is actively involved in decisions and fully supports the proposal. Testimony from key figures in the community is also useful, if their endorsement letter does not appear ritualistic.

In this section or, if you wish, in a separate section, indicate the capability of the organization to sustain the program beyond the grant period. Foundations which give time-limited funding especially want assurances that the project will be sustained beyond their grant period. Among the options you would need to explore are the following: (1) the organization itself absorbing the project in its regular operating

Table 10-1. PROPOSAL WRITING GUIDE

Problem	Impact Objectives	Evaluation Indicators	Program Components: Activities and Tasks	Monitoring Indicators
Lack of jobs for delinquent youth	(1) To increase employment	Number of youth employed	Provide workshops	Number of youth attending workshops

budget; (2) revenue from client fees; (3) third-party payments, e.g., insurance payments; (4) special fund raising drives; (5) application for membership or special funding in a United Way or other federated fund raising programs; (6) a voluntary organization or government agency assuming costs. Although it may be difficult to anticipate sources of funding 2 or 3 years hence, it is of such crucial importance to funders (and to you) that you make a sincere effort to explore options as you prepare the proposal.

The Budget

Consider the following general guidelines in preparing the budget.

(1) The budget is important, but unless it reveals major weaknesses or is obviously overinflated, it will not be the primary reason for rejecting a proposal. If your idea is sound, the budget is negotiable.

(2) Different funders will require varying degrees of detail in the budget. Most governmental agencies require a great degree of detail and usually provide budget forms and instructions for their completion. Foundations and corporations are less structured in their requirements, but will want a budget that is well-thought out and complete.

(3) Some government agencies have special instructions for preparing the budget that are separate from the program guidelines or regulations. These instructions are continually begin revised. Use the most recent instructions available rather than delay the preparation of your budget. Allow time to make necessary changes if you find that a new set of instructions is to be issued shortly before the final application is due. Application instructions generally include information regarding budget forms, examples of how to calculate specific budget items, agency formulas for determining the maximum allowance in major budgetary categories, and allowable rates for consulting fees, per diem, and travel. Be prepared to document your needs when your costs exceed the agency formula.

(4) A good budget will directly relate to the objectives and activities. It is not something apart from, but is a part of, the project. Each budget item should be justified on the basis of its contribution to the potential accomplishments of the project. To prepare a budget, review each major activity

and estimate its expense. There should be a clear connection between activities and budget.

(5) The budget is an estimate of what the costs will be. Generally, you will have a degree of flexibility in spending, as long as you do not exceed the total amount of the grant. Requests for additional changes may be authorized by the funding sources. Such requests should be in writing. The response, also in writing, becomes a formal budget modification and changes the conditions of the grant. The degree to which you have adequately planned your budget reduces the number of changes that may be required and also establishes a degree of credibility necessary to obtain permission for needed modifications.

(6) Be as specific as possible. Be able to document for each major item in the budget the exact costs. Do not have a *miscellaneous* or *contingency* fund. If you have unusual expenses that are likely to be questioned by the funder, attach a budget explanation. For example, *consultation services* might need to be clarified. When it is necessary for you to create new positions, you should survey other agencies with similar jobs to justify salary scales. If you include items on the budget you cannot fully support and have to back down during negotiations, the integrity of your project may be open to question.

(7) If the organization can make donations to the project, then the budget should distinguish requested from donated funding. Donations can include such contributions as staff time and building space. All volunteer-donated time should be based on what the organization would actually pay for the service.

(8) The following format can be used for personnel:[14]

Number of Persons	Title	Monthly Salary	Percent of Time	Number of Months on Grant	Requested	Donated
2	Coordinators	$1,200	50%	12	$14,400	0

Include fringe benefits—worker's compensation, state unemployment insurance, social security, retirement, and others—as a separate category in the budget.

(9) Other direct costs include the following: space costs; rental, lease, or purchase of equipment; supplies; travel in and out of town; telephone, including installation; copying and printing. Add other categories if expenditures are significant. Give details for the basis of cost estimates.

(10)   Indirect costs are more difficult to determine than the direct costs of a project. But they are important to the financial well-being of your organization. Indirect expenses may include estimated portions of time spent on the project by other members of your regular staff: the director, the accountant, and the maintenance staff. They will also cover expenditures that are difficult to account for with precision, such as wear and tear on office equipment. Indirect expenses may or may not include such items as office rental or office equipment, depending on whether they can be isolated or are an integral part in the administration of your organization. Indirect costs may be included in the grant request (if they are allowable) by adding a certain percentage for indirect expenses to the direct costs of the grant. That percentage is usually determined by an analysis of your overall financial operations which is done by an experienced accountant. Many organizations that carry on extensive grant activity with federal agencies negotiate an acceptable percentage with one government agency and are then privileged to use the same rate on contracts with other government agencies. The federal government will allow indirect expenses arrived at either as a percentage of total salaries involved in the project or as a percentage (much lower) of the total direct cost of the grant. Check with your funder on indirect costs policies.

(11)   If you intend to serve a certain number of people, divide this number into the costs to see if the cost per client is reasonable. Even if *you* do not make this cost figure explicit in the proposal, funders often calculate this. Be prepared to defend the per capita cost.

(12)   Do not accept less money than you know you need for a successful effort just to get the grant. You receive no credit for good intentions if they are not accomplished. Accepting the accountability for a project without having the essential resources to follow through is irresponsible. Do not be so eager for funds that you will later regret taking on something that was so poorly funded only failure could result.

CRITERIA FOR JUDGING PROPOSALS

Funders will obviously vary in the criteria they use for judging a proposal. As indicated previously, government agencies will have specific and unique criteria for each grant. Foundation funders will tend to be more flexible in using criteria to judge grants. The following ideas are culled primarily from literature about foundation grants, but they should also be kept in mind if you are preparing a governmental grant.[15]

Competency of the Individuals Involved

Are those who have prepared the proposal considered highly competent?[16]

Are they dedicated to making their ideas a reality?

Do they have a successful track record?

Do they demonstrate a depth of knowledge about what is happening in their community and across the country?

Are they sufficiently aware of the complexity of the problem?

Participation of the Organization's Membership

Are board members familiar with the proposal, and have they approved it?

Is the board composed of the best possible combination of community and client representation and outside people who can be resources to the organization?

Is the board willing to provide some of the organization's own resources?

If applicable, has provision been made for client or consumer participation in the design and implementation of the project?

Desirability of the Project

Does the proposal make a strong case for the urgency of funding?

Is it clearly a high priority for the requesting organization and for the community?

If similar programs already exist, does the proposal acknowledge this and strongly convey why, nevertheless, one more program is necessary?

Is the project creative in proposing an innovative approach to dealing with a community problem?

If asking for renewal of a grant, has the project adequately demonstrated accomplishments?

If the project has fallen short of its accomplishments, does the proposal adequately explain why and what the organization intends to do about it?

Is the proposal in keeping with the funder's own priorities?

Feasibility of the Project

> Does the proposal illustrate how it will adequately cope with the problem it has identified, neither being too limited in its objectives, nor too grandiose in its claims?
>
> If it proposes to meet a long-standing problem, does the proposal have a well conceived rationale for how it expects to succeed?
>
> What specific ingredients and talents can it bring to bear on the problem?
>
> If the project is to continue, what assurances are there for ongoing funding?
>
> Based on research of programs in other communities, does the proposal indicate why it can succeed in the same way as others have?
>
> If others have failed, what modifications are proposed to insure success?

Possibility of Leveraging Funds

> Will it draw in other private or public funding?
>
> If the request is large, has the organization explored combining this request with requests to other funding organizations?
>
> If several funders are involved, can each funder's contribution be separately identified?

Continuity of the Project

> If funds are being requested for a start-up project, what are the assurances of the requesting organization or another group to continue it?
>
> If the proposal is a demonstration project, what is the likelihood it might be replicated if it proves successful?

Impact Potential

> Are the results likely to be transferable to other programs and other communities?
>
> Will the results have a significant impact on the community?
>
> Does the organization have a record of being able to involve other organizations and outside individuals to work together to achieve objectives?
>
> If the proposal purports to make institutional changes, what assurances can it offer that it will be able to succeed?

Dedication

If the proposal was previously rejected, has it been resubmitted with necessary modifications made?

Have the proposers invested a considerable amount of their own time in preparing the proposal?

Does the organization demonstrate a willingness and ability to obtain resources from its own community or constituency?

Clarity of Proposal

Is the proposal written clearly with professional jargon used selectively?

Are subheadings used to guide the reader?

Is the proposal concise?

Fiscal Soundness

Is the budget adequate to do the job, but not wasteful?

Are contingencies anticipated?

Does the operational budget of the organization appear sound?

Is the organization tax exempt (501) (c) (3)?

Record of Results

Will there be accurate recording of results to demonstrate the project's success?

Has appropriate evaluation advice been considered?

Will the funder be kept informed through written or verbal reports?

What do you do if your proposal is not funded? In true problem-solving style you would consider your options: resubmitting a revised proposal, abandoning the project altogether, or pursuing other avenues that might solve the problem, though with fewer resources. If, on the other hand, you have the good fortune to be funded, you would know that ahead possibly lie frustrations, crises, accountability for results, and worries about refunding.

As anyone who has been involved in community problems knows, the process is unending. The solving of one aspect of a problem sets the stage for working on another. You know the future cannot fully be predicted, but you are prepared to anticipate events, to be proactive in response to problems—in short, to have greater mastery over community problems which you want to affect.

Chapter 11

REVIEWING EFFORTS AND RESULTS OF
THE PROBLEM-SOLVING PROCESS

RATIONALE FOR EVALUATION

Organizations evaluate their programs continuously. Whenever organization members ask questions like, "Are we making a dent in the problem? Are we achieving what we set out to accomplish? Are we on target in carrying out our program?," they are seeking information to evaluate their programs.

If the motivation to seek answers to these questions is based on making an organization attractive to a funding body or the news media, then it will be tempted to gather information which shows it in a positive way, even though serious flaws may exist. If, however, an organization has gone through a process of pinpointing problems *it* wants to tackle, setting objectives *it* wants to achieve, and establishing a timetable *it* wants to meet, then self-evaluation can be enlightening and can lead to significant self-correcting action that can help move the organization into the future in an active and purposeful way. The advantage of self-appraisal is that it can uncover and resolve problems that might otherwise go untreated. The organization will be motivated to use evaluation for its own benefit and improvement.[1] Thus, evaluation is not the end of the problem-solving process but a starting point for refining and revising the planning processes that have preceded it.

Unless organizations undergo self-evaluation leading to self-correcting action, they will have a tendency to retain those objectives and those projects that have become obsolete and unproductive. As Drucker has stated,

> No institution likes to abandon anything it does. Business is no exception. But, in an institution that is being paid for its performance and results, the unproductive, the obsolete will sooner or later be killed off by the customers. In a (community) institution no such discipline is being enforced. The temptation is great, therefore, to respond to the lack of results by redoubling efforts. The temptation is great to double the budget, precisely because there is no performance.[2]

Objectives and results need to be audited so that organizations can abandon those that waste resources. In community organizations the absence of a market test removes the important discipline of sloughing off yesterday's successes. Through examining critically their successes and failures, organizations are able to continually make necessary modifications of their actions.

KINDS OF EVALUATION

The experimental design evaluation method uses sampling techniques, assignment of subjects to control and experimental groups, and control of exposure to treatment or intervention variables. The use of experimental methods presumably eliminates competing explanations for observed results and permits generalization of findings. With an experimental design the organization can be confident that it was the particular program and not other factors that made the difference in reducing such problems as delinquency, unemployment, or illegitimate pregnancy. This design seeks to establish a cause-effect relationship by precisely identifying those factors that contribute to success or failure.

But the chief drawbacks of experimental or quasiexperimental design—extensive research costs, the requirements for sophisticated techniques, restrictive time delays, and often inconclusive results unless conducted on a massive scale[3]—do not make it a feasible approach for most organizations or for their funding bodies. Organizations that want to claim unequivocally that their interventions have significantly reduced a problem may be required to undertake an experimental research design. Most other organizations that document the results of their efforts must live with the problem of being unable to fully prove that their efforts alone made the difference in changing a situation.

Another form of evaluation is less rigorous, but nevertheless more immediately useful in the decision-making process for those organizations that want to answer two basic questions: (1) Is the performance adequate to meet the objectives? (2) Are the objectives being met? This form of evaluation requires the organization to review its own progress in achieving its predetermined activity and impact objectives. Organizations in human services and community work are generally motivated to use self-assessment because of their need to do the following:

> make decisions about the best use of resources,
>
> make changes in objectives or activities,
>
> provide feedback to key people, particularly project administrators and funders.

If the groundwork has been previously laid in setting objectives and determining action plan activities and tasks, then the evaluation task will be made easier. The evaluation process consists of two parts: (1) monitoring activities and tasks, and (2) assessing the achievement of objectives.

MONITORING ACTIVITIES AND TASKS

Chapter 7 detailed the tasks that needed to be fulfilled, who was responsible for achieving them, and the time period by which they were to be achieved. Through a monitoring process the organization's leadership or management can determine, on an ongoing basis, whether and to what extent tasks are being carried out as planned. These are among the questions to be reviewed:

(1)   Effectiveness: Was the task (activity) accomplished?

(2)   Sufficiency of resources: Were needed resources adequate to do the job?

(3)   Efficiency: What was the actual cost compared to projected cost?

(4)   Timeliness: Were the tasks (activities) accomplished on schedule?[4]

An approach to monitoring tasks and activities is shown in the checklist in Figure 11–1. Another approach to monitoring is to use the modification in Figure 11–2. of the GANTT chart.[5]

Figure 11–2. makes a visual comparison of projected versus actual completion of tasks and forms the basis for making continuing revisions. Figure 11–2. illustrates that all the tasks commenced and were finished later than was originally projected.

Figure 11-1. CHECKLIST FOR MONITORING ACTIVITIES/TASKS

	Resources Effective?	Sufficient?	Efficient?	Timely?
Activity: Foster Care Manual				
Task 1				
Task 2				
Task 3				
Task 4				
Activity: Speakers' Bureau				
Task 1				
Task 2				
Task 3				
Activity: Recognition Dinner				
Task 1				
Task 2				

A major reason for monitoring tasks is to determine to what extent a program is progressing as planned and to consider what adjustments might need to be made. Among the questions that can guide in this decision-making process, if the planned tasks are not being implemented as scheduled, are the following:

(1)   Should the amount of current committee or staff time be modified?

(2)   Should new resources (staff, funding, volunteer leadership) be considered?

(3)   Should different tasks and activities be considered?

(4)   Should the target group be modified?

(5)   Should more efficient use be made of volunteer and staff time?

(6)   Should certain tasks and activities be abandoned to meet the schedule of more urgent ones?[6]

A final progress report on the manual preparation activity might appear as follows:

Due to unforseen demands on staff time, assignment of staff to work on the manual was delayed by 3 weeks. This, in turn, set back the timetable for preparation of the manual outline and reaction to drafts. Unfortunately, the manual was not put into the hands of many of the foster parents, as planned, until after they were recruited.

Figure 11-2. GANTT CHART

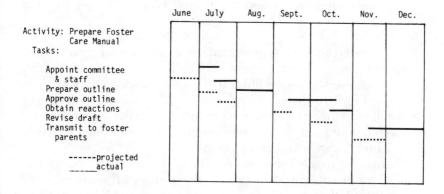

By observing that the staff appointment would be delayed beyond the initial projected time, organization management could be alerted that the completion date would be delayed, to the detriment of the project. Decisions could then be made to add more staff to speed up the progress or reduce time allotted to completion of other tasks. Monitoring activities and tasks thus permits the organization to make timely, crucial decisions in advance of a crisis.

Assessing Objectives

Whereas monitoring of tasks is performed on a continuous basis, assessing the achievement of objectives occurs on a less frequent, periodic basis. The purpose of the assessment is to help the organization compare intended results with actual outcomes. It will be recalled that objective statements should be written to foster subsequent evaluation by incorporating measurement indicators, as indicated below:

> to improve school performance (as indicated by teacher evaluation) of first offenders in 50% of the cases served in 1 program year;

> to improve personal adjustment (as determined by specifically constructed psychological tests of ex-mental hospital patients) in 75% of those served during 1 program year;

> to reduce the rate of recidivism of juvenile offenders (as measured by official police re-arrest data) by 50% during the next program year;

> to develop ongoing funding for the innovative delinquency pre-

vention project (as indicated by letters of commitment from the youth commission and the United Way) by the end of the second year.

As stated earlier in Chapter 2, in some instances it is necessary to devise instruments, called performance indicators, to measure results. In the objective statements illustrated above, these might be teacher assessment forms or psychological tests. Each organization will have to determine whether it will create its own or adopt existing performance indicators. With information thus collected the organization can compare planned with actual performance.

It may be recalled that in Chapter 9, one impact objective was written, "to increase by December 15 the number of potential foster parents by 30, thereby reducing monthly waiting lists." This example will be used to illustrate questions which can guide decision making related to the accomplishments of objectives.[7] If the organization *does achieve its objectives*, these questions could be asked:

(1) Given the nature of the problem and the resources that were available, were the objectives set too low?

Example: Is the recruiting of 30 foster parents unrealistically low in light of the need and the resources available to accomplish this objective?

(2) Was the cost worth the accomplishments?

Example: Is the per family recruitment cost of $300 worth the investment?

(3) Even though the objectives were achieved, does the basic problem remain essentially unchanged?

Example: Despite the addition of 30 foster parents per month, if the waiting list remains high, what should be done?

Recruit different kinds of foster families to more closely match children?
Increase objective from 30 to 50?
Develop new objective of reducing number of children requiring foster care (e.g., intensify work with natural parents)?

(4) Does solving this particular problem create other problems that must be dealt with?

Example: With the increase of 30 more foster parents per month, will more requests be made on the organization for services?

(5)   Has the achievement of these particular objectives interferred with the achievement of other objectives; if so, does the balance have to be redressed?

Example: As a result of assigning staff from other units (e.g., adoptions services) to foster care recruitment, other units are having difficulty in meeting their objectives. Can this be justified?

If the organization *does not achieve its objectives,* these questions could be asked:

(1)   Were adequate resources available to accomplish the tasks?

Example: Were enough staff resources given to the recruitment effort?

(2)   Were objectives set unreasonably high?

Example: Despite the desperate need for foster parents, would lowering the objective to 20 foster parents have been more realistic?

(3)   Was the timetable appropriate?

Example: Would a more reasonable date to achieve the objective be June of the following year?

(4)   Given the constraints and other demands, should the organization redirect its energies to other broad problem areas?

Example: Would staff time and energy be better invested in prevention programs so youngsters would not need foster homes, or in working with natural parents to reduce the amount of time in foster homes?

The review of success, partial success, or failure of objectives provides a springboard for further decision making. Because community organizations generally operate under less than ideal conditions, frequently objectives are either partially achieved, or some are achieved, but not others. Through the evaluation process, organization members become keenly aware that a discrepancy may exist between their aspiration level and actual outcomes.[8] They may not have been able to select the optimum solution for a given problem because of inadequate resources, political constraints, time presssures, or finances. Not being able to provide the optimum solution, they may have to settle on a second or third best approach. Confronted with this reality, organization members can either despair and do nothing, or they can use the opportunity to determine what changes in the problem-solving process they need to work on.

As Figure 11–3 illustrates, the problem-solving process is dynamic and subject to continuous revision: problems are analyzed, objectives are established, alternatives are developed through both rational and creative approaches, and action plans are designed and implemented. Monitoring and assessing results promote a review of whether or not changes should occur at any points along the process. Perhaps the problems need to be revised because the assumptions about what caused them are incorrect and therefore new causes have to be considered. Or perhaps because of changing conditions the organization needs to elect to work on other problems. Furthermore, objectives may need to be revised because they are set too low and are unchallenging, because they are set too high and are too difficult to achieve, or because though achieved, the problem remains, and new objectives need to be developed that are more on target. Perhaps a different strategy has to be considered to reflect changing circumstances. Finally, the activities and tasks may require alteration if they are insufficient and do not achieve objectives. It is through this continuous review and revision that an organization can take necessary corrective actions. Figure 11–3 illustrates this process.

The willingness to base decisions on a critical review of changing circumstances is at the core of the problem-solving process. For this attitude reflects a problem-solving style that is open to constantly changing conditions, flexible in adapting to particular situations, and willing to make modifications based on new situations. By accompanying a built-in review with flexibility, a community organization can avoid adhering to an approach which goes nowhere. It embraces the complex and kaleidoscopic nature of the real world in which everything is in flux. Thus the problem-solving process is never ending and ever challenging.

Figure 11-3. THE PROBLEM-SOLVING PROCESS

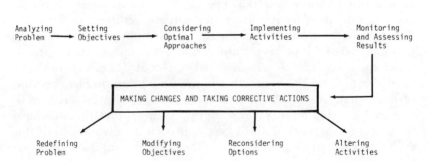

Epilogue

STRATEGIES FOR SURVIVAL

This Epilogue is written at a time when almost every community organization receiving local, state, or federal funding is faced with actual or potential cutbacks. Public agencies are not alone in experiencing cutbacks; voluntary organizations relying primarily on foundation, corporate, or United Way money are beginning to experience limits in funding because of increased competition. As more agencies feel squeezed, the queue for alternate funding sources grows longer. Almost all organizations concerned with community problems will be intensively concerned with survival in the foreseeable future.

The ability to survive and be a vital force for change will hinge in large part on an organization's ability to deal with current funding crises and, more importantly, to anticipate the future and plan ahead. Planning for the future is crucial if an organization is to survive in a turbulent, complex, and resource-limited world.

Developing strategies for the future is always desirable, even in periods when funding resources are strong and dependable, because conditions eventually change and all organizations must adapt to survive. In this time of diminished funding, strategic planning is absolutely essential to deal with unanticipated changes and to be in a position to take advantage of new opportunities. Those organizations that can do such strategic planning have the greatest potential for enduring.

Strategic planning is defined as developing a picture of what the organization wants to be; it is the framework that determines the nature and direction of an organization.[1] It answers the questions, "What is our basic area of work? Should it continue to be so? How should we accomplish our work?" A strategy, then, is a blueprint of the organization's game plan, indicating how an organization intends to get to where it wants to go.[2]

A mission statement is essential to the process of strategic planning. Reflecting the basic concept and character of the organization, the mission statement should identify (1) the nature of the service products, (2) the consumers or audience of the organization's activities, and (3) other special distinctive features of the organization. In the course of strategic planning, the mission statement may need to be revised.[3] For example, a rape counseling organization, after deliberation, might decide to broaden its mission from serving only those who have been victims of rape to educating the community on how to reduce the possibility of rape. An alcoholic counseling agency's mission might be altered to include working with those who use other drugs, in which case a name change might be in order.

The importance of the mission statement is that it makes clear to the organization and to the community the unique quality of the organization's contribution.

CRITICAL STRATEGIC PLANNING QUESTIONS

Because change is certain and the rapidity of change is accelerating, every community organization—no matter how strong—will have to engage in continuous review and adaptation. Changing circumstances are likely to prompt new directions, new opportunities, and new needs, sometimes resulting in an organization's discontinuing what it has been doing all along. Organization members should periodically ask the question, "If we were starting today, would we be doing what we are now doing?" Having reviewed its current mission and ways of carrying out its activities, it is in a better position to examine what the organization should become.

Asking critical questions can aid an organization in determining its future direction. Though demanding on members, the process of self-assessment provides significant insight during the exploratory phase of strategic planning. The following questions are fundamental in formulating a strategy:

Who are our primary consumers (clients, audience, customers)?
Why should consumers want our services?

Which services should be continued and which abandoned?

Who is our competition?

What programs in the community appear to be a duplication of what we offer?

Do our various programs mesh with each other? If not, should they do so?

How do others perceive our programs?

What are the opportunities for expansion, including different consumers, different geographic areas, different services or functions?

Do we have the skills and capabilities to handle new programs?

How will shifts in funding patterns influence our organizational directions?

Will the organization be able to take advantage of new opportunities?

Is the timing right for possible new directions?

The answers to these are not always clear, even for well established and successful organizations. Nor are the answers ever final because of changing circumstances in both the organization and the environment. In many organizations there may not be any one strategy, but rather there may be a collection of strategies—one for each major facet of the organization. Typically strategies evolve over time and are subject to continuous review and revision.[4]

STRATEGIC ALTERNATIVES IN AN ERA OF AUSTERITY

Beyond dealing with critical questions, in a period of austerity organizations should consider the following specific strategic planning alternatives.

Concentration Strategy

The advantage of concentrating on a single program, service, or population is that it generally permits an organization to do one thing well. The organization can achieve a high degree of efficiency and develop a distinctive and unique contribution to the community.

Strategic considerations for the single purpose organization become fine tuning issues: "How can we increase the number of people using our single program?" or, "How can we expand our service to the other geographic areas?"[5]

This strategy may prove detrimental if, having concentrated its efforts and its expertise in one area, an organization finds that it is out of fashion or its program has a low priority for funding. Concentration as a strategy is feasible when an organization may experience only a slight reduction in funding and is reasonably confident that its services or target populations will continue to be eligible for funding. The philosophy of this strategy might be summed up as, "If it ain't broke, don't fix it."

Diversification of Programs and Funding Strategy

A strategy of diversification may be embarked upon when funding from one source is uncertain, when competition increases because other organizations are beginning to offer the same service in the community, or when service demand declines. Diversification permits spreading the risk. It also has the advantage of providing staff and volunteers with something new and different to work on so they avoid becoming stale.

One major difficulty with a diversification strategy is the potential for the organization to take in more than it can digest. Every organization has to consider whether it has the time and the capability to take on new programs that create excessive demands and result in special strains. Organizations may have to discard some of their old efforts as they consider embarking on new ones.

Two kinds of diversification can occur in organizations. Concentric diversification preserves the organization's common unity; the additional program relates to already ongoing projects and builds upon knowledge, experience, and existing technology. For example, an organization that provides counseling services on alcoholism and has sufficient understanding about addictive behavior may decide to add counseling on drug abuse. An organization already active in advocating legislative changes for children may decide to add legislative advocacy for youth to its program repertoire.

Conglomerate diversification involves taking on an adjunct program that establishes a new and different direction, usually unrelated to existing programs. In business organizations conglomerates are intended to encance the profitability of the organization; in non-profit organizations a conglomerate strategy might develop out of a desire to enhance the survivability of an organization.[6] For example, a housing advocacy group may take on a drug counseling program because of the prospects of increased funding and community support, even though the new program may be related only in a very limited way.

Organizations pursuing a conglomerate diversification strategy should ask two questions: (1) "If we ran into difficulty would we know how to bail ourselves out?" and (2) "What is the least amount of diversification we need to be a viable organization?" The answer to these questions can help an organization avoid going willy-nilly in too many directions at one time.

Diversification as a strategy can occur in funding as well as in programs. In addition to developing the ability to write proposals for governmental, foundation, or corporate funding, as discussed in Chapter 10, organizations will increasingly seek other means to sustain their core budgets. In fact, as governmental funding diminishes, some organizations will be forced to seek funding from what may previously have been highly unusual sources. The following are some fund raising approaches non-profit organizations can consider to add to their financial strength.

(1)   *Special events* can attract new friends, enhance the public image of the organization, and raise needed money. Such events include raffles, telethons, banquets, dances, movie benefits, and walkathons. The best advice is this: select an event that is likely to be popular and one that the organization has sufficient resources to easily manage.[7]

(2)   *Direct mail order appeals* have the advantage of acquiring new friends and renewing the commitment of previous donors. They require investment of time and money, careful planning, and follow-up. The organization may either use its own list or buy mail lists. Simply stated, a direct mail package consists of a letter conveying the reason for the fund raising effort and a description of the organization.[8]

(3)   *Life income agreements* permit individuals who have a strong commitment to the organization to transfer cash, securities, or real estate to a non-profit organization in return for an assured income. Upon the death of the last beneficiary named in the agreement, the remaining assets become available to the organization. These agreements can take the following forms:

a. *A charitable gift annuity* is designed for the older person who wishes a guaranteed dollar return for life. The advantage to the donor is that a large part of the annual income is tax free.

b. *A deferred payment gift annuity* permits the donor to give currently an irrevocable gift, but defers receiving an income until a later time. The donor is permitted a sizeable deduction on his/her taxes at the time of the gift.

c. *A charitable remainder annuity* trust provides a guaranteed fixed income for life and freedom from investment responsibilities. This permits the donor to make a gift of assets while retaining income.

d. *A charitable remainder unitrust* also provides a lifetime income, but the recipient receives annual payments based upon a fixed percentage of the value of the gift assets.

e. *A pooled life income fund* permits pooling of the donor's gift with other gifts to receive a proportionate share of the "pooled fund."

f. *A living trust agreement* is a revocable gift that permits the donor to place cash with the non-profit organization that manages and invests the assets and pays income, minus a reasonable management fee.

(4) *Life insurance gifts* permit donors to name the non-profit organization as a contingent beneficiary (the one named to receive the proceeds in the event the primary beneficiary or beneficiaries do not survive the insured). A potential donor may also choose the organization as a co-beneficiary. Or a donor may choose to give the organization a paid-up insurance policy that he or she no longer needs, with possible tax benefits.

(5) *A bequest* or gift through a will can have the advantage of reducing taxes due in the total estate because it removes the property given from the taxable estate.

(6) A gift can be in the form of *appreciated securities*. If, for example, securities bought for $3,000 are now valued at $5,000, the $5,000 can be deducted as a gift for tax purposes.

The organization should obtain expert resource development and legal advice on these kinds of gifts.[9]

An organization wishing to embark on these resource development approaches should be aware of several major considerations. First, they may make considerable demands on the organization by requiring special funds and volunteer and staff time. Second, they may present new and special constraints different from those the organization may have experienced previously. For example, certain advocacy efforts may be constrained because of donor wishes. Third, the Economic Recovery Act of 1981 reduces some of the after-tax advantages of creating a charitable trust.

Joint Venture and Merger Strategies

In a period of fiscal austerity, some organizations will be joining together to do things they are unable to do on their own. Under a joint venture agreement (sometimes known as consortiums), two or more organizations jointly finance and operate a program. For example, two child care institutions could combine their efforts to sponsor a group home in the community. Neither might have been able to afford the full complement of staff or housing on its own. By pooling funds, staff, and volunteer expertise, the sponsoring organizations can more effectively provide their service. With cutbacks in funding, organizations may have to surrender some degree of autonomy in joint ventures if the services they want to provide are to continue.

Mergers are also likely to increase in a period of severe austerity. The previous two decades spawned many small agencies that now may have to merge as they struggle to survive. Because mergers involve giving up the precious commodity of an organization's control of its own destiny and the loss or alteration of its identity, most agencies enter merger discussions reluctantly and often out of a sense of desperation. But staying alive in a modified form may be preferable to complete annihilation.

Mergers do have some distinct advantages beyond saving a program or service that is too weak to stand alone. The merger of two or more agencies may reduce administrative costs, if this is agreed upon as an explicit goal of the merger. Moreover, the merged organization can provide greater specialization (accounting, personnel, administration) than might have been possible in a smaller agency. And the new organization is likely to have greater visibility and more power to negotiate financial support.

But several caveats should be kept in mind about mergers. First, merging two weak organizations will not necessarily result in one strong one. If the proposed merged organizations are poorly managed and underfinanced, then the new organization will start with severe and perhaps insurmountable problems. Second, retaining weak staff or obsolete programs in the merged organization also invites difficulties. Third, if the primary motivation for the merger is to provide a convenient mechanism for receiving funding, then a subcontracting agreement with a host agency may be more appropriate than a merger. Fourth, the merged organizations must have compatible goals and complementary functions; they have to fit together in a new unified whole. Finally, because not all problems can be anticipated and because the merger may be traumatic for both staff and volunteer leaders, those responsible for the merger must be willing to take corrective actions as problems arise.[10]

Divestment and Retrenchment Strategies

During these times of extraordinary financial cutbacks, organizations may have to take extraordinary measures to survive. Those organizations that have been built up over years of growth and expansion are faced with challenges to scale down their operations to fit their diminished financial resources. To stay afloat organizations may have to reduce their size and jettison programs. Zero based budgeting (ZBB) is a retrenchment strategy that can be used when an organization has to undertake stringent actions aimed at wringing out organizational slack and inefficiencies.

Most groups base their budgets on adding (or, infrequently, subtracting) incrementally to the previous year's budget. In times of growth, when more money is expected to be available, this typically means adding staff. Though it is orderly and fast, incremental budgeting does not invite intense examination of whether costs were worth the benefits. The underlying assumption is that budgeting of past programs has been equitable, and all programs should continue to receive the same or more funding. Because community organizations do not have the same pressure as profit-making organizations to justify costs in relation to profits, there may be a tendency to become complacent. For some organizations this has resulted in staff not functioning at full capacity or in continuing projects that evidence limited success.

When funds are curtailed during a period of austerity, the business-as-usual incremental budgeting is inappropriate. In its place ZBB should be considered. This requires a reevaluation of all programs of the organization; the underlying assumption is that everything done in the past must be justified. Nothing is taken for granted, as organizational members ask, "Can we justify this program at this particular funding level? Is there still a need? How does each particular program relate to our overall goals? Should a particular program be discontinued or funded at less than (or more than) the previous level?"[11]

ZBB requires scrutiny of the objectives of each program. If they have not been achieved, achieved at less than anticipated levels, or, despite previous successes, if new information reveals that they are not likely to be achieved in the future, then perhaps the program should be reduced or eliminated.

ZBB places special demands on the organization. It takes considerable time as it requires a comprehensive look at all facets of the organization. It requires periodic examinations of the organization's goals, objectives, and priorities. Furthermore, it may compel painful changes in personnel affected by cutbacks. But in a period of austerity, organizations will be required to abandon even some worthwhile programs in the interest of retaining the most effective and efficient ones. Thus, ZBB serves to reorient the organization's thinking. Instead of concentrating on a small percentage of increments or decreases, as with incremental budgeting, ZBB forces the organization to scrutinize the management of the entire operation and to ferret out programs that have been continued only through inertia.

Though the intent of ZBB is admirable, political and organizational realities may require that it be modified and not applied in its purest form.[12] Depending on the extent of retrenchment, many organizations resort to a modified version of ZBB by establishing degrees of cutbacks. Reviews of the budget might require an answer to this question: "What would be the effect of budgeting at a 70 percent (80 percent) (90 percent) level on the delivery of our organization's programs?" Requiring answers to this question forces program proponents to assess in hard, realistic terms the extent to which they would achieve their objectives with reduced budgets.

ZBB may identify programs that must be divested. A divestment strategy to eliminate a program may prove better than trying to provide it with less resources than can adequately do the job.[13] Moreover, this strategy can result in eliminating non-essential, ancillary programs to keep the core program. An organization, for example, may have to divest itself of training workshops to preserve its essential mission of offering counseling services.

A retrenchment strategy is also difficult, but nevertheless essential, for survival. Cutting back on costs (travel, conferences, printing) may be necessary to deal with budget constraints. Substituting volunteers for staff, subcontracting projects, developing automated procedures, placing staff on a part-time schedule, eliminating salary increments—these and other methods are used to cut costs. Unfortunately some cost savings may be more harmful in the long run to the organization than their short-run advantages. For example, knowledgeable and highly trained personnel may be laid off, thus preventing the organization from later taking advantage of new opportunities that cannot be handled as well by less experienced personnel. Low morale may occur if staff forego raises or have to compete for dwindling funds. On the positive side, retrenchment may result, under some circumstances, in consolidating programs that have elements of duplication and in requiring staff and volunteers to be conscious of whether they are using their time productively.[14]

These major strategy approaches—concentration, diversification, mergers, divestment, and retrenchment—are among the ways organizations must cope now and in the future. The key to all of them is the ability to deal consciously, purposefully, and proactively to new events. These approaches require building on success and reducing failures through strategic planning. In short, organizations will have to develop the ability to respond dynamically to a very challenging and turbulent world.

PROBLEM SOLVING CONCEPTS AND METHODS CHECKLIST

FORMULATING THE PROBLEM (CHAP. 1)

Have you refined the problem by

—gathering relevant information?
—defining key words in the problem statement?
—breaking the problem into its component elements by asking basic questions?
—avoiding a prematurely narrow view of the problem?
—determining different perspectives of the problem?
—identifying key factors that affect the problem?
—developing a problem focus?
—identifying the consequences of the problem?

Have you considered

—concentrating on problems in sequence or simultaneously?
—establishing priorities on the basis of the importance of the problem and potential for success?

Setting Objectives (Chap. 2)

Have you sharpened objective statements by

—preparing organizational purposes and goals?
—distinguishing objective statements from problem statements?
—distinguishing operating, activity, and impact objectives?
—formulating each impact objective so that it contains a strong verb, one result, and is realistic?
—developing performance indicators?
—specifying the desired situation to be changed, target population, extent of change, and time period?
—reporting results by using a ratio format?

Decision Making in Organizations (Chaps. 3 and 4)

Have you attempted to improve the decision-making process by

—defining the functions of the group?
—preparing criteria for membership?
—distinguishing between constructive and destructive conflict?
—identifying the responsibilities of the chairperson?
—determining the appropriate decision-making powers of leader and group?
—clarifying staff assistance to boards of trustees and to committees?
—developing a consensus approach that permits disagreement?
—asking questions to facilitate discussions?
—using, when appropriate, parliamentary procedure in pure form or in combination with consensus?
—recording the session?

Generating Ideas Through Creative Thinking (Chap. 5)

Have you tried to stimulate new ideas by

—establishing a climate of thinking the unthinkable?
—using brainstorming or nominal group technique?

—using analogies to promote novel ideas?
—considering a checklist of key verbs (e.g., magnify, reduce, reverse)?
—reframing the issue?

AVOIDING TRAPS OF THE PROBLEM-SOLVING PROCESS (CHAP. 6)

Have you avoided certain traps in the problem-solving process by watching out for

—conclusions based on invalid premises?
—circular reasoning?
—oversimplification of cause-effect relationship?
—uncritical use of analogous thinking to justify solutions?
—promising grandiose solutions?
—delimiting the scope of the solution?
—reducing the pain of the problem without actually solving it?
—overemphasizing the rational problem-solving process?

DEVELOPING ALTERNATIVE ACTION PLANS (CHAP. 7)

Have you attempted to anticipate future events and consequences by

—developing a decision-tree approach for uncertain events?
—preparing contingency plans for projected events?
—developing contingency plans based on anticipated consequences?
—applying critical questions to a potential action plan that examines its feasibility?
—using force field analysis that examines the positive (driving) and negative (restraining) forces affecting an action plan?
—determining ways in which the action plan will be accepted?

COLLABORATING AND NEGOTIATING WITH OTHER ORGANIZATIONS (CHAP. 8)

Have you enhanced your collaborative efforts by

—determining that a particular undertaking can truly benefit by involving other organizations?

—assessing the specific benefits and specific costs to your organization?

Have you improved your negotiating capability by

—clarifying what you want to accomplish?
—obtaining all the essential information on the subject and the people with whom you will be dealing?
—preparing your case?
—anticipating the response of your opponents?
—developing a fall-back position?
—being aware of the many ways you could be manipulated?
—considering strategies appropriate to your organization and the solution?
—knowing how to resolve a stalemate?

DEVELOPING ACTION PLANNING CHARTS (CHAP. 9)

Have you considered ways to implement the alternative selected by

—preparing assignment charts?
—developing activity and task schedules?
—relating tasks and activities to objectives?
—displaying activities and tasks on GANTT, PERT, or narrative network charts?
—preparing project development flow charts?
—designing alternative choice charts?

OBTAINING FUNDS FOR PROBLEM-SOLVING PROJECTS (CHAP. 10)

Have you improved your chances of obtaining funds by

—making sure you are aware of the risks inherent in obtaining outside funding?
—knowing the procedures for matching potential foundations with your project?
—understanding the steps to obtain government grants?
—including relevant items in a summary statement?
—documenting the need?
—setting measurable objectives?
—specifying activities and tasks?
—describing evaluation procedures?

—indicating capability of the organization?
—submitting a defensible budget?

REVIEWING EFFORTS AND RESULTS OF THE PROBLEM-SOLVING PROCESS (CHAP. 11)

Have you reviewed results, keeping the following in mind?

—monitoring tasks and activities by considering effectiveness, sufficiency of resources, efficiency, and timeliness?
—modifying the GANTT chart to show comparison of projected with actual implementation of scheduled tasks?
—making crucial decisions based on relevant questions if the organization falls behind schedule?
—assessing objectives based on specifically designed measurement indicators?
—making crucial decisions based on relevant questions if the organization does not achieve what it set out to do?
—developing a flexible approach that responds to a changing and complex world?

Appendix B

PROBLEM SOLVING EXERCISES

The following exercises can be used in connection with the review of each chapter. The group leader or instructor can, with the group, determine whether all or some of the exercises should be carried out.

CHAPTER 1: FORMULATING THE PROBLEM

(1) Divide into groups of six to eight people; each group identifies a problem that may not yet be viewed as a widespread community problem. List ways that could be used to attract broader community interests.

(2) Based on the problems identified in (1) (or in any other problem selected by the group), identify sources of information on the problem(s).

(3) Divide the groups into six to eight people; each group then divides into A and B teams, and carries out the following exercises:

    (a) Team A develops an initial general problem statement, purposefully using vague and abstract terms; team B revises this problem statement. Then switch responsibilities: team B prepares the general statement; team A revises the problem statement.

(b) Each team develops a specific hypothetical community problem statement using the following for the basis of the problem statement:

What is the problem?
Where does it exist?
Who is affected by it?
When does it occur?
To what degree is it felt?

The other team reviews and critiques the problem statement. Is it sufficiently precise?

(c) Team A identifies a problem from the perspective of a particular agency or organization; team B takes the same problem and prepares a statement from a different organizational perspective.

(d) Team A develops a problem statement that contains within it a premature solution; team B broadens the statement to permit other solution possibilities. Teams reverse assignments.

(4) Taking a general issue (e.g., housing, employment), each group lists several problem categories and then, from these problem areas, identifies one or more contributing factors.

(5) Taking the same problem, each group identifies consequences.

(6) Each group takes those problems it has considered and determines priority rankings by voting, basing their ratings on the factors of importance and probability of success.

Chapter 2: Setting Objectives

(1) Working in groups of six to eight and keeping in mind the importance of specifying observable results, improve the following hypothetical objectives:

(a) "To provide social services to persons over age 60."

(b) "To assist trainees to achieve higher paying positions."

(c) "To increase the advocacy capability of the organization's members."

(d) "To improve coordination between our organization and X organization."

(e) "To increase understanding between the agency's board and staff."

(f) "To establish outreach offices as soon as possible."

(g) "To enhance the well-being of alcoholics."

(h) "To meet with city officials about establishing half-way houses for runaway youth."

(2) Working again in groups of six to eight, consider a problem previously discussed and defined.

(a) Develop a general goal statement for the hypothetical organization.

(b) Develop one or more objectives; if useful, identify whether they are operating, activity, or impact objectives. If feasible, indicate (1) desired situation, (2) target population, (3) extent, and (4) time frame in the objective statement.

(c) Identify indicators of performance.

(d) Use, if feasible, the ratio format described in the text to show how results will be reported.

CHAPTER 3: DECISION MAKING IN ORGANIZATIONS: FUNCTIONS, STRUCTURES, AND PARTICIPANTS

(1) Divide into groups of six to eight people. Based on problems discussed previously, divide into pairs to carry out the following assignments:

(a) One pair prepares a charge to the task force; be as specific as possible.

(b) Another pair determines the membership of a task force. Give a rationale for why each person was selected and what each person's contribution would be to the group effort.

(c) Another pair defines the role and responsibilities of staff to the task force.

(d) Another pair prepares a description of the chairperson's role and develops the agenda for the first meeting.

(2) Within each group, discuss areas of potential conflict between participants.

(3) Within each group, select different points along the decision-making continuum and discuss or role play how a chairperson and group would interact on the problem you have selected.

(4) Working in pairs within your group, develop how you would function as staff working with a committee on the previously selected problem. One pair might select a facilitative style; a second pair, an entrepreneurial style; and a third pair, an advocacy style.

CHAPTER 4: FACILITATING THE DECISION-MAKING PROCESS

(1) In groups of six to eight, take a problem topic previously selected and spend 15 to 20 minutes attempting to arrive at a consensus on a possible solution. Someone in the group should play devil's advocate. The chairperson and others in the group should promote the discussion by using various questions suggested in the text. Someone in the group should be assigned to record the session on flip chart paper, if possible.

(2) In groups of six to eight (or the entire group, if desired) pick a topic and conduct a meeting using parliamentary procedure.

CHAPTER 5: GENERATING IDEAS THROUGH CREATIVE THINKING

(1) Divide into groups of six to eight. Each group takes a problem initially discussed and, through brainstorming, develops as many possible solutions as possible within 10 minutes.

(2) Selecting a different problem, each group generates a list of solutions employing nominal group technique. Using one of the suggested voting procedures, narrow the list to three or four potential solutions.

(3) Taking the same or a different problem, each group develops a creative solution by using analogous thinking. Use the checklist suggested in the chapter to stimulate ideas.

(4) Each group takes a problem it has previously considered and, by reframing the issue, promotes a different approach.

CHAPTER 6: AVOIDING TRAPS OF THE PROBLEM-SOLVING PROCESS

(1) In groups of six to eight, team A and team B members develop examples or statements that reflect the following:
   (a) conclusions or solutions that do not necessarily follow from the underlying premises or assumptions (non sequitur thinking),
   (b) circular reasoning,
   (c) oversimplifying cause-effect relationships,
   (d) using analogous thinking to prove a point,

(e)   grandiose plans,
(f)   delimiting the scope of the problem solution,
(g)   palliative solutions.
The two teams of each group alternate in presenting a statement and identifying which trap it belongs to.

CHAPTER 7: DEVELOPING ALTERNATIVE ACTION PLANS

(1)   In groups of three to four prepare a decision tree on one or more of the following events:
   (a)   The percent of people who would (would not) be upset if a committee report did recommend (did not recommend) abortions be made available to low-income women. Indicate possible results.
   (b)   The likelihood of the juvenile court accepting (not accepting) a screening device that would identify mentally retarded juveniles. Indicate possible results.
   (c)   The likely repose of a community if a neighborhood (settlement) house developed plans to facilitate a bussing program to racially integrate students.
   (d)   The group itself identifies an issue, an uncertain event, and likely results that could be diagrammed on a decision tree.
(2)   In small groups develop contingency plans for the following possible situations:
   (a)   "If X foundation does not fund our project, then we will. . . ."
   (b)   "If we have to reduce our budget by 10 percent, then we will. . . ."
   (c)   "If staff goes on strike, then we will. . . ."
   (d)   "If, despite merits of our plan, we receive strong opposition from residents, then we will. . . ."
(3)   In small groups, determine a possible solution to a problem and anticipate advantages and disadvantages. If the group cannot determine a proposal, consider the following situation:
A respected group of Scandanavian professionals has decided to establish a Scandanavian Family Counseling Agency. What are the pros and cons for this proposal?
(4)   Using force field analysis, determine the driving and restraining forces affecting a problem situation.
(5)   Consider several alternatives to a particular problem pre-

viously discussed. Use the chart of critical questions to consider a preferred approach.

(6)   After selecting an action plan, consider specific potential resistances and how these would be overcome.

CHAPTER 8: COLLABORATING AND NEGOTIATING WITH OTHER ORGANIZATIONS

(1)   Divide into groups of six to eight. Each person is a representative of one of the following organizations: Child Advocacy, United Way, League of Women Voters, Welfare Rights, Catholic Charities, Mental Health Manufacturers' Association, and Rotary. Role play how each representative would respond to the question, "Will your organization support an increased tax levy to provide local mental health services? If so, how?"

(2)   Working in groups of six to eight, divide into two teams. Team A represents a community organization or advocacy group; team B, public officials or administrators. Mutually select a topic, such as request for increased funds or change in procedures. Each team determines its negotiating strategies and its case. Anticipate the position of the other side, and prepare fall-back positions.

(3)   Assuming, after 20 minutes discussion, that a stalemate has occurred, mutually explore ways to break the deadlock. Analyze afterwards what was effective and what was not in negotiations.

CHAPTER 9: DEVELOPING ACTION PLANNING CHARTS

(1)   Based on an action plan previously selected, do the following:
(a)   Develop an assignments chart.
(b)   List activities and tasks that need to be carried out using both forward planning and reverse order planning procedures.
(c)   Prepare a GANTT chart.
(d)   Prepare PERT or narrative network charts (optional).

(2)   Assuming each group has identified a project that will require several reviews and revisions by different bodies, prepare a project development flow chart.

(3)   Assuming each group has identified a project that requires clients to be processed through a series of yes/no decision points, prepare an alternative choice chart.

CHAPTER 10: OBTAINING FUNDS FOR PROBLEM-SOLVING PROJECTS

(1) Working in small groups, identify a project requiring special funding. Based on your decision to obtain either foundation or governmental funding, follow the steps suggested in the text to locate a funder.

(2) Develop a proposal by assigning specific tasks to members of the group. Critique each other's contribution. Be prepred to make changes in the proposed outline if this makes sense. (Alternative assignment: members are responsible for writing their own proposals.)

(3) Select a panel of funders for each proposal. Panel members will have read carefully the proposals in advance of the meetings with the proposal writer(s), who will attempt to convince the funders. The group as a whole can be given responsibility to select 20% of the proposals for actual funding.

CHAPTER 11: REVIEWING EFFORTS AND RESULTS OF THE PROBLEM-SOLVING PROCESS

(1) Assume that some of the tasks of major activities you developed previously are not completed as planned. Prepare a hypothetical GANTT chart that shows when schedules were actually completed.

(2) For each task that was not completed on time, give a hypothetical monitoring report.

(3) Review objectives that had been developed earlier to determine methods of measuring tangible results. If they had not been developed previously, identify what measurement indicators could now be used.

(4) Assuming objectives developed earlier were (not) achieved, what questions should be considered for decision making?

REFERENCES

CHAPTER 1

1. Charles H. Kepner and Benjamin B. Tregoe, *The Rational Manager* (New York: McGraw-Hill, 1974), pp. 18–20.
2. Ann Glampson, Tony Scott, and David N. Thomas, *A Guide to the Assessment of Community Needs and Resources* (London: National Institute for Social Work, 1977), pp. 7–50.
3. Richard L. Purtill, *Logical Thinking* (New York: Harper & Row, 1972), pp. 9–11.
4. Ralph Brody and Arlene Kaukus, "Community Problem Solving Through Setting Objectives," *Journal of Asian-Pacific and World Perspectives* (July 1977): 19–32; Michael Doyle and David Straus, *How to Make Meetings Work* (Los Angeles: Wyden Books, 1974), p. 225.
5. Marvin Rosenberg and Ralph Brody, *Systems Serving People: A Breakthrough in Service Delivery* (Cleveland, Oh.: School of Applied Social Sciences, Case Western Reserve University, 1974), p. 2.
6. Doyle and Straus, *How to Make Meetings Work*, p. 221.
7. Ibid., p. 214.
8. Paul Mali, *Managing by Objectives* (New York: Wiley Interscience, 1972), p. 41; Kepner and Tregoe, *The Rational Manager*, p. 63.
9. Ralph Brody, *Guide for Applying for Federal Funds for Human Services* (Cleve-

land, Oh.: School of Applied Social Sciences, Case Western Reserve University, 1974).

10. Brody and Kaukus, "Community Problem Solving Through Setting Objectives," pp. 20–3.

CHAPTER 2

1. Ralph Brody and Holly Krailo, "An Approach for Reviewing Program Effectiveness," *Social Work* 23 (May 1978):226–32.
2. Robert MacDicken et al., *Toward More Effective Management,* Kirschner Associates, Inc., U.S. HEW, Office of Human Development, Administration on Aging, 1975, p. 72.
3. Office of Budget and Management, State of Ohio, *Measuring Program Results* (Columbus, Oh., 1975); see also United Way Services, *Program Planning and Performance Measurement System* (Cleveland, Oh., 1979), pp. 62–3.
4. Brody and Krailo, "An Approach for Reviewing Program Effectiveness," pp. 227–8.
5. Ibid., p. 228.
6. Anthony P. Raia, *Managing By Objectives* (Glenview, Ill.: Scott, Foresman, 1974), p. 24.
7. Robert Elkin and Darrel J. Vorwaller, "Evaluating the Effectiveness of Social Services," *Management Controls* (May 1972):104–11.
8. Peter F. Drucker, "What Results Should you Expect? A Users Guide to MBO," *Public Administration Review* (January–February 1976):18.

CHAPTER 3

1. Harleigh B. Trecker, *Citizens Boards at Work* (New York: Association Press, 1970), p. 135; Peter B. Schoderbek, *The Effective Use of Committees* (Alexandria, Va.: United Way of American, 1979), p. 2.
2. Charles Handy, *Understanding Organizations* (Baltimore: Penguin Books, 1976), p. 174.
3. See Michael Doyle and David Straus, *How to Make Meetings Work* (Los Angeles: Wyden Books, 1974), pp. 159–63; Handy, *Understanding Organizations,* p. 146
4. The idea that form follows function is adapted from a work on studies of General Motors, DuPont, Standard Oil of New Jersey, and Sears Roebuck: Alfred Chandler, Jr., *Strategy and Structure* (Garden City, N.Y.: Doubleday, 1966).
5. Adapted from Trecker, *Citizens Boards at Work,* p. 144 and Theodore

Caplow, *How to Run Any Organization* (Hinsdale, Ill.: The Dryden Press, 1976), pp. 59–61.

6. Edgar H. Schein, *Process Consultation: Its Role in Organization Development* (Reading, Mass: Addison Wesley Publishing, 1969), pp. 31–45.

7. Handy, *Understanding Organizations*, p. 244 and Trecker, *Citizens Boards At Work*, p. 216.

8. Handy, Ibid., p. 212.

9. Ibid., pp. 220–22.

10. Caplow, *How to Run Any Organization*, p. 171.

11. Ibid., p. 173.

12. Adapted from Schoderbek, *The Effective Use of Committees*, pp. 5–7; Caplow, *How to Run Any Organization*, pp. 57–8; Trecker, *Citizens Boards at Work*, p. 162; Schein, *Process Consultation: Its Role in Organization Development*, p. 40.

13. John Morse and Jay Lorsch, "Beyond Theory Y," *Harvard Business Review* (May–June 1970):61–8.

14. Adapted from Robert Tannenbaum and Warren Schmidt, "How to Choose a Leadership Pattern," *Harvard Business Review* (May–June 1973).

15. Trecker, *Citizens Boards at Work*, p. 79.

16. Adapted from Peter B. Schoderbek, *The Board and Its Responsibilities* (Alexandria, Va.: United Way of America, 1979), pp. 7–9.

17. Ibid., p. 19.

18. Trecker, *Citizens Boards at Work*, p. 87.

19. Harry Fagan, *Empowerment* (New York: Paulist Press, 1979), p. 62.

CHAPTER 4

1. Edgar H. Schein, *Organizational Psychology* (New York: Prentice-Hall, 1970), pp. 45–68; Jay Hall, "Decisions, Decisions, Decisions," *Psychology Today* (November 1971):51–4, 86–8.

2. Irving L. Janis, "Groupthink," *Psychology Today* (November 1971):43–6, 74–6.

3. O. Garfield Jones, *Parliamentary Procedure at a Glance* (New York: Appleton-Century, 1949).

4. General Henry M. Robert, *Robert's Rules of Order* (Chicago: Scott, Foresman, 1943).

5. John C. Glidewell, *Choice Points* (Cambridge, Mass.: The MIT Press, 1976), p. 77.

6. For a variation of this recording approach, see Michael Doyle and David Straus, *How to Make Meetings Work* (Los Angeles: Wyden Books, 1974), pp. 139–42.

Chapter 5

1. See Edward DeBono, "Information Processing and New Ideas—Lateral and Vertical Thinking," in *Guide to Creative Action*, ed. Parnes et al. (New York: Charles Scribner's Sons, 1977), pp. 195–200; Edward DeBono, *New Think*, (New York: Basic Books, 1968).
2. George M. Prince, "The Operational Mechanism of Synectics," in Parnes et al., *Guide to Creative Action*, p. 156.
3. Abraham Maslow, *Toward a Psychology of Being* (New York: D. Van Nostrand, 1968), pp. 135–45.
4. DeBono, *New Think*, p. 89.
5. Rollo May, *The Courage to Create* (New York: W. W. Norton, 1975).
6. DeBono, *New Think*, pp. 85–7.
7. May, *The Courage to Create*, p. 93.
8. DeBono, *New Think*, p. 113.
9. In DeBono's *New Think*, p. 197, this moving from one point to another in a haphazard manner and then allowing the points to coalesce into a pattern is called "lateral thinking."
10. See Thomas J. Bouchard, "Whatever Happened to Brainstorming?" in Parnes et al., *Guide to Creative Action*, pp. 189–92; Morris Stein, *Stimulating Creativity, Vol. 2* (New York: Academic Press, 1975), pp. 25–38, 268–70.
11. This material on nominal group technique is summarized from Andre L. Delbecq et al., *Group Techniques for Program Planning* (Glenview, Ill.: Scott, Foresman, 1976).
12. W. J. Gordon, "On Being Explicit About Creative Process," in Parnes et al., *Guide to Creative Action*, p. 172.
13. Ibid., p. 173; Stein, *Stimulating Creativity, Vol. 2*, pp. 187–9.
14. For a more detailed description of methods to evoke analogous thinking in problem solving, see George M. Prince, "The Operational Mechanism of Synectics," in Parnes et al., *Guide to Creative Action*, pp. 155–60; George M. Prince, *The Practice of Creativity* (New York: Collier Books, 1970).
15. Adapted from Alex Osborn, "Applied Imagination," in *The Psychology of Efficient Thinking*, ed. Zbigniew Pietrasinski (New York: Pergamon Press, 1969), pp. 129–39.
16. Paul Watzlawick et al., *Change* (New York: W. W. Norton, 1974), pp. 92–109.

Chapter 6

1. Richard L. Purtill, *Logical Thinking* (New York: Harper & Row, 1972), pp. 56–9.
2. Ibid., pp. 62–3.

3. Ibid., p. 80.
4. Ibid., p. 60.
5. Paul Mali, *Managing by Objectives* (New York: Wiley Interscience, 1972), p. 99.
6. Gerald Zaltman and Robert Duncan, *Strategies for Planned Change* (New York: John Wiley & Sons, 1977), pp. 34–8; Paul Watzlawick et al., *Change* (New York: W. W. Norton, 1974), pp. 40–1.
7. Austin J. Freeley, *Argumentation and Debate* (Belmont, Calif.: Wadsworth Publishing, 1961), p. 100.
8. Mali, *Managing by Objectives*, p. 100.
9. Purtill, *Logical Thinking*, pp. 70–3; Freeley, *Argumentation and Debate*, pp. 93–6.
10. Watzlawick et al., describes the ultimate, all-embracing solution as the utopia syndrome, *Change*, pp. 47–61.
11. Robert Adrey, *The Social Contract: A Personal Enquiry into the Evolutionary Sources of Order and Disorder* (New York: Atheneum, 1970), p. 3.

CHAPTER 7

1. Paul Mali, *Managing by Objectives* (New York: Wiley Interscience, 1972), p. 140.
2. The decision-tree procedures are adapted from business literature for use by human services and community organizations. See the following for a more detailed review of decision trees: Paul Mali, *Managing by Objectives*, pp. 140–5; Harold Koontz and Cyril O'Donnell, *Essentials of Management* (New York: McGraw-Hill, 1974), pp. 107–8; John Magee, "Decision Trees for Decision Making," *Harvard Business Review* (July–August 1964):126–38; Steven C. Wheelwright and Spyros Makridakis, *Forecasting Methods for Management* (New York: John Wiley and Sons, 1973) pp. 162–76.
3. Adapted from Max Richards and Paul Greenlaw, *Management Decision Making* (Homewood, Ill.: Richard D. Irwin, 1966), pp. 304–11.
4. The questions and chart were stimulated by Mac Dicken et al., *Toward More Effective Management*, (Kirschner Associates, Inc.), U.S. HEW, Office of Human Development, Administration on Aging, 1975, pp. 151–6.
5. See Fremont Kast and James Rosenzweig, *Organization and Management* (New York: McGraw-Hill, 1967), pp. 590–3; Anthony P. Raia, *Managing by Objectives* (Glenview, Ill.: Scott, Foresman, 1974), p. 154.
6. Koontz and O'Donnel, *Essentials of Management*, p. 130.
7. Gerald Zaltman and Robert Duncan, *Strategies for Planned Change* (New York: John Wiley & Sons, 1977), p. 14.
8. Raia, *Managing by Objectives*, p. 156.

CHAPTER 8

1. Norton E. Long, "The Local Community as an Ecology of Games," in *Perspectives on the American Community*, ed. Roland Warren (New York: Rand McNally, (1966), pp. 54–69; William J. Reid, "Inter-Organizational Coordination in Social Welfare: A Theoretical Approach to Analysis and Intervention," in *Readings in Community Organization Practice*, eds. Ralph M. Kramer and Harry Specht (Englewood, N.J.: Prentice-Hall, 1969), pp. 178–9.
2. Martin Rein and Robert Morris, "Goals, Structures, and Strategies for Community Change," in *Readings in Community Organization Practice*, eds. Ralph M. Kramer and Harry Specht (Englewood Cliffs, N.J.: Prentice-Hall, 1969), p. 198.
3. William J. Reid, "Inter-Organizational Coordination in Social Welfare: A Theoretical Approach to Analysis and Intervention," p. 177.
4. Ibid., p. 179.
5. Sol Levine and Paul E. White, "Exchange as a Conceptual Framework for the Study of Interorganizational Relationships," *Administrative Science Quarterly* 5 (March 1961):583–601.
6. Frank Baker and Gregory O'Brien, "Intersystems Relations and Coordination of Service Organizations," *American Journal of Public Health* 61 (January 1971):130–7; Eugene Litwak and Lydia F. Hylton, "Interorganizational Analysis: A Hypothesis on Co-ordinating Agencies," *Administrative Science Quarterly* 6 (March 1962):pp. 395–420.
7. William J. Reid, "Inter-Organizational Coordination in Social Welfare: A Theoretical Approach to Analysis and Intervention," p. 181.
8. Martin Rein and Robert Morris, "Goals, Structures, and Strategies for Community Change," p. 195.
9. Ibid., p. 197.
10. Adapted in part from Sheldon P. Gans and Gerald T. Horton, *Integration of Human Services: The State and Municipal Levels* (New York: Praeger, 1975), pp. xviii–xix.
11. Gerald I. Nierenberg, *Fundamentals of Negotiating* (New York: Hawthorn Books, 1973), p. 4.
12. Stephen M. Davidson, "Planning and Coordination of Social Services in Multiorganizational Contexts," *Social Service Review* (March 1976):132.
13. Nierenberg, *Fundamentals of Negotiating*, pp. 23, 27, 183.
14. Ralph Brody and Kay Cremer, *Organizing for Social Change* (Cleveland, Oh.: The Institute of Urban Studies, Cleveland State University, 1970), p. 178.
15. Chester L. Karras, *The Negotiating Game* (New York: T. Y. Crowell Publishing, 1970), pp. 184–5.
16. Harry Fagan, *Empowerment* (New York: Paulist Press, 1979), pp. 17, 18.

17. Willard C. Richan and Marvin Rosenberg, "The Advo-Kit: A Self-Administered Training Program for the Social Worker Advocate" (Cleveland, Oh.: School of Applied Social Sciences, Case Western Reserve University, 1971), p. 7.
18. Nierenberg, *Fundamentals of Negotiating*, p. 60.
19. Richan and Rosenberg, "The Advo-Kit," p. 10.
20. Fagan, *Empowerment*, p. 58.
21. Richan and Rosenberg, "The Advo-Kit," p. 10; Nierenberg, *Fundamentals of Negotiating*, p. 67; and Fagan, *Empowerment*, p. 58.
22. Nierenberg, *Fundamentals of Negotiating*, p. 15.
23. Karras, *The Negotiating Game*, p. 174.
24. Nierenberg, *Fundamentals of Negotiating*, p. 169.
25. Ibid., p. 175 and Karras, *The Negotiating Game*, p. 175.
26. Nierenberg, *Fundamentals of Negotiating*, pp. 171–5.
27. Brody and Cremer, *Organizing for Social Change*, p. 178; Richard H. Hall, *Organizations: Structure and Process* (Inglewood Cliffs, N.J.: Prentice-Hall, 1972), pp. 88–9.
28. Karass, *The Negotiating Game*, p. 178.
29. Nierenberg, *Fundamentals of Negotiating*, pp. 175–8.
30. Richan and Rosenberg, "The Advo-Kit," p. 10.
31. *Public Welfare Committee Report*, Cleveland, Oh.: Federation for Community Planning, September 1979.
32. For a variety of legislative advocacy approaches see Ralph Brody, Richard Chesteen, and Marcie Levy, *The Legislative Process: An Action Handbook for Ohio Citizens' Groups* (Cleveland, Oh.: Federation for Community Planning, 1979), pp. 55–75.
33. Davidson, "Planning and Coordination of Social Services in Multiorganizational Contexts," pp. 125–33.
34. Richan and Rosenberg, "The Advo-Kit," p. 3.
35. Karass, *The Negotiating Game*, pp. 191–3.
36. Harry Specht, "Disruptive Tactics," *Social Work* (April 1969):7.
37. Zbigniew Pietrasinski, *The Psychology of Efficient Thinking* (New York: Pergamon Press, 1969), p. 87. Pietrasinski cautions against habitually applying the same strategy indiscriminantly to problem solutions.
38. Karass, *The Negotiating Game*, p. 187.
39. Nierenberg, *Fundamentals of Negotiating*, p. 183.
40. Ibid., p. 113.
41. Richan and Rosenberg, "The Advo-Kit," p. 1.
42. Nierenberg, *Fundamentals of Negotiating*, pp. 183–95.

CHAPTER 9

1. Adapted from Anthony P. Raia, *Managing by Objectives* (Glenview, Ill.: Scott, Foresman, 1974), p. 77.

2. Adapted from Dorothy P. Craig, *Hip Pocket Guide to Planning and Evaluation* (Austin, Tx.: A Learning Concepts Publication, 1976), pp. 60–7; Robert MacDicken et al., *Toward More Effective Management* (Kirschner Associates, Inc.), U.S. HEW, Office of Human Development, Administration on Aging, 1975, pp. 75–82.
3. Adapted from Craig, *Hip Pocket Guide to Planning and Evaluation*, p. 64; MacDicken et al., *Toward More Effective Management*, p. 76.
4. MacDicken et al., *Toward More Effective Management*, p. 77.
5. Harold Koontz and Cyril O'Donnell, *Essentials of Management* (New York: McGraw-Hill, 1974), p. 382; Craig, *Hip Pocket Guide to Planning and Evaluation*, p. 70.
6. For a more detailed discussion of PERT, including techniques for quantifying critical path times, see the following: James F. Buddle, *Measuring Performance in Human Services* (New York: AMACOM, 1979), pp. 85–102; Donald A. Krueckeberg and Arthur L. Silvers, *Urban Planning Analysis: Methods and Models* (New York: John Wiley and Sons, 1977), pp. 231–55; Robert J. Thierauf and Richard A. Grosse, *Decision Making Through Operations Research* (New York: John Wiley and Sons, 1970), pp. 114–28; Edward P. Ward, *The Dynamics of Planning* (Oxford: Pergamon Press, 1970), pp. 267–72; Policy Management Systems, Inc., *A Programmed Course of Instruction in PERT* (Washington, D.C.: Office of Economic Opportunities, 1969); Koontz and O'Donnell, *Essentials of Management*, pp. 383–6.
7. Adapted from D. M. Wheatley and A. W. Unwin, *The Algorithm Writer's Guide* (London,: Longman Grp., Ltd., 1972); Edwardo Roberto, *Strategic Decision Making in a Social Program* (Lexington, Mass.: D. C. Heath, 1975), pp. 101–4.

CHAPTER 10

1. Ralph Brody, *Guide for Applying for Federal Funds for Human Services* (Cleveland, Oh.: School of Applied Social Sciences, Case Western Reserve University, 1974), pp. 3–6.
2. Norton J. Kiritz, "Program Planning and Proposal Writing," *The Grantsmanship Center News* (May-June 1979):34; Timothy Saasta, "How Foundations Review Proposals and Make Grants," *The Grantsmanship Center News* (reprint issue 1978):6.
3. Jack Shakley, "Exploring the Elusive World of Corporate Giving," *The Grantsmanship Center News* (July-September 1977):35–48.
4. Saasta, "How Foundations Review Proposals and Make Grants," pp. 6–7.
5. Discussion with Jeanne Bohlen, Field Representative, Foundation Center, Cleveland, Oh., March 18, 1980.
6. Karl Borden, *Dear Uncle: Please Send Money—A Guide for Proposal Writers* (Pocatello, Id.: Auger Associates, 1978), pp. 19–50; *Grantsmanship Center News*, "Basic Grantsmanship Library" (March-April 1979):67.

7. Lee F. Jacquette and Barbara I. Jacquette, *What Makes a Good Proposal,* Washington, D.C.: The Foundation Center, August 1977; Kiritz, "Program Planning and Proposal Writing," p. 37.
8. Kiritz, "Program Planning and Proposal Writing," p. 45.
9. Borden, *Dear Uncle: Please Send Money—A Guide for Proposal Writers,* p. 85.
10. Ibid., pp. 86–90; Kiritz, "Program Planning and Proposal Writing," p. 50.
11. Almost all proposal consultants use this approach in writing proposals. See Barry Mastrine, "How to Develop an Effective Funding Strategy," *The Grantsmanship Center News* (November-December 1976):1–12; Borden, *Dear Uncle: Please Send Money—A Guide for Proposal Writers,* pp. 64–72; Kiritz, "Program Planning and Proposal Writing," pp. 52–55; and Brody, *Guide for Applying for Federal Funds for Human Services,* pp. 16–19.
12. Kiritz, "Program Planning and Proposal Writing," pp. 60–1.
13. Borden, *Dear Uncle: Please Send Money—A Guide for Proposal Writers,* pp. 108–12; Kiritz, "Program Planning and Proposal Writing," pp. 39–44.
14. Kiritz, "Program Planning and Proposal Writing," p. 72.
15. Jacquette and Jacquette, *What Makes a Good Proposal,* pp. 1–7; Robert A. Mayer, "What Will a Foundation Look For When You Submit a Grant Proposal," reprint from *The Foundation Center Information Quarterly* (October 1972); Steven Beasley and Timothy Saasta, "Anatomy of a Grants Process: Federal Funding for Health," *The Grantsmanship Center News* (March-April 1978); the Cleveland Foundation, "Guidelines for Grant Getting," reprinted in *The Grantsmanship Center News* (1978):14; *Health and Welfare Planning Association Newsletter* (Pittsburgh, Pa.), "Approach Foundations Creatively" (November 1979):4.
16. The director of one large community foundation observes, "It always comes down to kind of a gut reaction whether I think this person has the kind of commitment to the idea and the ability to carry it out." See Saasta, "How Foundations Review Proposals and Make Grants," p. 9.

CHAPTER 11

1. See Ralph Brody and Holly Krailo, "An Approach for Reviewing Program Effectiveness," *Social Work* 23 (May 1978):230; Peter F. Drucker, "What Results Should You Expect? A Users' Guide to MBO," *Public Administration Review* (January-February 1976):12–39; and Theodore Caplow, *How to Run Any Organization* (Hinsdale, Ill.: The Dryden Press, 1976), p. 203.
2. Peter F. Drucker, "Managing the Public Service Institution," *Public Interest* (Fall 1973):59.
3. Carol Weiss, *Evaluative Research* (Englewood Cliffs, N.J.: Prentice-Hall, 1972), p. 5.
4. Adapted from Robert MacDicken et al., *Toward More Effective Management,* Kirschner Associates, Inc., U.S. HEW, Office of Human Development, Administration on Aging, 1975, p. 241.

5. Ibid., p. 220.

6. Ibid., pp. 231–6; Norton J. Kiritz, "Program Planning and Proposal Writing," *Grantsmanship Center News* (May-June 1979):60–5.

7. Adapted from Brody and Krailo, "An Approach for Reviewing Program Effectiveness," pp. 230–1.

8. Max Richards and Paul Greenlaw, *Management Decision-Making* (Homewood, Ill.: Richard D. Irwin, 1966), p. 29.

EPILOGUE

1. Benjamin B. Tregoe and John W. Zimmerman, *Top Management Strategy*, (New York: Simon and Schuster, 1980), p. 17.

2. Arthur A. Thompson, Jr., and A. J. Strickland, Jr., *Strategy Formulation and Implementation*, (Dallas: Business Publications, Inc., 1980), p. 20.

3. Ibid., p. 55.

4. Ibid., pp. 56–80; Tregoe and Zimmerman, *Top Management Strategy*, pp. 82–98.

5. Thompson and Strickland, *Strategy Formulation and Implementation*, pp. 102–5.

6. Ibid., pp. 105–13.

7. Jeffrey L. Lant, *Development Today: A Guide for Nonprofit Organizations*, (Cambridge, Mass.: J.L.A. Publications, 1981), pp. 93–105; Bernard P. Taylor, *Guide to Successful Fund Raising for Authentic Charitable Purposes*, (South Plainfield, N.J., 1976).

8. Lant, *Development Today*, pp. 107–16.

9. Robert F. Sharpe, *The Planned Giving Idea Book*, (Nashville: Thomas Nelson Publishers, 1978), pp. 79–165; Lant, *Development Today*, pp. 7–92.

10. Thompson and Strickland, *Strategy Formulation and Implementation*, pp. 116–26; James P. Cole, "Factors in Mergers of Voluntary Agencies," *Social Casework* (July 1975), pp. 427–32.

11. Robert Leduc, "Financial Management and Budgeting" in *The Nonprofit Organization Handbook*, ed. Tracy D. Connors, (New York: McGraw-Hill, 1980), pp. 6/47–62.

12. Aaron Wildovsky, *Politics of the Budgetary Process*, (Boston: Little Brown & Co., 1979), pp. 202–21.

13. Thompson and Strickland, *Strategy Formulation and Implementation*, pp. 127–9.

14. Ibid., pp. 126–7.

BIBLIOGRAPHY

Adams, James L. *Conceptual Blockbusting.* San Francisco: W. H. Freemon, 1974.

Adrey, Robert. *The Social Contract: A Personal Enquiry into the Evolutionary Sources of Order and Disorder.* New York: Atheneum, 1970.

Alexis, Marcus and Wilson, Charles Z. *Organizational Decision-Making.* Englewood Cliffs, N.J.: Prentice-Hall, 1974.

Baker, Frank and O'Brien, Gregory. "Intersystems Relations and Coordination of Service Organizations." *American Journal of Public Health* 61 (January 1971) :130–7.

Beasley, Steven and Saasta, Timothy. "Anatomy of a Grants Process: Federal Funding for Health." *The Grantsmanship Center News,* March-April 1978, pp. 20–8.

Blake, Robert and Mouton, Jane. *Group Dynamics—Key to Decision-Making,* Houston, Tx.: Gulf Publishing, 1961.

Bohlen, Jeanne. "Finding Your Way Around the Foundation Materials— Outline of a Sample Foundation Search." Cleveland: Foundation Center (no date).

Borden, Karl. *Dear Uncle: Please Send Money—A Guide for Proposal Writers.* Pocatello, Id.: Auger Associates, 1978.

Bouchard, Thomas J. "Whatever Happened to Brainstorming." In *Guide to Creative Action,* edited by Sidney J. Parnes, Ruth G. Noller, and Angelo M. Biondi, pp. 189–92. New York: Charles Scribner's Sons, 1977.

Brody, Ralph. *Guide for Applying for Federal Funds for Human Services* Cleveland, Oh.: School of Applied Social Sciences, Case Western Reserve University, 1974.

Brody, Ralph, Chesteen, Richard, and Levy, Marcie. *The Legislative Process: An Action Handbook for Ohio Citizens' Groups.* Cleveland, Ohio: Federation for Community Planning, 1979.

Brody, Ralph and Cremer, Kay. *Organizing for Social Change.* Cleveland, Oh.: The Institute of Urban Studies, Cleveland State University, 1970.

Brody, Ralph and Kaukus, Arlene. "Community Problem Solving Through Setting Objectives." *Journal of Asian—Pacific and World Perspectives,* July 1977, pp. 19–32.

Brody, Ralph and Krailo, Holly. "An Approach for Reviewing Program Effectiveness." *Social Work* 23 (May 1978) : 226–32.

Buchanan, Paul C. "A Guide to Effective Problem Solving." Xeroxed (no date), pp. 1–19.

Buddle, James F. *Measuring Performance in Human Service.* New York: AMA-COM, 1979.

Caplow, Theodore. *How to Run Any Organization.* Hinsdale, Ill.: The Dryden Press, 1976.

Chandler, Alfred, Jr. *Strategy and Structure.* Garden City, N.Y.: Doubleday, 1966.

Cleveland Foundation. "Guidelines for Grant Getting." *The Grantsmanship Center News Reprint,* 1978, p. 14.

Cole, James P. "Factors in Merging of Voluntary Agencies." *Social Casework,* July 1975, pp. 427–32.

Craig, Dorothy P. *Hip Pocket Guide to Planning Evaluation.* Austin, Tx.: A Learning Concepts Publication, 1976.

Davidson, Stephen M. "Planning and Coordination of Social Services in Multiorganizational Contexts." *Social Service Review,* March 1976, pp. 117–37.

DeBono, Edward. "Information Processing and New Ideas—Lateral and Vertical Thinking." In *Guide to Creative Action,* edited by Sidney J. Parnes, Ruth B. Noller, and Angelo M. Biondi, pp. 195–200. New York: Charles Scribner's Sons, 1977.

—.*New Think.* New York: Basic Books, 1968.

Delbecq, Andre L., Van de Ven, Andrew, and Gustafson, David H. *Group Techniques for Program Planning.* Glenview, Ill.: Scott, Foresman, 1976.

Downs, George. "Conceptual Issues in the Study of Innovation." *Administrative Science Quarterly.* 24 (December 1976) :702–13.

Doyle, Michael and Straus, David. *How to Make Meetings Work.* Los Angeles: Wyden Books, 1974.

Drucker, Peter F. "Managing the Public Service Institution." *Public Interest,* Fall 1973, pp. 43–60.

—. "What Results Should You Expect? A Users' Guide to MBO." *Public Administration Review,* January-February 1976, pp. 12–39.

Elkin, Robert and Vorwaller, Darrel J. "Evaluating the Effectiveness of Social Services." *Management Controls*, May 1972, pp. 104–11.

Erving, David. "Discovering Your Problem-Solving Style." *Psychology Today* 11 (December 1977) :69–74.

Fagan, Harry. *Empowerment*. New York: Paulist Press, 1979.

Freeley, Austin J. *Argumentation and Debate*. Belmont, Calif.: Wadsworth Publishing, 1961.

Gans, Sheldon P. and Horton, Gerald T. *Integration of Human Services: The State and Municipal Levels*. New York: Praeger, 1975, pp. xvii–xix.

Glampson, Ann, Scott, Tony, and Thomas, David N. *A Guide to the Assessment of Community Needs and Resources*. London: National Institute for Social Work, 1977.

Glidewell, John C. *Choice Points*. Cambridge. Mass.: The MIT Press, 1976.

Gordon, W. J. "On Being Explicit About Creative Process." In *Guide to Creative Action*, edited by Sidney J. Parnes, Ruth B. Noller, and Angelo M. Biondi, pp. 172–74. New York: Charles Scribner's Sons, 1977.

Gore, William J. and Dyson, J. W. *The Making of Decisions—A Reader in Administrative Behavior*. London: Free Press of Glencoe, Collier-MacMillan Ltd., 1964.

Grantsmanship Center News. "Basic Grantsmanship Library." March-April 1979, pp. 67–74.

Hall, Jay. "Decisions, Decisions, Decisions." *Psychology Today*, November 1971, pp. 51–4, 86–8.

Hall, Richard H. *Organizations: Structure and Process*. Inglewood Cliffs, N.J.: Prentice-Hall, 1972.

Handy, Charles. *Understanding Organizations*. Baltimore: Penguin Books, 1976.

Health and Welfare Planning Association Newsletter. "Approach Foundations Creatively," November 1979, Pittsburgh, Pa., pp. 1–5.

Houle, C. O. *The Effective Board*. New York: Association Press, 1960.

Jacquette, Lee F. and Jacquette, Barbara I. *What Makes a Good Proposal*. Washington, D. C.: The Foundation Center, August 1977, pp. 1–7.

Janis, Irving L. "Groupthink." *Psychology Today*, November 1971, pp. 43–6, 74–6.

Johnson, Robert M. "We Turned You Down Because. . . ." *The Grantsmanship Center News Reprint*, 1978 (from the November-December issue of *The Foundation News*), pp. 12–3.

Jones, O. Garfield. *Parliamentary Procedure at a Glance*. New York: Appleton—Century, 1949.

Karrass, Chester L. *The Negotiating Game*. New York: T. Y. Crowell Publishing, 1970.

Kast, Fremont and Rosenzweig, James. *Organization and Management*. New York: McGraw-Hill, 1967.

Kepner, Charles H. and Tregoe, Benjamin B. *The Rational Manager*. New York: McGraw-Hill Book, 1974.

Kiritz, Norton J. "Program Planning and Proposal Writing." *The Grantsmanship Center News Reprint.* 1974, pp. 1–8.
—. "Program Planning and Proposal Writing." *The Grantsmanship Center News,* May-June 1979, pp. 33–79.
Koontz, Harold and O'Donnell, Cyril. *Essentials of Management.* New York: McGraw-Hill, 1974.
Kramer, Ralph M. and Specht, Harry. *Readings in Community Organization Practice.* Englewood Cliffs, N.J.: Prentice-Hall, 1969.
Krueckeberg, Donald A. and Silvers, Arthur L. *Urban Planning Analysis: Methods and Models.* New York: John Wiley and Sons, 1977, pp. 3–28, 231–55.
Lant, Jeffrey L. *Development Today: A Guide for Nonprofit Organizations.* Cambridge, Mass: JLA Publications.
Levine, Sol and White, Paul E. "Exchange as a Conceptual Framework for the Study of Interorganizational Relationships." *Administrative Science Quarterly* 5 (March 1961) : 583–601.
Liduk, Robert. "Financial Management and Budgeting." In *The Nonprofit Organization Handbook* edited by Tracy D. Connors, pp. 6/47–62. New York: McGraw-Hill, 1980.
Litwak, Eugene and Hylton, Lydia F. "Interorganizational Analysis: A Hypothesis on Co-ordinating Agencies." *Administrative Science Quarterly* 6 (March 1962) :395–420.
Long, Norton E. "The Local Community as an Ecology of Games." In *Perspectives on the American Community,* edited by Roland Warren, pp. 54–69. New York: Rand McNally, 1966.
MacDicken, Robert, Trankel, Joanne, Peterson, Morris, and Callahan, William. *Toward More Effective Management.* Kirschner Associates, U.S. DHEW, Office of Human Development, Administration on Aging, 1975.
Magee, John. "Decision Trees for Decision Making." *Harvard Business Review,* July-August 1964, pp. 126–38.
Mager, Robert F. *Goal Analysis.* Belmont, Calif.: Lear Sieger/Fearon Publishers, 1972.
Maier, Norman R. F. "Assets and Liabilities in Group Problem Solving: The Need For an Integrated Function." *Psychology Review,* 1967, pp. 239–49.
Mali, Paul. *Managing by Objectives.* New York: Wiley Interscience, 1972.
Margulies, Newton and Wallace, John. *Organizational Change Techniques and Applications.* Glenview, Ill., and Brighton, England: Scott, Foresman, 1975.
Maslow, Abraham. *Toward a Psychology of Being.* New York: D. Van Nostrand, 1968, pp. 135–45.
Mastrine, Barry. "How to Develop an Effective Funding Strategy." *The Grantsmanship Center News,* November-December 1976, pp. 1–12.
May, Rollo. *The Courage to Create.* New York: W. W. Norton, 1975.
Mayer, Robert A. "What Will a Foundation Look for When You Submit a Grant Proposal." Reprint from *The Foundation Center Information Quarterly,* October 1972.

McConkey, Dale. *MBO for Non-Profit Organizations*. New York: AMACOM, 1975.

—. "20 Ways to Kill Management by Objectives." *Management Review*. October 1972.

Morse, John and Lorsch, Jay. "Beyond Theory Y." *Harvard Business Review*, May-June 1970, pp. 61–8.

Murdick, Robert G. and Ross, Joel E. *Information Systems for Modern Management*. Englewood Cliffs, N.J.: Prentice-Hall, 1972.

Nierenberg, Gerald I. *Fundamentals of Negotiating*. New York: Hawthorn Books, 1973.

Norman, Richard. "Organizational Innovativeness." *Administrative Science Quarterly* 16 (June 1971):203–15.

Office of Budget and Management, State of Ohio. *Measuring Program Results*. Columbus, Oh., 1975.

Parnes, Sidney Jr. "Idea-Stimulation Techniques." In *Guide to Creative Action*, edited by Sidney J. Parnes, Ruth B. Noller, and Angelo M. Biondi, pp. 193–4. New York: Charles Scribner's Sons, 1977.

Parnes, Sidney J., Noller, Ruth B., and Biondi, Angelo M. *Guide to Creative Action*. New York: Charles Scribner's Sons, 1977.

Pietrasinski, Zbigniew. *The Psychology of Efficient Thinking*. New York: Pergamon Press, 1969.

Policy Management Systems, Inc. *A Programmed Course of Instruction in PERT*. Washington, D.C.: Office of Economic Opportunity, 1969.

Prill, George. "Creative Meetings Through Power Sharing." *Harvard Business Review*, July-August 1972, pp. 47–54.

Prince, George M. "The Operational Mechanism of Synectics." In *Guide to Creative Action*, edited by Sidney J. Parnes, Ruth B. Noller, and Angelo M. Biondi, pp. 155–60. New York: Charles Scribner's Sons, 1977.

—. *The Practice of Creativity*. New York: Collier Books, 1970.

Policy Management Systems, Inc. *A Programmed Course of Instruction in PERT*. Washington, D.C.: Office of Economic Opportunities, 1969.

Public Welfare Committee Report. Cleveland, Oh.: Federation for Community Planning, September 1979.

Purtill, Richard L. *Logical Thinking*. New York: Harper and Row, 1972.

Raia, Anthony P. *Managing by Objectives*. Glenview, Ill.: Scott, Foresman 1974.

Reid, William J. "Inter-Organizational Coordination in Social Welfare: A Theoretical Approach to Analysis and Intervention." In *Readings in Community Organization Practice*, edited by Ralph M. Kramer and Harry Specht, pp. 176–84. Englewood Cliffs, N.J.: Prentice-Hall, 1969.

Rein, Martin and Morris, Robert. "Goals, Structures, and Strategies for Community Change." In *Readings in Community Organization Practice*, edited by Ralph M. Kramer and Harry Specht, pp. 188–200. Englewood Cliffs, N.J.: Prentice-Hall, 1969.

Richan, Willard C. and Rosenberg, Marvin. "The Advo-kit: A Self-Administered Training Program for the Social Worker Advocate." Cleveland, Oh.: School of Applied Social Sciences, Case Western Reserve University, 1971.

Richards, Max and Greenlaw, Paul. *Management Decision Making.* Homewood, Ill.: Richard D. Irwin, 1966.

Robert, General Henry M. *Robert's Rules of Order.* Chicago: Scott, Foresman, 1943.

Roberto, Edwardo. *Strategic Decision Making in a Social Program.* Lexington, Mass.: D.C. Heath, 1975.

Rosenberg, Marvin and Brody, Ralph. *Systems Serving People: A Breakthrough in Service Delivery.* Cleveland, Oh.: School of Applied Social Sciences, Case Western Reserve University, 1974.

Saasta, Timothy. "How Foundations Review Proposals and Make Grants." *The Grantsmanship Center News Reprint,* 1978, pp. 1–11.

Schein, Edgar H. *Organizational Psychology.* New York: Prentice-Hall, 1970, pp. 46–58.

—. *Process Consultation: Its Role in Organization Development.* Reading, Mass.: Addison Wesley Publishing, 1969.

Schoderbek, Peter B. *The Board and Its Responsibilities.* Alexandria, Va.: United Way of America, 1979.

—. *The Effective Use of Committees.* Alexandria, Va.: United Way of America, 1979.

Shakley, Jack. "Exploring the Elusive World of Corporate Giving." *The Grantsmanship Center News.* July-September 1977, pp. 35–58.

Sharpe, Robert F. *The Planned Giving Idea Book.* Nashville: Thomas Nelson, 1978.

Specht, Harry. "Disruptive Tactics." *Social Work* 14 (April 1969) :5–15.

Stein, Morris. *Stimulating Creativity, Vol. 2.* New York: Academic Press, 1975.

Tannenbaum, Robert and Schmidt, Warren. "How to Choose a Leadership Pattern." *Harvard Business Review,* May-June 1973, pp. 162–80.

Taylor, Bernard P. *Guide to Successful Fund Raising for Authentic Charitable Purposes.* South Plainfield, N.J.: *Groupwork Today,* 1976.

Taylor, Charles W. "Panel Consensus Technique: A New Approach to Decision-making." In *Guide to Creative Action,* edited by Sidney J. Parnes, Ruth B. Noller, Angelo M. Biondi, pp. 201–5. New York: Charles Schribner's Sons, 1977.

Thierauf, Robert S. and Grosse, Richard A. *Decision Making Through Operations Research.* New York: John Wiley and Sons, 1970.

Thompson, Arthur A. and Strickland, A. J., III. *Strategy Formulation and Implementation.* Dallas: Business Publications, Inc., 1980.

Trecker, Harleigh B. *Citizen Boards at Work.* New York: Association Press, 1970.

Tregoe, Benjamin B. and Zimmerman, John W. *Top Management Strategy.* New York: Simon and Schuster, 1980.

United Way Services. *Program Planning and Performance Measurement System.* Cleveland, Oh., 1979.

Ward, Edward P. *The Dynamics Of Planning.* Oxford, England: Pergamon Press, 1970.

Warren, Roland. "Types of Purposive Social Change at the Community Level." In *Readings in Community Organization Practice,* edited by Ralph M. Kramer and Harry Specht, pp. 205–22. Englewood Cliffs, N.J.: Prentice-Hall, 1969.

Watson, G. and Glaser, E. M. "What We Have Learned About Planning for Change." *Management Review* 54 (1965) :34–46.

Watzlawick, Paul, Weaklane, John H., and Fisch, Richard. *Change.* New York: W. W. Norton, 1972.

Weiss, Carol. *Evaluative Research.* Englewood Cliffs, N.J.: Prentice-hall, 1972.

Wheatley, D. M. and Unwin, A. W. *The Algorithm Writer's Guide.* London: Longman Grp., Ltd., 1972.

Wheelwright, Steven C. and Makridakis, Spyros. *Forecasting Methods for Management.* New York: John Wiley and Sons, 1973, pp. 162–84.

White, Douglas, J. *Decision Methodology.* London: John Wiley and Sons, 1975.

Wildavsky, Aaron. *Politics of the Budgetary Process.* Boston: Little Brown and Co., 1979.

Zaltman, Gerald and Duncan, Robert. *Strategies for Planned Change.* New York: John Wiley and Sons, 1977.

INDEX